HOPE AND HEARTBREAK IN TORONTO

HOPE AND HEARTBREAK IN TORONTO

LIFE AS A MAPLE LEAFS FAN

PETER ROBINSON

DUNDURN
TORONTO

Editor: Allison Hirst
Project Editor: Michael Carroll
Design: Jesse Hooper
Printer: Webcom

Library and Archives Canada Cataloguing in Publication

Robinson, Peter, 1972-
     Hope and heartbreak in Toronto : life as a Maple Leafs fan / by Peter Robinson.

Issued also in electronic format.
ISBN 978-1-4597-0683-5

     1. Hockey fans--Ontario--Toronto. 2. Toronto Maple Leafs (Hockey team). I. Title. II. Title: Life as a Maple Leafs fan.

GV848.T6R63 2012   796.962'6409713541   C2012-904460-1

1   2   3   4   5   16   15   14   13   12

We acknowledge the support of the **Canada Council for the Arts** and the **Ontario Arts Council** for our publishing program. We also acknowledge the financial support of the **Government of Canada** through the **Canada Book Fund** and **Livres Canada Books**, and the **Government of Ontario** through the **Ontario Book Publishing Tax Credit** and the **Ontario Media Development Corporation**.

Care has been taken to trace the ownership of copyright material used in this book. The author and the publisher welcome any information enabling them to rectify any references or credits in subsequent editions.

J. Kirk Howard, President

VISIT US AT
Dundurn.com | Definingcanada.ca | @dundurnpress | Facebook.com/dundurnpress

Dundurn
3 Church Street, Suite 500
Toronto, Ontario, Canada
M5E 1M2

Gazelle Book Services Limited
White Cross Mills
High Town, Lancaster, England
LA1 4XS

Dundurn
2250 Military Road
Tonawanda, NY
U.S.A. 14150

For Jody
You've enabled a man who hasn't quite grown up
to chase his boyhood dream

CONTENTS

FOREWORD

THIS BOOK EXPLORES HOW THE MIND OF A TORONTO MAPLE LEAFS fan works. I experienced this passion firsthand, and I still hear from many of those people who bleed the blue and white. It is almost like the love parents have for their children, in that it has no conditions or boundaries. There have been heart-wrenching moments on the ice over the past forty-five years, but this book opens the door to some of the stories that weren't covered by the mainstream media, but which still grab your attention — like Mike Sundin's overtime heroics or a sprawling, series-clinching save by "Cujo."

Anybody who passionately follows a sports team will understand the feelings that resonate through these pages, how their daily lives are influenced by the ups and downs of their team during the season.

This book reminded me of those crazy times I enjoyed as a player in Toronto. One that sticks in my memory is the night I left the Air Canada Centre after we beat the New York Islanders in Game 7 of the 2002 playoffs. I remember walking outside after the game. The traffic around the ACC was like a parking lot, but probably the happiest parking lot in Toronto's traffic history. People were jumping out of their cars to high-five pedestrians and others stuck in the traffic melee. That showed me the thirst for success the Leafs Nation has and the large space those individuals reserve in their hearts for the lucky twenty players who wear the blue-and-white jersey each and every game night.

I understood many of the qualities that define a Leafs fan, having had the chance to wear the cherished Leaf crest on my chest for almost six years, but this book helped me to grasp the lengths to which fans will go in order to realize their dream of watching a Leafs game live.

Alyn McCauley
Former Toronto Maple Leafs forward (1997–2003)
and Los Angeles Kings scout

June 2012
Kingston, Ontario

ACKNOWLEDGEMENTS

I WISH TO THANK THE MANY PEOPLE WHO HELPED ME IN THIS project; but first, some context.

I was finishing the manuscript as the Leafs were beginning an epic slump that would see them fall out of the NHL playoff race for the seventh consecutive season. The ugly slide cost head coach Ron Wilson his job. More telling was the anger that exploded amongst the team's fan base — myself included — and the declining reputation of Leafs GM Brian Burke among the team's supporters that took hold during this time. Having come undone as they did also scuttled any suggestion of a hopeful parting theme in this book. No one expected the 2011–12 version of the Leafs to win the Stanley Cup, but there was real hope up until about Valentine's Day that the team would make the playoffs and provide genuine optimism for the future.

We all know how that turned out, and as painful as the lost 2011–12 season became, it meant that there would never be a better time to examine the sheer extent of emotions experienced when you're a Leafs fan. There have been many quality books and stories written about the hockey team, but they tend to reflect the journalists' take on the various goings-on at Air Canada Centre. The intent of this book is to provide a fan's perspective on the joys, as few as there have been, and overwhelming angst involved in following the team. To that end, none of the traditional methods of covering a hockey team were followed in putting together this book. Instead, I assumed the vantage point of a fan sitting in Air Canada Centre, not in its press box. To me, and I would hope that readers also feel this way, that's a key difference.

That said, many people deserve a heartfelt thank-you for helping me with the completion of this book.

First, to the staff at Dundurn, many thanks to you for taking a chance on a first-time author, but most of all for the professionalism and expertise in finishing the project. Like Dundurn, my agent Brian Wood rolled the dice with a neophyte. He was an immense help in getting the ball rolling.

James Ansley, Jason Logan, and Stephen Hubbard are three very dear friends who have all helped me — James and Jason directly with the manuscript, and Stephen for his many years of helpful advice and affording me writing opportunities. Wendy Thomas has also been of great assistance on both this book and also during many, many years in my regular work. I would like to express my gratitude to Cliff Kivell, who has been the publisher of many magazines that I've edited and has always been generous in allowing me to work on other projects. I'm also grateful for the help of Gord French and Britney Mackey at various points along the way.

Long ago, I had a elementary school teacher named Jack Williams who I've since lost touch with. I haven't seen him in decades, but he planted the seed for much of my life's work to this point.

My father, Ron, has always supported me even though I gave him ample reason for him to want to clobber his middle child, especially during the first half of my life. Thanks, Dad.

There is not nearly enough space here to list all the entertaining characters I've met down at the Air Canada Centre; but I would like to make special mention of John Wilczynski and Sean Davis for being such great guys to watch games with and to spin the yarn with on the golf course.

In closing, I will leave you with words written by a man named David Lowe around the same time the Leafs were going into the tank in early 2012. They were forwarded on to me by a relative and I pass them on here simply because they are perhaps the most fitting of any saying or metaphor I've seen: "Being a Leafs fan is the worst relationship I have ever been in."

It can't be that bad, can it?

SACRED BONDS

On the evening of December 9, 2010, a man named Angus Ronalds pushed his son, Riley, through the concourse of the Air Canada Centre in a wheelchair. Earlier that year he had buried his wife, the mother of their two young children, after she died from a rare form of cancer. Within weeks, Riley, his oldest child, was stricken with the same type of cancer, which has a tendency to attack much more aggressively in successive generations.

The pain and sorrow that Mr. Ronalds must have been going through is unimaginable. His son had just weeks to live, but aggressive chemotherapy had allowed him to realize a few dying wishes: going to Disney World, and celebrating one last Christmas and his birthday.

That night the two were fulfilling another one of those wishes as they attended a Leafs–Flyers game. In the moments leading up to game, I approached Angus and re-introduced myself. I had been to his wife Heidi's funeral earlier that year but I could tell that he didn't recognize me (my wife and Heidi had taught together at a Toronto-area public school).

"He's terminal," said Angus of Riley's condition when I asked. "We're just enjoying what time we have left together."

Little Riley died shortly after his fifth birthday, on February 1, 2011.

♣　　♣　　♣

It's a question that confounds many people across the hockey world and even some who consider themselves Leafs fan: Why? What is it about a hockey team that makes Angus Ronalds's story so common, even with its extraordinary and utterly sad details? Ronalds wasn't the first father to bring his terminally ill son to see a Leafs game, and he certainly won't be the last.

The team has been mostly a losing or mediocre club on the ice for the past four decades and is owned by a largely faceless patchwork of corporate interests. So why does the club have such a hold on its fans? It is supposed to be in the business of winning hockey games, yet business has thrived *despite* the fact that the team has never been so unsuccessful on the ice in its near century of existence.

With the possible exception of the LA Lakers and one or two National Football League and Major League Baseball teams, there is no North American sports franchise that can count on unconditional support from its fans the way the Leafs can. But all those others franchises, aside from possibly the Chicago Cubs, win.

So what is it that makes the Toronto Maple Leafs so popular?

To a certain degree the need for us to share a common goal or interest with others keeps fans coming back in any sport. That's been especially true in the past fifty years or so because sports have in many ways filled a void that was previously taken up by the sheer struggle to survive.

It's a vexing question — why do we need to support anyone? Is it a primal need, a longing to belong to a group? Whatever the answer to that question, many professional sports teams in leagues around the world have stepped into that void created as our lives have evolved for the better. But beyond that, there is still something different when it comes to the Leafs. They have crept into, if not their collective fans' soul, at least into that grey area that lurks between it and our DNA.

They are there and they're not leaving.

Given everything Leafs fans have been through — the Harold Ballard years, the inexorable, corporately funded march toward and obsession about fattening the bottom line that started soon after, and now the post-lockout drought — if they were going to take their leave, they would have done it long ago. These otherwise intelligent people, who, frankly, ought to know better, wouldn't even consider switching their allegiance. The bond is so strong, it's almost scary.

A few years ago, a particular man in his fifties died from cancer. In every way, he was an average Toronto-area man except that he died too young. A passionate Leafs fan, he had been a solid hockey player in his youth and a quality recreational player right up until soon before he passed away. Not a religious man, he was seen off from this world in a secular tribute; anyone who wanted to speak was invited to say a few words. One man stepped forward. Clearly shaken, he swallowed hard, pulled out a beer and cracked it open, and raised it in a toast to his friend: "You were the best fucking defenceman I ever seen," he said. He then took a drink over his friend's Maple-Leafs-flag-draped casket and sat back down.

Another example: back in the early 1990s I was attending my then-girlfriend's high school prom. The tuxedo I wore to the festivities for some reason came without cuff links. I borrowed some from a friend, who had gotten them from his father as a birthday gift. His father was in the early stages of MS, a disease that claimed his life about a decade later. "Robinson," my friend said to me as he was showing me how to put them in my shirt, "I'm not going to be getting too many more gifts from my father, so make sure they get back to me."

The cuff links were adorned with the Maple Leafs logo, a simple gift from a father to his son that meant infinitely more than the few dollars they cost. Back then, still a teenager, there was little in my life that I took seriously, but I made sure I got those cuff links back to my friend.

About ten years later, his father having died two years before, that same friend and I were in a Toronto bar watching Canada defeat the U.S. and win gold at the Salt Lake Olympics. In the glorious moments that followed that victory — it came fifty years to the day since Canada had last won Olympic men's hockey gold — I glanced over at my friend. I could see tears in his eyes. I instantly knew that he was thinking about his dad and how much he would have liked to watch that game with him. Both having been Leafs supporters, if my friend is fortunate enough to witness a Toronto Stanley Cup win in his lifetime, I know the first thing he will think about is his father.

The bonds go beyond death.

As any Canadian knows, the story is pretty much the same across the hockey-obsessed nation. It's difficult to imagine the scenes that will unfold when a Canadian team finally breaks the two-decade hex that the country's NHL clubs have experienced since the Montreal Canadiens last won the Cup in '93.

Leaving Canada Hockey Place on February 28, 2010, after watching Canada defeat the U.S. to win the men's hockey gold medal at the Vancouver Olympics, I had one overriding thought: I hope to live a charmed enough life to experience the same thing someday when the Leafs win the Stanley Cup.

Aside from getting married and the birth of my children, I haven't experienced that feeling of sheer joy I did in Vancouver that day. I can't imagine feeling it again, aside from being able to witness seminal moments in my own children's lives.

But what if the Leafs did win the Stanley Cup? When and if that day finally comes, it goes beyond words to describe how happy I will be. That would be especially true if I could experience it with my son, who I hope, selfishly perhaps, grows up to be a Leafs fan.

As we all know, Sidney Crosby scored the winning goal in Vancouver. Permanently etched in my mind, as it is for so many other Canadians, is the image of Crosby crouched down, looking almost in disbelief as he waited for his teammates to pile on top of him. It was as if for the first time in his life, Sid the Kid's remarkable physical gifts had failed him and he just sat there, overcome with the moment. That image is now on par with the grainy black and white pictures of Paul Henderson's goal in Moscow in 1972 and Mario Lemieux's in Hamilton in 1987.

Imagine if the Leafs ever win the Stanley Cup in a similar manner. What kind of iconic image of the goal scorer will live on? And who will that goal scorer be? As unbelievable as it sounds, he could be playing on the Leafs right now. Or he could be a little boy who goes to bed every night in some place like Peterborough, or Penticton, or Pardubice dreaming of doing it.

If it ever happens, there will be a lot of people, both alive and no longer with us, who can rest in peace.

2

LONG WALK IN THE NHL DESERT

LIKE A LOT OF ENLIGHTENING MOMENTS, MINE CAME TO ME AT THE oddest of times. I was overseas in Germany in the spring of 2001, desperately trying to find a venue to watch the Leafs play the New Jersey Devils in a conference semifinal playoff matchup. I was covering the men's world hockey championship, a work trip that sounded agreeable in theory, but in practice it was proving painful and not particularly lucrative. It was also conflicting directly with the NHL playoffs.

Done work for the night, I was winding my way through a collection of back streets that were notable for their medieval feel and the Second World War bomb damage that was still faintly visible on some of the buildings. The time difference between Europe and North America would let me watch the pivotal Game 5 of the Leafs–Devils series if I could only locate the bar where it was alleged it was to be shown. During my search, I began to realize that my meandering had taken me to an area near Hanover's main train station to a small neighbourhood bathed in the dull glow of red lights. I had ended up in the area reserved for the city's houses of ill repute.

Visible through a floor-to-ceiling window in front of me, I saw a middle-aged man bound and gagged. Beside him was, to use a word of my father's generation, a buxom blonde woman who could be no other nationality but German. As I watched, she began whipping the hapless man. Worse, she seemed to be enjoying it.

I'm not sure what he thought — he had a leather mask on — but I presume that, given that the whole episode was taking place in full view of people walking by, he had elected to be subjected to this public humiliation.

I still recall thinking "What on God's green earth could be the point of such an exercise?" and "How could it possibly be enjoyable for either of them?" But then it hit me: I was a Leafs fan going to extraordinary measures to try to find the game on television in a faraway land. Ultimately I knew, or ought to have known, the result would leave me asking similar questions of myself. It may not involve being clad in leather restraints, but the invisible shackles of my addiction were just as emotionally painful.

In the complicated world of team/fan relations, the Leafs don't use a device normally reserved for four-legged beasts of burden; instead, their method of inflicting pain on its followers could be better described as death by a thousand cuts. That's what it's been akin to — a lifetime of anticipation, a bit of teasing, oftentimes utter incompetence, and, ultimately, failure. There have been reasons to be optimistic. Until the long post-lockout run of playoff misses, the Leafs could be called the most successful Canadian team in the era that ran from the 1992–93 season, which is generally assumed to be about the point that hockey started to undergo a massive transformation, until the spring of 2004, before the work stoppage.

Calling the Leafs the best Canadian team in that span does require a small leap of faith because the Montreal Canadiens won the 1993 Stanley Cup and both the Calgary Flames and Vancouver Canucks came within a game of doing the same in 2004 and 1994 respectively. The Leafs also missed the playoffs twice during that time, but that was hardly a rare event for Canadian teams, who all struggled to a degree keeping up to hockey's changing economics. But, on balance, I would say that Toronto was the best Canadian team during that span because the Leafs did make it to the conference final four times. The club was generally assumed to be a good bet to win at least one playoff round every year it did make the playoffs. Not an impeccable record of success, but not table scraps either.

The time since the NHL lockout ended in 2005 has been an inexcusable failure because the Leafs can't make the post-season. Their record during the 1980s and early 1990s was about the same, and often worse, though the masses kept pouring into Maple Leaf Gardens just like they do now at Air Canada Centre.

So, in the wider view, since 1967 they haven't exactly been Three Stooges bad because of the ten-or-so years of competence, but also nowhere near the rarefied air they occupied up until they last won the Stanley Cup. The problem is that I don't remember those halcyon days when the Leafs more or less went blow-for-blow with the Montreal Canadiens. This is because I was still several years away from sucking in my first breath. You have to be about fifty years old to even remember a Leafs Stanley Cup win and older to have appreciated its significance at the time. The rest of us are left to grasp at small victories. And, boy, can we ever cling to those!

If loving the Leafs is like an addiction, then the four visits to conference finals since 1993 are the proverbial crack houses. The last one came in 2002, and if I allow myself to dream, it was like it was yesterday. The Leafs played twenty games over a period of six weeks and had to fight tooth-and-nail for everything as the team was decimated by injuries and came up against two very determined squads in the first two rounds. First it was the New York Islanders and then the Ottawa Senators, both of them falling to the Leafs in seven games. But the Leafs were ultimately stopped by the Carolina Hurricanes in six games in the Eastern Conference final.

Given the way the playoffs broke that year, it may have been the best opportunity the club would ever have to win the Stanley Cup. Top seeds Boston and Philadelphia had been eliminated in the first round and their nemesis the previous two post-seasons, New Jersey, also exited at that stage.

There is a saying in sports that it's often not the teams you beat but the ones you don't have to that determines championships. With that credo in mind, 2002 should have been the Leafs' year. It wasn't, of course, and as more time has passed, I've slowly grown to accept that perhaps the rest of the NHL had a point when the Leafs that season were referred to as the most hated team in the league.[1]

I don't necessarily agree, but I now understand what riled others, particularly in other parts of Canada. Leafs winger Darcy Tucker had hands-down his best year as an NHL player, but he was also not afraid to push the boundaries too much and too often. His low-bridge hit on the Islanders' Michael Peca in Game 5 of the first-round series was the perfect example of the Leafs' penchant for just tickling the grey area between what was allowed and what shouldn't be. The snapshot lives on as perhaps the best modern-day example of what ails the Leafs. Tucker, a player of reasonable ability, but also one with some flaws, going low on Peca was cheap, plain and simple. Replays then, as they do now, clearly showed Tucker looking to the referee right after making contact to see if he was going to be penalized. Players who honestly believe they've done nothing wrong generally don't glance back to see if they've been caught.

Pictures from that game involving Tucker and Peca also show a disturbing sign that has remained a bugaboo for the Leafs franchise: acres of empty seats in the lower platinum section, even though it was an intense and important playoff game. Then, as now, the well-moneyed areas of the ACC are full of people who didn't seem too bothered watching all the action, no matter how critical the game may be.

It's no small asterisk that Peca never played another game that series: the Tucker hit ended his season. Peca and Tucker later patched things up when Peca came to Toronto, a nice gesture by both men.

But the run ended for the Leafs that year in one of those split-second blurs that so often define playoff hockey. Alex Mogilny, with eight goals scored that post-season, helped allow one in overtime that would kill the Leafs season. He let Carolina Hurricane forward Martin Gelinas walk to the Leafs net, where Gelinas took a pass from teammate Josef Vasicek,[2] and then deposited the puck behind Leafs goaltender Curtis Joseph.

That was it. That night, as I left the Wheat Sheaf Tavern just up the road from the ACC — I had feverishly tried to get tickets for the game but the prices were approaching several hundred dollars a seat — I distinctly recall thinking that the Leafs had made the final four on four occasions over the past ten years. It wouldn't be long before they would be back. Right?

Since that day in 2002 the Leafs have won just one playoff series. What constitutes success these days is the hope that they are still in the playoff chase come late March. It has not been easy to be a Leafs fan in the decade since that warm spring night in Toronto. Even back then, loving the Leafs meant being in bed with the team that was the most hated in the NHL, or so went the prevailing wisdom of the day.

I can only wonder that if the Leafs had behaved a bit more honourably that season and in others leading up to it, fate would have been kinder to the hockey club and its long-suffering fans. Looking back, I do believe the label was somewhat unfair (just as I'm sure Vancouver Canucks' fans think a similar tag their team has inherited recently is unjust). Respected hockey man Pat Quinn was the Leafs' coach and general manager at the time and he was also the man behind the bench of Team Canada at the Salt Lake City Olympics and later the 2004 World Cup and 2006 Turin Olympics. If Wayne Gretzky, in charge of Team Canada, installed Quinn as his coach, then surely the Leafs couldn't be nearly as bad as some of the worst parts of their reputation suggested.

I also used to cringe at the characterization that Leafs fans treated even small victories as though they were steps on the path to planning a Stanley Cup parade. The decade-long run of reasonable success really did give Leafs fans a sense of entitlement, an expectation that things would not only stay the same but that they would likely get even better. Back in 2002, I, like pretty much all my Leafs Nation brethren, thought that the numerals 1-9-6-7 signified Canada's Centennial year. I'm not sure I even think about Canada's 100th birthday when I see "1967" written anywhere now. I know precisely what it means: the last Stanley Cup victory for the Leafs.

Lost in the desert of missed playoffs and early springs, Leafs fans now grasp wins in pretty much the same way as their detractors used to say they did way back when, when all those unseemly comments really weren't true. The Leafs won an average of thirty-four games in the five seasons between the fall of 2007 and the spring of 2012. If you extend that period back two additional years to include the first seven seasons since the NHL lockout wiped out the 2004–05 season, the number nudges up to an average of thirty-six wins per year. Those stats, especially the number from the past five years (because it's more reflective of the Brian Burke managerial regime) really hits home. Most people who are gainfully employed get paid every two weeks. That means twenty-six times a year. The comparison struck me because a Leafs victory now really does feel like payday, that's how rarely it happens.

I'm not sure fans need the Leafs to win the Stanley Cup to make all this longing fade away. The NHL, like all the professional sports leagues, is an incredibly difficult milieu to cast your lot in. There are thirty teams, and only one wins the championship each year. Former Maple Leaf Sports and Entertainment head Richard Peddie used to shamelessly exploit this fact to justify the Leafs' lack of success. What Peddie ignored is the one simple thing that Leafs fans want, and that's a chance to feel good again. Make the playoffs, win a round or two, make spring synonymous with playoff hockey again. Those four springs in Toronto — 1993, 1994, 1999, and 2002 — when the Leafs made it to the penultimate round made everyone feel alive. Of course, you wished it lasted a bit longer, but Toronto was gripped with a belief, a feeling that was in the air. It was as if the warm spring air was somehow connected to the hockey team; as if the Leafs were helping us breathe. Everyone, even those who wouldn't know a hockey puck from a grapefruit, believed in the Leafs. Get to that stage often enough and the Leafs will eventually win the Stanley Cup and the numerals 1-9-6-7 will go back to meaning Canada's Centennial.

❦　　❦　　❦

I believed back in 2001 in Germany, as well. I eventually found that bar in Hanover and watched as the Leafs took on the New Jersey Devils in an Eastern Conference semifinal series. Tomas Kaberle scored the winner with less than a minute left in the game. The result put the Leafs in control with a three-games-to-two lead heading back to Toronto.

I wound my way back to my guesthouse in Hanover, wanting to tell the first person I saw on those deserted streets how happy I was. I didn't care that they would have been German and likely didn't give two shakes of lederhosen about a hockey game taking place across the Atlantic Ocean, especially since the world championship was going on in the city. It was middle-of-the-night late and even the bawdy houses were closed down, not that the pleasure on offer in them could have approached what I was feeling as I skipped back to my room.

A few days later, with the Devils having won Game 6 to tie the series at three games apiece, I arrived back in Toronto literally an hour before the puck drop in the decisive seventh. My then-girlfriend, now-wife, scooped me up at the airport and we drove straight to a sprawling sports bar in Toronto's west end to watch the game. Things were looking good when Steve Thomas scored to give the Leafs a 1–0 lead — I'm not sure the world could have been a better place. On this warm night in May the Leafs were on the verge of winning a playoff series that would have meant they were one of just four teams vying for the Stanley Cup.

You know what happened next. Thomas's goal was the last one of that Leafs season as the Devils poured in four in the second period on their way to a 5–1 win.

The pain seared through me. All I could think about was that guy in the window a few days earlier.

3

MAY 25, 1993

I CAN STILL HEAR THE CLICK OF THE TICKETMASTER MACHINE. And I remember the date: the morning of May 25, 1993. I had just finished an overnight shift working on the cleaning crew at the Honda plant in Alliston, Ontario. Dropped off at home by the contractor who drove us to work each day, I rushed in, grabbed my bike, and made a beeline for the Kozlov Centre, the main ticket outlet in my hometown of Barrie, Ontario.

Back in the days before Internet searching and even before the wristband policy that helped regulate crowds trying to get sports and concert tickets, it was possible to try your luck simply by lining up. It was completely hit and miss, of course, and during that glorious Leafs playoff run that spring there were times when not a single person of the dozens who lined up early each morning was getting a ticket.

For some reason the line was moving on the morning of Game 5 of the Campbell Conference Final. The rhythmic clicking of the machine spitting out tickets continued as I neared the front of the line. Every ticket that was being issued was decidedly low-end: high greys, standing room — the bottom of the barrel, seating-wise. With a limit of two each, my friend in front of me landed a pair. Then it was my turn.

I got the last ticket, a grey in the second-to-last row of the Gardens. I know it was the last one on offer because as the machine tried to punch out a second one it stopped with the ticket still half inside the machine.

"I'm sorry," said the agent.

I didn't care. I was going to the Gardens that night. The second ticket that sat stuck in the machine had been earmarked for anyone

I could find who was willing to pony up, as I recall, $40 for the seat. I would be sitting alone, but I had a seat and a ride down to Toronto with my friend who had secured the pair in front of me.

That spring in the Toronto area was unlike anything anyone could have imagined even six months earlier. It was the first prolonged playoff run by the Leafs in fifteen years and a by-product of the hiring of Pat Burns as coach and one of the most lopsided trades in the history of the NHL. Doug Gilmour and a collection of other players, including defenceman Jamie Macoun and role player Kent Manderville, had come to Toronto from the Calgary Flames for Gary Leeman and spare parts.

I had an odd perspective on the trade because the Calgary general manager at the time was Doug Risebrough. Risebrough's late mother and my father were brother and sister, making us first cousins. Though we were separated in age by almost two decades, his playing career with the Montreal Canadiens and later with the Flames provided a happy sidelight to my obsession with hockey, both playing and watching it, while growing up. I don't profess to know Risebrough — I've had no more than ten meaningful conversations with him in my life. The one enduring memory I have of his days with the 1970s Canadiens dynasty is playing checkers with our shared grandmother and great-grandmother in their home in Collingwood, Ontario, because a photo of him with the Stanley Cup always hung nearby in the kitchen. But many people knew of the connection, and it always meant my buddies asked about him when I was a really young kid growing up. After Risebrough had won four Stanley Cups with the Canadiens as a player, my friends and I were a bit older and the family connection with a real-life NHL player basically lost its appeal.

However, not long after Gilmour came to Toronto it was obvious that the old silver fox, Cliff Fletcher, the former Flames GM, had fleeced his protégé, Risebrough, in the trade. Suddenly anyone who had vague memories of us being cousins had an opinion on Risebrough, and often not a flattering one. I defended Risebrough, though I've since learned to keep my mouth shut around people from Calgary.

Courtesy of Graig Abel.

DOUG GILMOUR'S TRADE TO TORONTO IN 1992 WAS THE SINGLE BIGGEST EVENT TO REVERSE THE DAMAGE OF THE HAROLD BALLARD ERA, WHICH HAD ENDED TWO YEARS EARLIER.

Deep down, of course, I was giddy that Gilmour was lighting it up in Toronto.

Leeman, on the other hand, struggled in Calgary playing under defence-orientated Flames coach Dave King and he was unable to replicate the splendid offensive form he had shown in Toronto.[1]

Gilmour was a catalyst, scoring 127 points during the regular season, a Leafs record that will likely never be broken. Though it's always difficult to compare accomplishments across different sports and eras, Gilmour's Hart Trophy nomination and his Selke Trophy win from that season could be the best performance by a Toronto athlete in modern times.

Beyond Gilmour, the guidance of Burns, and an impressive supporting cast led by Wendel Clark and others, most notably fifty-goal man Dave Andreychuk, who had been acquired by Fletcher in his various wheelings and dealings, the Leafs were suddenly a very good team. Deep down the middle, with a solid defence, playing in front of a very capable young goaltender in Felix Potvin, in the space of a year the Leafs had gone from being also-rans trying to shake off the doldrums of the Harold Ballard era to a legitimate Stanley Cup contender.

I've never forgotten the sudden transformation, and I even think that the quick 1993 reversal still plays a role in how Leafs fans of today think that a turnaround is possible in the space of a few weeks; because it felt like back then, that the team became Cup contenders almost overnight.

Seven-game wins over Detroit (a massive upset) and St. Louis set up a series with the Wayne Gretzky–led Los Angeles Kings, a matchup that even non-Toronto fans and media have acknowledged as being one of the best played in the post-expansion-era NHL. Say what you want about over-the-top Hogtown hubris, every hockey fan should have the opportunity to experience two weeks like those that took place in late May in Toronto in '93.

With the teams having split the first four games, the critical fifth contest would go a long way in determining who would win the series. I was in possession of a single ticket that was burning a hole

Courtesy of Graig Abel.

THE 1993 PLAYOFF SERIES AGAINST THE ST. LOUIS BLUES WAS THE DEMARCATION LINE SIGNALLING A NEW ERA OF FAN EXCITEMENT IN TORONTO. LOOKING BACK, IT ALSO ILLUSTRATES THE GENUINE ENTHUSIASM OF THE CROWD THAT HAS BEEN LOST IN THE MOVE TO THE AIR CANADA CENTRE.

in my hand. A call in to work begging off sick was made, a short nap followed, and then I was on my way to Maple Leaf Gardens.

❖   ❖   ❖

Maple Leaf Gardens is now a grocery store. People rave about how functional a space it is as shoppers buy their groceries amidst telltale indicators of the place's previous incarnation. I can't bring myself to visit, because the idea of it being a retail space is just as offensive as the Montreal Forum now being a cinema. I eventually will take a stroll around, and I plan to take my son in much the same way my own father took me for the first time to a Leafs game versus the Chicago Black Hawks on October 10, 1981. The building sits in its original location and is still recognizable for its yellow brick and the white dome that stretches skyward. Flying over Toronto, it's possible to pick it out fairly easily, a short diagonal line just northeast of the CN Tower. Inside, the gold-red-green-grey seat configuration (with blue replacing green on the ends) is so memorable that I still recognize the colour combination when I spot it in a painting or on someone's clothing.

Courtesy of Graig Abel.

MAPLE LEAF GARDENS AS IT LOOKED NOT LONG BEFORE IT CLOSED; THE BUILDING IS NOW A GROCERY STORE AND RECREATION FACILITY FOR NEARBY RYERSON UNIVERSITY.

Sporting arenas built in the pre–Second World War years have an indelible effect on those who walk through them. It's tough to pin down why, but it likely has something to do with the fact that people of that era lived much more simply. Even wealthy people rarely had homes that were much bigger than what a typical family has now. When a big, ornate structure was erected, especially a sports venue, people noticed and never forgot it. Churches had that effect, and they, too, inasmuch as they continue to survive, remain notable pieces of architecture. Near the Gardens, St. Michael's Cathedral stands just south on Church Street, and the Royal York Hotel fits the bill though it lies quite a bit farther to the southwest. All three still grab the attention of passersby, so it's not hard to imagine Toronto in the pre-war years and how much St. Mike's, the Royal York, and the Gardens dominated the downtown. The Gardens still dominates my early hockey and childhood memories in much the same way.

The assault on the senses started as you disembarked from the subway and started to climb the stairs at College Station. It wasn't so much the location as it was the sense of place. The scene around the Gardens was like a pagan Christmas. Street vendors, scalpers, crowds filing here and there — both those going to the game and others just hanging out — and the restaurants. PM Toronto was a nondescript eatery with little in the way of appeal, either for what was on the menu or its décor, but if you made the trip to the Gardens, getting a table at that bar just east of the Gardens was like getting an audience with the Pope.

A small sliver of the Gardens ice was always visible from the street, the goal area that the Leafs attacked twice each game, and a small area immediately in front of the net. If you stood at just the right spot on Carlton Street and peered through the various obstacles — mostly heads bobbing to and fro — you could take in the action from this vantage point.

Once the game was on, that other thing the area around the Gardens was known for started to show its face. The various prostitutes and drug dealers who worked the area to the east between Church and Jarvis would start to show up around the time of the first intermission and only temporarily move away as the hockey hordes made their way out of the building at the end of the game. Toronto's thriving gay village started in earnest slightly north of the Gardens, though the "gaybourhood" has expanded and the building now essentially serves as its southwest border.

More than anything, the Gardens was like a cathedral of dreams. Going there was like going to a house, not necessarily of God himself, but of His creation. It's where the Leafs played, where Wendel Clark and Darryl Sittler, all the way back to Ace Bailey, Charlie Conacher, and Busher Jackson suited up. It wasn't a Hollywood set; it was *our* very own Hollywood. To go there, sit in the seats, and watch, you could feel the ghosts of those who had been there before you. If you sat and listened, you could almost hear the memories within those walls echoing. The seats, the concessions, the stairs, even the distinct urinal troughs, everything had a personality all its own. Consider these facts: When I glimpse a bag of peanut shells now, I still think of the ones I saw at the Gardens as a kid. When I was on holiday in Mexico a few years ago and room service drinks came with a removable elastic-sealed plastic top, I instantly remarked to my wife that it looked as though they had taken the idea from how the Gardens served drinks in paper cups. The Gardens has provided many such touchstones for me and others.

The Air Canada Centre may be one of North America's best entertainment facilities, but that's the point: it's a facility for entertainment. The Gardens was a shrine, though it was a hockey arena, and from the second you walked through the doors you never forgot it. If someone could bottle the Gardens smell — and boy, did Maple Leaf Sports and Entertainment try to take advantage of every commercial opportunity relating to Gardens' memories when it closed — I would recognize it the second it was released into the air. I'm sure countless others could as well.

Ask any NHL player who grew up in Ontario and even beyond where his favourite place to play was and virtually every single one would give you a simple two-word answer: the Gardens. Even Wayne Gretzky stated so time and time again.

We now know, sadly, of the shocking acts going on down at the intersection of Church and Carlton. Almost a hundred boys were sexually abused there by a small group of Gardens staff members. When the abuse came to light in 1997 shortly before the arena closed its doors, the revelation stained its legacy. Reconciling those horrible crimes with the dreams of my youth was not easy, and the situation certainly did give me pause to reconsider. But over time the disgust faded away and I, like so many others, have rediscovered the feeling of growing up in awe of the place. Even now, when I walk the short distance from the intersection of College and Yonge, where the street straightens out and gives way to Carlton, I get chills as the Gardens comes into view.

Game 5 of the 1993 NHL Campbell Conference final between the Leafs and Los Angeles Kings, played at the Gardens on May 25, was the second-best sporting event I have ever witnessed live. The only game that possibly surpasses it for excitement was the gold medal final at the Vancouver Olympics between Canada and the U.S., February 28, 2010. I think I'm just forcing myself to believe that the Olympic final was more exciting because the stakes in the Canada–U.S. game were much, much higher. As important as any NHL conference final is, neither the Leafs nor Kings were going home series winners after Game 5 back in 1993. Also, two conference finals take place every year. That description may make it sound run-of-the-mill, but I would argue the 1993 example is the most memorable hockey game to take place in Toronto in modern hockey history — because the Leafs won. Four nights later Gretzky came back and quashed the dreams of the fans and the team that he grew up watching. Game 7 was far more important, but it all ended so badly.

With the sixth contest set for Los Angeles two days later, Game 5 was a virtual must-win for the Leafs. The night started with the crowd cheering as they were informed that Mark Osborne had been scratched from the Leafs lineup. Osborne, one-third of the so-called

B-O-Z line that also included Bill Berg and the late Peter Zezel, had some issues scoring goals that post-season even though Zezel had set him up with dozens of glorious chances. The guy sitting next to me that night — and if he said it once he said it a million times — thought that had Osborne been able to convert half his scoring chances, the Leafs would have already won the series in a sweep. Osborne was scratched because his wife had given birth; Kent Manderville had taken his place. These days, Osborne is a frequent presence on Leafs TV telecasts, and though I think he was a decent NHL player, every time I see him on the Leafs TV set near the ACC west escalator, I think of that long-ago night when Leafs fans cheered his omission from the lineup.

Just before the puck drop, I ran into no less a figure than Gary Bettman as I was about to ascend the Gardens escalators to my assigned seat. I had just read a fairly positive review in *The Hockey News* that day about Bettman's first hundred days on the job as NHL commissioner. Like the review, I believed that Bettman had done a good job, and, giddy in the excitement of the moment, I shook his hand and congratulated him. Bettman sheepishly thanked me but looked as if he thought I was not in complete control of all my mental faculties (I swear, I was). To this day, my friends, a few of whom are conspiracy types who believe Bettman is somehow out to get Canadian hockey fans, won't let me forget doing it.

The game is both a blur and an event where even marginal details remain burned into my mind. Both men are no longer with us, but I can still see the mullets of Leafs coach Pat Burns and Peter Zezel swaying in the wind as though they are both very much alive. Even less glamorous Leafs such as Mike Krushelnyski are embedded in my brain. That same guy beside me — the Osborne fan — had hung the unofficial nickname of "Casual Cruiser" on Krushelnyski in some sort of backhanded nod to his effortless skating ability. And it was true: Krushelnyski's cruising up and down his wing is one of the details that a setting such as the Gardens framed so perfectly. I saw Krushelnyski play in an NHL old-timers game in Barrie almost two decades later, and I instantly recognized that fluid stride the moment

I saw it — it hadn't changed a bit since he played at the Gardens that night, even if the man himself was older and greyer.

If the same game took place at Air Canada Centre, or any of the other leading arenas of the present-day NHL, it wouldn't have matched the atmosphere that night in the Gardens. I was sitting in one of the last rows of the building and it was as if I could reach out and touch Glenn Anderson when he swatted in the winning goal out of mid-air. The dome almost flew off the Gardens. With nowhere for the sound to go but bounce right back at you, the noise was paralyzing and liberating all at the same time. The Leafs had one step to go before a dream Stanley Cup final with the Montreal Canadiens. The air around the Gardens that night was so thick with excitement, you could taste it. But a guy in zebra stripes with bad hair poured hemlock into the Leafs cup of dreams. The bitter aftertaste still stings.

4

KERRY FRASER

REFEREES.

They are often cited as having the most difficult and thankless job in all of sports. That said, there are times, however rare, when a ref wholeheartedly earns the scorn heaped on them by fans, players, and media alike.

If you follow or play hockey long enough, you'll start to notice the offending individual in many ways — the mannerisms, the way he skates, the way he waves off calls. Depending how much hockey you played as a youngster and how high a level you managed to make it to once you got a little older, you picked up on these annoying ref-isms more as you went along.

It first hit me how grating certain refs could be when I was playing AAA rep hockey as a kid. A few just seemed to have a sense of superiority about them when they entered the arena. Aside from teenagers or early-twenties types who toil as minor-hockey refs, or others who handle rec league games for pocket money, most zebras, if they were honest with themselves, would admit they'd rather be playing the game than calling it. Seriously, would you rather play in the National Hockey League, or be one of the guys who are noticed only if he makes a mistake?

And there's the rub. It really takes guts to skate around knowing full well that virtually every time you blow the whistle half the people on the ice will be annoyed, the other half asking "What took you so long?"

If you were around in the 1980s, you'll recall the styles of the day called for a lot of hair. And although the fashion crossed ages and classes, nowhere was it more consistently and slavishly followed than in hockey and all its subcultures.

"Hockey mullets" survive as one of the most entertaining Google searches at work that won't get you fired.

Along with shorter hair, much has changed over the years relating to how games are called in the NHL. The biggest change has been the addition of a second referee. But a strong personality and a healthy dose of self-belief remain key prerequisites for managing all the competing forces and personalities on the ice.

Let's be honest, it takes stones the size of billiard balls to tell a raving John Tortorella that he has it all wrong. It takes even bigger ones to make a split-second call that you know may turn the tide of a game. Skate a mile in a ref's skates and you would very quickly understand how difficult a job they have. Still, there is always a niggling sense that a few refs are just a little too smart, not unlike the uniformed police officer who develops that strange habit of always taking a stroll at your local pub when most of his brethren can't be bothered.

And then there is Kerry Fraser. Fraser has never had a shortage of self-belief and he apparently missed the memo that hairstyles from the 1980s are no longer *de rigueur*. And if there is one man who makes the collective blood of Leafs fans boil, it is undeniably Fraser.

Let's start with the hair. Mullets were bad enough but perfectly explainable. It wasn't just hockey players — everybody from schoolboys to actors had them way back when they were fashionable. But Kerry Fraser lives in a world where bouffants are perpetually cool. According to the *Oxford Dictionary*, *bouffant* means "puffed out" — kind of a mullet on steroids, in other words. Marie Antoinette is credited with inventing the hairstyle when she was the French queen; her bouffant died, of course, along with the rest of her when her head became dislodged. If Leafs fans had their way, the punishment inflicted upon Fraser for the events of May 27, 1993, would make the guillotine look dignified by comparison.

It was Game 6 of the Campbell Conference Final and the Leafs had a 3–2 lead in their best-of-seven series after their overtime exploits two days earlier. One more Leafs victory was all it would take to set up a dream Stanley Cup Final between Toronto and the Montreal Canadiens.

Courtesy of Graig Abel.

KERRY FRASER WAS ONE OF THE NHL'S MOST RESPECTED OFFICIALS, AND HE NOW DABBLES IN MEDIA COM-
MENTARY. LEAFS FANS WILL NEVER FORGET HIS GAFFE IN GAME 5 OF THE 1993 CAMPBELL CONFERENCE FINAL,
HOWEVER. THE PERFECTLY MANICURED HAIR ONLY ADDED TO THE ANGST.

Playing in Los Angeles, the Leafs' Wendel Clark had completed a hat trick, scoring late to tie the game 4–4 and forcing overtime. With the Leafs' Glenn Anderson having drawn a penalty late in regulation, they took to the ice knowing they had to kill off the Kings power play to prevent the series returning to Toronto for a Game 7.

Wayne Gretzky, largely an inert presence to that point in the game, was starting to find his mojo. Both Gretzky and the Leafs captain, Doug Gilmour, were on the ice when Gretzky attempted to shoot the puck toward the Toronto goal. The shot was blocked before it reached goaltender Felix Potvin, and Gretzky and Gilmour reacted instinctively, heading toward the deflected puck.

Gretzky missed the puck and clipped Gilmour on the chin. Gilmour went down in a heap, bleeding, and play was whistled dead. No one doubted the hit was unintentional but it was equally beyond doubt that Gilmour was fouled, perhaps grievously so given the blood pouring from his chin.

The television footage shows Fraser, who would normally drink in the thick air of the spotlight on such occasions, looking like a child scared out of his wits. He later claimed that he had asked Gilmour

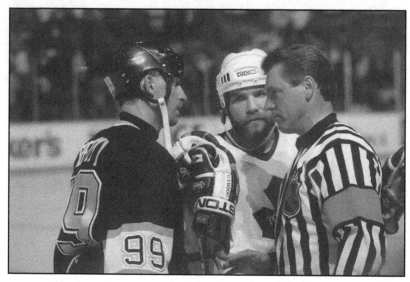

Courtesy of Graig Abel.

THE WAYNE GRETZKY LED LOS ANGELES KINGS AND WENDEL CLARK'S LEAFS ENGAGED IN AN EPIC PLAYOFF BATTLE IN LATE MAY 1993.

what happened and that the Leafs captain had told him Gretzky had clipped him on the "follow-through." It was a critical distinction because in the early 1990s, like now, hitting an opposing player while "following through" shooting the puck was not normally a penalty.

There was also some doubt at the time as to whether Gilmour was struck by the deflected puck or by Gretzky's stick, to the point that the NHL offices cited the confusion as part of the league's official explanation for why a penalty wasn't called.

Replays of the incident — widely available on YouTube in raw video but also in many hilarious spoof formats — show Fraser feverishly consulting with his linesmen Kevin Collins and Ron Finn. Linesmen are allowed to call stick infractions, or at very least advise the referee that an offence had taken place.

Although admitting that it was a missed call all these years later, Fraser maintains that he never saw the infraction. There is one huge problem with his recollection: the replay clearly shows that he had an unobstructed view to the incident. Fraser never saw Gilmour being fouled because his head was turned toward the Leafs goal anticipating the puck arriving there. Gretzky and Gilmour were reacting to the puck being blocked before getting to the net but Fraser failed to pick up on it. To put that oversight into perspective, even Bob Cole, who has been missing broadcast calls in his own unique manner for the past thirty years, could see that the puck never made it to Potvin's crease.

Fraser simply missed what at the very least should have been a minor penalty. That miss, combined with the official explanation from the NHL office, which was clearly at odds with the so-called following-through argument, burns the collective soul of Leafs Nation to this day.

Perhaps even more telling was the look on Gretzky's face at the time. Like all superstar athletes, Gretzky had an understated swagger. When he was on the ice, his face rarely changed from that of a determined, singularly focused athlete. But the look on Gretzky's face as Fraser and his two confederates deliberated was more like a worried schoolboy than a confident superstar. The only other expression that approached the one Gretzky wore for a brief moment that night came almost five years later when he was left on the bench during a shootout at the 1998 Winter Olympics as Canada lost to the Czech Republic.

During the *Hockey Night in Canada* broadcast of the game, analyst Harry Neale asked, "Wouldn't this be something if Wayne Gretzky was thrown out for a high stick?" It would have been *something* all right, but Fraser made no call. And so it turned out to *be* nothing and Gretzky remained on the ice without so much as a minor penalty as Gilmour went to the Leafs dressing room to be stitched up.

With seconds left in that same Kings power play, the game's greatest-ever player took a nice feed from Luc Robitaille and deposited the puck behind Potvin to win the game.

The Kings lived to fight another night and sent the series back to Toronto for the deciding Game 7. Two nights later Gretzky scored three more times to clinch the series for the Kings with another 5–4 win. Gretzky later called it the best game of his incomparable career.

For the Leafs, their best opportunity to win the Stanley Cup since 1967 swung, literally, on a missed call. And by a man who, for all his later regret, gave off an air of indifference, an unspoken "Do you really think that I, a man of such brilliance, could miss something so important?"

There are Leafs fans out there who, without a shred of evidence, claimed that this was all part of a big conspiracy perpetrated by the head office to deny a Leafs–Habs final, which would have run counter to their plans of expanding the game into sunnier climes. These fans, who are otherwise sensible human beings, swore that the "fix" was in that night — a claim that gathered some steam when Don Cherry hinted that he, too, believed something fishy had happened.

There are no shortage of Leafs fans, often perched on a bar stool and with the help of one too many drinks, who still feel the need to regale those around them with their theory that NHL commissioner Gary Bettman may have been involved. It's enough to make 9/11

Truthers blush, and it's all codswallop, of course, but it gives you a sense just how much the thought of Kerry Fraser still stings, even now, two decades later.

WAYNE GRETZKY AND DOUG GILMOUR SHAKE HANDS AT THE CONCLUSION OF THE KINGS' VICTORY IN GAME 7.

✦   ✦   ✦

Though it was the most blatant example, that 1993 missed call by Kerry Fraser was not the only one that has cost the Leafs over the years. The next incident came late in the 2006–07 season, when the Leafs were battling the New York Islanders (and others) for the final playoff spot in the Eastern Conference. That night Fraser inexplicably put himself in the midst of another season-defining incident.

Fraser was officiating the game, which took place on Long Island. In a play that Leafs Nations conspiracy theorists compare to the Gilmour incident almost fourteen years earlier, captain Mats Sundin scored what appeared to be a goal off a scramble in front of Isles goalie Rick DiPietro. Standing to the left of the Isles net, Fraser waved it off; Sundin, never one to argue just any call, protested this one profusely.

The scene would have been comical if it wasn't so utterly infuriating. Sundin, almost a foot taller than Fraser, yanked out his mouthguard and passionately stated his case. Fraser didn't budge.

The Leafs, it should be said, blew a two-goal lead and should have won even without the disputed goal. But had Sundin's goal been allowed, it would have restored the Leafs two-goal cushion. Though there was no sure thing in that topsy-turvy season of 2006–07, especially with the unpredictable Andrew Raycroft in goal, Toronto very likely would have won the game had Sundin's goal counted. Instead, New York tied it up during regulation time and the Isles' Randy Robitaille scored the lone shootout goal to win it for his team.

The Leafs' dropped point for losing in a shootout was bad enough. The two points that would have been denied to the Islanders had the Leafs been able to win in regulation time ended up being a killer. That's because New York was able to mount a late-season charge bolstered by picking up Ryan Smyth at the trade deadline a week after the contentious Fraser-officiated game.

Six weeks and twenty-one games later, the Isles edged out the Leafs for the eighth and final playoff spot in the Eastern Conference. The final margin? A single point.

Blessedly, Fraser was never much of a factor as far as the Leafs were concerned for the three seasons that remained of his NHL officiating career.

About two and a half years later, Fraser was playing out the string in what was his final season as an NHL official. The Leafs hosted the Buffalo Sabres on November 30, a Monday night.

The Leafs had been playing fairly decent hockey to that point. Phil Kessel, acquired in a training camp trade though he was recovering from surgery at the time, had been back for close to a month and was the catalyst for some improved play. In fact, the Leafs were riding a mini two-game win streak when the Sabres made the short trip up to Toronto.

The Leafs dominated in every category except for the score sheet as Sabres goalie Ryan Miller turned away thirty-eight shots in an eventual 3–0 shutout victory by Buffalo. Throughout the game, Fraser seemed almost a bit bored with it all.

By this point, Fraser's head had been covered by a helmet for almost four full seasons.[1] Never one to let an opportunity slip by to remind Leafs fans who he was, he skated out at the start of the third period with his helmet in his hands. How we wished his head was still in it.

The sight was a perfect reminder of what we had been subjected to for all those years before he was forced to don a helmet. His hair was immaculate, the sheen of gel visible even to those in the 300 level. The mould of his head looked like someone had placed an old Butch Goring helmet and crazy-glued it to his cranium.

Fraser juggled his helmet in his hands — it looked as if he was doing it to the beat of the music playing — before donning his *chapeau* for the final period.

Fraser was scarcely heard of again as far as the Leafs were concerned, working his final game at the ACC the following April without so much as a peep in the way of official recognition. Not recognizing a long-serving official in his final game in a marquee building was a rarity, but in this case it was completely the right thing, given the anger Fraser still elicits.

But, for me, there was one final indignity. Eleven months later, the Leafs were playing a road game in Philadelphia on October 23, 2010, a Saturday night. The Leafs' 4–0 start that fall had come crashing down, and they were never really in the game against the Flyers, eventually losing 5–2, their third consecutive setback. With Mrs. Robinson and the kiddies safely tucked in to bed, I'd gone downtown to meet a friend. The scene around Front Street was clearly missing the remnants of the hockey crowd that typically added some spice to the atmosphere.

As I had some time to kill as I waited for my friend, I decide to head up to Fionn MacCools, an Irish bar across the street from the Rogers Centre, to watch the late game on *Hockey Night*. As I walked along an unusually quiet street — had it been a typical Leafs Saturday night tilt the hockey hordes would have been cramming the sidewalks — I saw a solitary poster that cried out to be read. It was just north of the intersection of Blue Jays Way and Front Street and had been placed across a temporary wall that guarded a building site despite it being clearly marked "Post No Bills."

As I got closer, I saw it was an advert for Fraser's upcoming book signing. Now retired, Fraser had written *Final Call* about his time in the NHL. It turned out that a meet-and-greet and book signing with Fraser had just taken place, about two hundred metres up the street. At Wayne Gretzky's restaurant. How fitting.

5

CRAIG MUNI'S GHOST

WHAT IS LARRY MURPHY DOING HOISTING THE STANLEY CUP? I MUST still be drunk.

It seems like a lifetime ago, but I will never forget it: Larry Murphy winning the Stanley Cup just months after I had concluded that he was the single most overrated player in the history of the Toronto Maple Leafs.

It was June 1997 and I was in Bangkok, the nerve centre of backpacker travel in Southeast Asia and, as that song from the mid-1980s said, a place that can make you feel really humble. *The Hangover Part II* later detailed how easy it is to forget what happened the night before in that city.

But there was no forgetting the image in front of me: Murphy clad in a Red Wings jersey celebrating winning hockey's Holy Grail with surefire Hall of Famer Steve Yzerman having just accepted the trophy for the very first time.

The alcohol was exiting through my pores, helped along by my angst at what I was witnessing on the television screen and accelerated by the crippling Bangkok heat.

I had left the winter chill in Canada in February, when Murphy was still a Toronto Maple Leaf and an increasingly frustrating presence with every game. Two days before leaving for what turned into an eighteen-month around-the-world sojourn, I had taken in one last Leafs game down at Maple Leaf Gardens: a Leafs–Senators tilt that featured, literally, the two worst teams in the NHL at the time. The Leafs were on a slide, with Pat Burns having been fired the season before and Mike Murphy put in charge of a hockey club that was well past its expiry date. A 2–1 loss to the Sens, with Tie Domi of all people scoring the lone Leafs goal, meant the Leafs were dead last in the NHL.

For me, it was a perfect time to be leaving. Travelling in those days meant leaving behind many habits — mine centred on the fate of the Leafs. The Internet was only in its infancy and live streaming and other online technological advances that could have made it possible to track events back home were still well off.

It had been a good run for the Leafs for a while, with two conference final appearances and four straight playoff showings. But obsessing over how they were going to stem the inevitable decline was getting a bit tedious as I was finishing up my university studies. A few weeks in New Zealand and then in Australia was all it took for me to forget about the Leafs and the various machinations that were taking place back home. I was quickly realizing that the world through the bottom of a pint glass and my reflection in it looked pretty much the same in both New Zealand and Australia as it did in Toronto.

Wanting a bit of a different experience, I flew from Australia to Thailand in the second week of June. I hadn't gone completely cold turkey, though — I had managed to gather very fragmentary information before leaving that the Detroit Red Wings had a 3–0 stranglehold on the Stanley Cup Final over the Philadelphia Flyers. To that point, North American sports wasn't really shown much in the Southern Hemisphere, but I would soon find out that games were, oddly perhaps, widely available in Asia. I arrived in Bangkok between Game 3 and Game 4 and had made the rookie traveller's mistake of miscalculating the time difference by a few hours while trying to pin down when Game 4 would be showing.

When I awoke in Bangkok that morning, instead of arriving at a Khoa Shan Road bar in time for the game, I got there just as Yzerman was being interviewed by Ron MacLean literally minutes after the Wings had won the Cup by sweeping the Flyers. The camera frame showed Stevie Y and MacLean, with Yzerman offering his condolences to Don Cherry, whose wife, Rose, had just died. Murphy and his trademark angular smile were soon peering out of the screen. He looked a little like someone who had crept out onto the ice from the crowd and slipped on a Red Wings jersey, or maybe it just seemed that way, because a few short months before, Murphy winning the Stanley Cup seemed just as impossible.

♣   ♣   ♣

Murphy, Jamie Macoun, and Hal Gill all have drawn the ire of Leafs fans over the past fifteen years or so, ranging from white-hot anger to mere grumpiness at the mention of their names. And all were basically run out of town. All three were defencemen, which, given that they were playing on such bad teams when they fell out of favour, likely offers a hint of why they became the focus of everyone's anger.

But all three also did something else when they left Toronto: they won the Stanley Cup.

It could be that there is a different form of so-called Blue and White disease, the affliction that occurs when certain players suddenly develop a higher opinion of themselves when they end up in Toronto. Perhaps this is a different strain of the same virus, one that paralyzes certain players' abilities and is cured only when they leave town.

There has to be some explanation. I distinctly recall arriving at Maple Leaf Gardens on April 16, 1996, for a Leafs playoff game against the St. Louis Blues. The Leafs had been through a season of turmoil: Pat Burns had been fired and the little-known Nick Beverly had taken over on an interim basis. The Leafs were at the end of their time as a solid NHL team. Doug Gilmour and Wendel Clark had regressed just a hair, but more importantly their supporting cast wasn't nearly as adept at stepping up the way they had in the two previous runs to the Campbell Conference finals. The final standings hadn't been decided until the final game of the season a few nights earlier when the Leafs had beaten the Edmonton Oilers to move all the way up to the conference fourth seed. Heading into that game, there had been some serious questions about whether the Leafs were even going to make the playoffs. Tickets were relatively easy to come by once the final opening-round matchups were set, and I managed to scoop up a pair in the very last row of the greys for the Game 1 opener.

The pall in the arena subsided only briefly when Clark steamrolled over some poor, unfortunate Blues player not long after the puck dropped. But soon after, the Leafs looked to be just a step behind the Blues, who had Wayne Gretzky in their lineup after he had been traded there from the Los Angeles Kings about six weeks before. Gretzky put on a clinic, registering three assists and keying a 3–1 win. The home fans had difficulty accepting the loss because it was hard to face the fact their team simply wasn't good enough after the previous playoff runs that were still fresh in their minds. And so they began searching for a scapegoat.

"Come on down, Larry Murphy."

Before leaving on my trip, the last thoughts I had had of Murphy involved imagining trying to inflict pain on his blond head in order to stop the stress he was causing me as I watched him play for the Leafs. Granted, Murphy was a much better player than, say, Macoun, and he had come to the Leafs after winning the Stanley Cup twice with the Pittsburgh Penguins. Previous to that, Canadian hockey fans had fond memories of him because he helped set up Mario Lemieux when he scored the Canada Cup–clinching goal in 1987. But there was something not quite right about Murphy; though he was a local Toronto lad, he appeared to have picked up something oddly American, or foreign, playing in places such as Los Angeles and Washington. Even though he replaced a Russian — Dmitri Mironov — in the Leafs lineup, there was a sense that he was an outsider, an intruder, not long for Toronto. Murphy just didn't seem to fit with his home city and its fans. It likely had something to do with his salary, as players' paycheques were starting to grow fatter by the mid-1990s and Murphy was making more than $2-million a year. Murphy's play during his first season in Toronto, statistically speaking, was fine, and he notched 61 points, only marginally behind his numbers in Pittsburgh, a club that had much more offensive firepower headed up by Lemieux. But there was something missing. He had been touted as a puck-moving defenceman, which the Leafs had needed even during their impressive playoff runs to the conference final. Murphy, as the point totals suggested, had done okay in that role, but there was also the worrying sight of him looking helplessly behind him as speedier opposition forwards blew past. That image tended to stick out more than the still-impressive offensive game he brought to the table.

Worse, on this early spring night when the Leafs needed him to stop up most, Murphy simply wasn't up to the task, or so it appeared. By the time the Leafs fell behind the Blues, virtually every time he touched the puck, Murphy was booed mightily. I will confess I was not shy in joining in the chorus.

The Murphy–Toronto marriage was destined to not end well. In the next season the Leafs were spiralling out of the playoff race and on their way to the aforementioned cellar. Players such as Gilmour and Dave Andreychuk had already been dealt away before Murphy headed down to Detroit.

And now here I was watching the aftermath in an exotic locale that seemed just as foreign as the thought of Murphy becoming a Stanley Cup champion again. Given that the Leafs were never going to win anything that spring, it just seemed, well, annoying that Murphy got the opportunity to leave Toronto unscathed. Worse, the fact he kind of slid into such a good situation in Detroit after failing to prevent such a bad one in Leafs-land was enough to make you want to punch Murphy's lights out.

On the other hand, Bob Rouse had joined the Red Wings three years earlier and was long embedded on their blue line, so it was both not surprising and even a bit gratifying to see the dependable former Leaf on the television screen that day in Bangkok.

A year later, both Murphy and Rouse acquired a third member of the former Leafs club: Jamie Macoun. I was back in Southeast Asia, this time in Bali, watching it all unfold on television again. Like Bangkok, Bali's charms are extensive, not the least of which are the liberal cultural norms and wide abundance of sports (and other things) available. I was in Kuta Beach in an Irish pub watching the Red Wings take control of the Western Conference final over Dallas. (Four years later the same pub was the site of a "diversion" bomb to the massive one that killed more than two hundred people just up the street at the Sari Club.)

Courtesy of Getty Images.

LARRY MURPHY (LEFT) AND JAMIE MACOUN BOTH LEFT THE MAPLE LEAFS AND IMMEDIATELY WON A STANLEY CUP WITH DETROIT. THIS PICTURE SEEMED UNIMAGINABLE EIGHTEEN MONTHS BEFORE IT WAS TAKEN IN 1998.

Watching with me was a Kiwi friend, Mark, a car salesman from Wellington who had never been out of New Zealand before. To say he was caught up in the moment of being on the lash in Southeast Asia was like saying I was gobsmacked that Macoun, whom I honestly believed to be the worst defenceman in the NHL when I left Canada eighteen months earlier, was on the verge of winning the Stanley Cup. During the past year, I had gleaned through agate type in Australian newspapers that Macoun had ended up in Detroit. As much as I disliked Murphy, I positively hated Macoun. As I looked up at the screen, it was surreal he could be playing a key role on a team well on its way to another Stanley Cup win. It was him all right, right down to the cookie duster moustache.

"That guy looks like my dad's mate," said Mark, when I pointed out Macoun and the reason for my disbelief. "And I say his mate because my mom would have never let my dad wear a moustache like that."

Back before I had left on my trip, Macoun's tendency to cross-check the living daylights out of opposing forwards had become even more painful for Leafs fans than it was for the unfortunate players on the receiving end of them. A good stay-at-home defenceman since arriving as part of the Gilmour trade in 1992, Macoun appeared to have made the decision to wear flippers instead of skates — he slowed down almost overnight. His laying the lumber on opponents was no longer oddly endearing. That's because the cross-checks seemed to be coming more and more frequently just as the soon-to-be-injured opposition forward was scoring a goal.

The cross-checking just topped it all off. Back in Macoun's time with the Leafs, a defenceman had to know the black art of using his stick for something other than shooting or passing. Macoun learned the craft perhaps better than any defenceman in the NHL and it was a central feature of his more than 1,100 games. It was an amazing run for a kid who grew up just north of Toronto and didn't even get drafted by an NHL team.

By that point in his career, Macoun was so stay-at-home he barely crossed over centre ice into the opposition zone. It was also long before Movember made it acceptable for thirty days a year to adorn your upper lip with hair, especially when it lacked the charm of Lanny McDonald's legendary 'tache. Despite winning a Stanley Cup with the Calgary Flames in 1989, Macoun was not an agreeable sight on the ice either, as his natural skating stride made him look like a disabled car heading for the exits of a demolition derby.

Your typical hockey fan, especially in Toronto, is generally not interested in the folly of blaming defencemen for all things bad when teams start to slip. That's especially true when you're talking about a man who isn't exactly easy on the eyes. In fact, Macoun had the faint appearance of dressing up for Halloween but being caught equidistant between Tom Selleck and Ned Flanders.

That Macoun and Murphy became lightning rods for criticism was understandable, because fans tend to want to apportion blame when things aren't going well. But the fact that so many out-of-favour Leafs moved on and often did very well when they appeared to be on their last legs in Toronto is a phenomenon that has had me screaming Craig Muni's name since the late 1980s.

"Jamie Macoun is the worst defenceman in the NHL," said a young kid of about seventeen beside me during my last game at the Gardens before I left on my trip. It was just one of thousands of comments I've heard from people around me in my time attending Leafs games. Most are instantly forgotten, but I've always remembered this particular barb because I had attempted to defend Macoun before the young man convinced me otherwise. That sentiment stuck with me and the negative thoughts never left me after watching live that night how much Macoun struggled to keep up with an Ottawa team that wasn't exactly flush with talent.

Bali's famous Arak drink tends to blur the lines between reality and fiction. That afternoon, watching the grainy television pictures of the three former Leafs well on their way to winning the Stanley Cup, I poured back the Arak to keep myself from crying. I was spurred on by the liberal amounts of beverage, the game, and Murphy, Macoun, and Rouse's presence in it, and so I decided it was time for a mental overview of what had happened to the Leafs over the past two seasons since I had been away.

Burns's long-ago firing had confirmed that the jig was up for that wonderful group of Leafs players that had gotten to two conference finals, even if I was still in denial before I left Canada. It's perhaps logical that a few players are suddenly cast in the role of heel, as Macoun and Murphy were by the frustrated masses. But for one of the game's greatest coaches, Scotty Bowman, to find a use for them, and then go on to win the Stanley Cup? Had you told the average Maple Leafs fan that night at the Gardens in 1996 that Macoun and Murphy were going to be hoisting hockey's premier trophy over their heads, you would have been asked where you bought such effective medicinal enhancements, something far more powerful than Arak.

Holy, shit, this guy thinks both Murphy and Macoun are going to win the Stanley Cup — where in the hell is he getting his gear from?

Not only did it happen, it happened twice for Murphy.

Sitting in that sweltering Bali bar in the midday heat, I allowed myself dark moments of anger just recalling their names. At the time they were still two playoff rounds away from sipping champagne together out of the Stanley Cup, but the foreboding was thick in my mind.

It remains one of the great confounding mysteries how two men were so despised in the centre of the hockey universe where they both grew up, only to travel a relatively short distance down Highway 401, over the Ambassador Bridge, and suddenly ceased being, well, useless.

Scotty Bowman really is a genius.

Bowman was not involved in what followed a little more than a decade later, but Hal Gill also offered an interesting study in how a guy can spend large amounts of time in Toronto looking, well, like a taller version of Macoun *sans* moustache. Gill was a likable enough guy. Towering over everyone — 6'7", 250ish pounds — he moved precisely as you would expect someone of those dimensions would. Brought in by John Ferguson Jr. in 2006 to try to upgrade a team that had missed the playoffs the previous year for the first time since the fire sale that saw both Murphy and then Macoun leave, there was no way the lumbering Gill was going to somehow transform himself into something he had never been up to that point in his almost decade-long NHL career. But don't tell that to Leafs fans. Gill wasn't so much disliked in Toronto as he was discounted. When you're playing for a bad team — and this precise point could have applied to Macoun ten years earlier — steady, yeoman's work at the back end isn't appreciated. It's especially not appreciated when your one enduring image is that of a hulking beast helplessly chasing faster opposition forwards in your own zone. Gill was a taller version of Macoun without the cross-checks.

To be fair, Gill did okay killing penalties and taking a regular shift, but he sometimes handled the puck as though it was a hand grenade. Though even the very best defencemen are bound to make the occasional bobble in their own zone, Gill's share of them seemed to come only in the games that the Leafs desperately needed to win — like the one on December 5, 2006, against the Atlanta Thrashers, when Gill wore the goat horns in a game that the Leafs should have won easily. The Leafs were up 2–0 heading into the third period against a team that was showing signs of slowly breaking out of its expansion funk but certainly wasn't there yet. The Thrashers scored five third-period goals, taking a pin to the fragile air of anticipation inside the Air Canada Centre. The eventual 5–2 loss saw Gill managing a gaggle of giveaways and ill-timed penalties. From my seat in the first row of the greens, my despair was broken up by a little boy of about seven or eight nudging me out of the way in order to lean over the balcony with two thumbs down while booing the Leafs.

The lumbering Gill continued to trudge around his own zone for little more than a year before he was dealt by Cliff Fletcher to the Pittsburgh Penguins for a second-round pick. Gill looked every bit as awkward in Pittsburgh but strangely was much more competent than in Toronto. He filled a solid depth role for the Penguins for the remaining season-plus he played there. His forty-four playoff appearances in Pittsburgh were two more than he had to that point in his career and exceeded by forty-four how many post-season games he played for the Leafs. Gill, like Macoun and Murphy before him, soon hoisted the Stanley Cup. For Gill, it came after his second season in Pittsburgh, and he'd even played a key role in the Pens getting to the final the previous year.

Where does Craig Muni fit into this? Well, the Toronto native grew up around the same time as Macoun and Murphy. A year younger than those two, he was drafted by the Leafs twenty-fifth overall in 1980, twenty-one picks after Murphy was taken by the Los Angeles Kings (Macoun was passed over in the same draft). He never broke in with the Leafs, who instead were concentrating their efforts on ruining the careers of young defencemen Jim Benning and Fred Boimistruck, while others such as Jim Korn, Bob McGill, and Gary Nylund barely managed to escape Harold Ballard's zoo with their careers intact. Lucky for Muni he played just nineteen games for the Leafs and was signed by the Edmonton Oilers in 1986. When he got to Edmonton he stepped right into a lineup that included Wayne Gretzky, Mark Messier, and Paul Coffey and which had just won its second consecutive Stanley Cup. Muni was part of the Oilers third and fourth straight triumphs and stayed on when Edmonton won another in 1990 without Gretzky, who had been traded to Los Angeles by that time.

Muni, of course, wasn't good enough to play for the Leafs in the 1980s, a time when they were one of the NHL's worst teams. They let him go to Edmonton for nothing.

And what did the Leafs get in return for dealing Murphy, Macoun, and Gill many years later? Alex Ponikarovsky is the only prospect or draft pick that even played for the team.

6

INTERNATIONAL WALLFLOWERS

It's doubtful that many Toronto Maple Leafs fans gave either of the two separate events of Tuesday, December 14, 2010, a second thought. That night the Leafs beat the Edmonton Oilers on the road to record their second consecutive victory and twenty-eighth point of the season. It left the team with a 12–14–4 record, or roughly the same winning percentage the club could be expected to have during much of their prolonged walk through the wilderness in the post-lockout era.

But there was a significant event that *did* happen to two Leafs prospects earlier that day. It was symbolic of a malaise that has plagued the club for ages. Jesse Blacker and Brad Ross, both Leafs draft picks, were sent packing from the final evaluation camp of the Canadian world junior team. Blacker, a defenceman then playing for the Owen Sound Attack, and Ross, a pesky Portland Winterhawks forward, received the dreaded early-morning phone call in their hotel room that comes along with being cut. They were sent home during the first round of cuts after a few days of practices and intrasquad games at MasterCard Centre of Excellence, a west Toronto rink that, of all things, is also the Maple Leafs practice venue.

Two teenage prospects being let go from their World Junior team is no big deal, right? Maybe it's not important if viewed in the context of that one year. But it becomes quite relevant when you take the wider view and realize how often the Leafs simply don't measure up when it comes to hockey competitions such as the World Juniors, Olympics, and Canada/World Cups.

The World Juniors tends to be a good barometer of a prospect's future because if a young player is on his way to becoming an elite professional, there is a very good chance that he will play in at least one World Junior Championship. Because the tournament is generally regarded as a tournament for nineteen-year-olds and players are typically drafted in the year they turn eighteen, their prime opportunity to play for their country comes in the season or two after they are selected by an NHL club. Therefore, the evaluation process that players go through to make their respective teams also serves as an unofficial report card on NHL clubs' scouting departments.

Though not a hard-and-fast analysis, it's a pretty good way to grade the job NHL teams are doing drafting players. And based on the results from the past twenty years, the Maple Leafs have not done well. There has been one exception in the relatively recent past — Halifax, 2003. Canada had a good team that year, eventually finishing second, losing 3–2 to Russia in the gold medal game — a fair result from a Canadian perspective, but also if you were a Leafs fan. The rights to five players who played key roles for Canada — Brendan Bell, Carlo Colaiacovo, Matt Stajan, Kyle Wellwood, and Ian White — were owned by the club. All five eventually made the Leafs roster over the next few seasons. In fact, both Colaiacovo and White could now be called quality NHL defencemen, though they became that type of player *after* leaving Toronto.

Aside from that one year, there remains another one when the Leafs were well represented by two different goaltenders, but the way things eventually shook out nullified any potential benefit. It was 2006 and the two best goaltenders at the World Junior that year belonged to the Leafs: Team Canada's Justin Pogge and Finland's Tuukka Rask. Eventually, Rask was dealt for Andrew Raycroft, and Pogge never developed into the solid NHL goaltender the Leafs thought he might. The Leafs general manager at the time, John Ferguson Jr., gambled that Pogge was the better of the two prospects and it blew up in his face. Go figure.

Aside from 2003 and 2006, the Leafs' representation on the Canadian squad has been pretty thin. A cynic watching the action that took place in Alberta in 2012 could snicker and point out that Canadian defenceman Dougie Hamilton should have been Leafs property — he was selected by the Boston Bruins with one of the two first-round picks that Toronto sent to Beantown in the Phil Kessel trade.

And what about Leafs prospects playing for other nations? Well, it's not much better. During the 2012 World Juniors played in Calgary and Edmonton, the Leafs had but a single prospect, Swedish defenceman Petter Granberg, a solid if unspectacular player who eventually won gold with the rest of his teammates. In fact, Granberg was on the ice when countryman Mika Zibanejad scored the overtime winner against Russia. As a result, Granberg's image was widely shown on highlights and in newspaper and website pictures in the aftermath of Sweden's first gold medal at the event in some thirty years. Zibanejad, who belonged to the Ottawa Senators, is a much brighter prospect, but at least Granberg was able to bask in the glow of his much more celebrated teammate.

In the past three decades of World Junior tournaments, Colaiacovo and Swedish defenceman Kenny Jonsson are the only elite World Junior performers whose rights were owned by the Leafs during the competition who remained with the Leafs to start their NHL careers. Jonsson, like Colaiacovo, became a very solid NHL player, but he, too, was traded away, in the move that brought Wendel Clark back to Toronto in 1996.

Two other defencemen whom the Leafs owned the rights to — Finn Janne Gronvall and Swede Pierre Hedin — played well enough to earn World Junior all-star honours at two different tournaments in the 1990s. But neither ended up playing regularly in the NHL. Hedin had his moments, but as a smallish, slick defenceman, he came along at a time when the NHL game, and especially Pat Quinn, the Leafs coach at the time, demanded much bigger players. After a year of playing on the Leafs' AHL affiliate in St. John's, no doubt puzzled at the Newfoundlanders' accents just as much as the Leafs' indifference at playing him on the big club, Hedin hightailed it back to Sweden. Not exactly the big one that got away, but Hedin's story could have been different had he come along a few years later.

All told, if you accept the premise that the World Juniors tend to identify the best teenage hockey players in the world, the Leafs have acted like a middle-aged schoolteacher with little or no interest in the best and brightest pupils before him; at very least, they've done an incredibly bad job identifying them.

And that's just the World Juniors. The Leafs' contribution to other elite world hockey competition has been just as modest. The lone significant NHL tournament where the Maple Leafs had a wide representation was at the 2002 Winter Olympic Games in Salt Lake City when Toronto hit the proverbial mother lode: Curtis Joseph (Canada), Tomas Kaberle (Czech Republic), Alex Ponikarovsky (Ukraine), Robert Reichel (Czech Republic), Mikael Renberg, Mats Sundin, and Mikael Tellqvist (all Sweden) represented their respective countries; Alex Mogilny would have played for Russia had he not been hurt just before the NHL schedule broke for the Olympics. Aside from that rather impressive contingent, Maple Leafs' involvement in other significant tournaments has been rather modest.

Of course, both Leafs and Team Canada fans of a certain age will never forget Paul Henderson's Summit Series winner in 1972 or Darryl Sittler's goal four years later in the Canada Cup. Both men played for Toronto at the time of those dramatic tournament-clinching goals.

Much has changed in the international arena since the 1970s; the world game is now a much more mature and different beast and it has left Leafs players largely out in the cold. The result? When a major competition is going on, Toronto fans can sit back and watch dreamy-eyed. Those taking part are almost assuredly not Maple Leafs.

Aside from the Henderson and Sittler examples cited above, the most memorable Canadian hockey moments of recent times are any combination of the three Canada Cup triumphs between 1984 and 1991 and the two Olympic gold medals won by the men's team in 2002 and 2010. Non-Canadian triumphs in that era of note: the U.S. victory in the 1996 World Cup of Hockey and the Czech and Swedish triumphs at the 1998 and 2006 Olympics, respectively. Leafs involvement? Aside from Sundin's pivotal role in Sweden's long-overdue win, that sound you're hearing is crickets (defenceman Aki Berg played for 2006 silver-medal winners, Finland).

Even the U.S. "Miracle on Ice" team, a squad that later sent so many players to the NHL after winning Olympic gold at Lake Placid in 1980, had nary a Leafs prospect on it.

But there is a quaint ritual that takes place at the Air Canada Centre after successful World Junior tournaments and also after the Salt Lake Olympics. It's the honouring at centre ice of the returning Canadian heroes, gold medals draped around their necks. The glint from the gold baubles almost takes the sting from the salt in the wounds being felt as the players are introduced. On many occasions during Canada's World Junior run of gold medals from 2005 to 2009, Leafs fans were even forced to endure more than a few young Canucks walking out to centre ice knowing full well that (1) this kid is going to be beating us some day (see Richards, Mike) and (2) prospects like these kids are what *other* teams have, not us.

But, like so much of the Leafs history, even when there are rare moments to celebrate, there is almost always an asterisk, a tinge of the bittersweet. For example, in 2002, when Curtis Joseph was

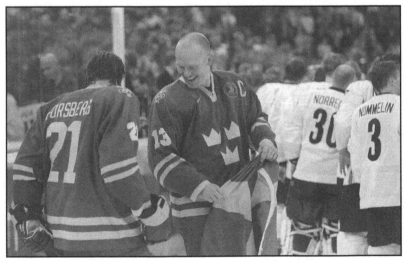

Courtesy of Getty Images.

MATS SUNDIN NEVER WON A STANLEY CUP, BUT HE LED SWEDEN TO THE 2006 OLYMPIC GOLD MEDAL. SUNDIN'S ROLE IN THAT VICTORY IS THE MOST NOTABLE INTERNATIONAL PERFORMANCE BY A LEAF SINCE DARRYL SITTLER'S 1976 CANADA CUP WINNING GOAL.

honoured for returning from Salt Lake City with his Olympic gold medal, and then-Maple Leafs head coach Pat Quinn was likewise feted for his masterful job leading the boys wearing that *other* Maple Leaf to victory.

Joseph had been given the starter's job in Salt Lake — a questionable move given the small matter of Martin Brodeur's multiple Stanley Cup victories in New Jersey and the fact he had beaten Joseph the previous two springs in head-to-head playoff battles. Giving his netminder in Toronto the nod over a player as accomplished as Brodeur showed remarkable loyalty by Quinn. One problem: Cujo got funnelled almost from the moment the puck was dropped in the first game versus Sweden. The Swedes, chock full of their so-called golden generation, all in their prime in 2002, shook off an early allowed goal and made Canada look like, well, sorry Swedish hockey fans, Belarus.

The images of Sundin running roughshod over a Canadian team coached by Quinn and with Joseph in goal was about as surreal as hockey played in June at the ACC. Joseph, Quinn, and Sundin were the three key cogs in what was one of the best post-1967 Maple Leafs

Courtesy of Graig Abel.

CURTIS JOSEPH RARELY BECAME UNHINGED IN TORONTO, BUT HE WAS ALSO NEVER COMFORTABLE IN TEAM CANADA'S NET DURING THE 2002 OLYMPICS AND LOST THE STARTING JOB. HIS PERFORMANCE LIKELY HAS-TENED HIS EXIT FROM THE LEAFS.

teams, and now they were opposing one another, with the Swedish captain helping turn Quinn's exterior so red that the big Irishman appeared as if he was about to explode.

It all worked out, of course. Canada found its stride a few days later, Sweden fell to the aforementioned Belarus, and Quinn eventually led the team to an extremely memorable gold medal win over the U.S. with Cujo firmly stuck to the bench and Brodeur between the pipes.

Back in Toronto, both men went to collect their congratulations, and the awkward moment at centre ice had the feeling of father and son running into each other in the coat check of a strip joint.

It wasn't Quinn's fault. He gave his guy a chance and he failed to do anything with it. When Brodeur was given his long-overdue opportunity, he ran with it and helped the country win its first men's hockey gold in fifty years. Joseph? Though his character was never in question — the man has never lost his humble appeal — it was plainly obvious that if he could have kept his mask on that night, he would have.

In the end, the Leafs dispatched Carolina in the game following the ceremony — ironic, because it was precisely the same Hurricanes who defeated the Leafs in six games in the Eastern Conference final later that spring. Joseph played well both during the first game back and the rest of the season, but then left for greener pastures, signing with Detroit because he felt they offered him a better chance to win a Stanley Cup. Well, umm, of course, but Cujo never won a Cup in the Motor City like so many former Leafs had done previously.

And so there you have it. What should, or could have been a crowning moment for the Maple Leafs and their fans — celebrating an Olympic gold medal, the pursuit of which had gripped both the city and country for a fortnight — only hastened the exit of arguably the team's best player; certainly its best puck-stopper in the post-1967 era. The prolonged melodrama that played out from March through to early July was a little like watching your cute ex-girlfriend leave town with an aging rock star because she couldn't get along with your dad.

There was an instance of that niggling feeling of discord in the ACC on the night after another major competition. March 2, 2010, offered no touchstone moments in the history of the Toronto Maple Leafs franchise. But it did remind its fans how completely and utterly inferior the team was that year relative to the action that had taken place during the previous two weeks. The Vancouver Olympics were about as proud a moment not involving military action that Canada has ever felt. It was like celebrating New Year's for seventeen consecutive days, the hangover part nicely taken care of by a bunch of golden Caesars that Canadian athletes kept on serving up.

The Leafs, of course, had an understated role in the events of the men's hockey competition. The chief decision-makers for the Leafs, general manager Brian Burke and head coach Ron Wilson, had the same roles for the U.S. team. This was just as bizarre then as it seems now. If an alien had descended from outer space in the lead-up to the Games, he would have been excused for thinking that earthlings had an odd sense of fair play.

"Wait," you could almost imagine an alien saying, "how come the head coach and the GM from one of the NHL's worst teams are in charge of one of the best national teams? And the same two guys also run a Canadian NHL team even though they are American and putting together the American team at the biggest hockey event to ever take place in Canada?"

Well, yes, of course, and those two men did a fabulous job for their country. If only they could have replicated that success with their day jobs in Toronto (Wilson, we now know, paid with his job for not even coming close). Wilson — the memory must still haunt him — showed why he is considered a good hockey coach everywhere else but Toronto by leading the Americans to within a hair's breadth of the gold medal. But, thank God, Canada prevailed.

Two days after the overtime final won by Canada 3–2, Wilson was back behind the bench for a Leafs home game versus — no kidding — Carolina again. Even if you don't like Ron Wilson, you couldn't fault him if he'd thought he had been kidnapped and placed behind the Leafs bench. He wasn't, of course, and his personal coaching nightmare resumed in a Tuesday night encounter that will not be remembered for the ages. In Vancouver, Wilson had Zach Parise, Patrick Kane, Ryan Kesler, Bobby Ryan, and Ryan Suter at his disposal, along with many others of the world's elite, including the best goaltender on the planet at the time in Ryan Miller. Back at his regular gig, Wilson had the luxury of Colton Orr, Jamie Lundmark, Freddy Sjostrom, Christian Hanson, and Garnet Exelby. Wilson must have felt like he had driven home in a Ferrari and woken up with a Ford Pinto in the garage.

The Leafs did their level best to make their coach and general manager feel right at home again, which is to say that they played like complete donkeys, losing 5–1 and eliciting a number of sarcastic barbs from Wilson to the media after the game. Under normal circumstances, the game was about as exciting as you would expect from a mid-week tilt between two non-playoff teams coming off a long break. When compared to events of the previous seventeen days, it was like seventeen years of uninterrupted white noise.

"Welcome home, coach. Are you happy to see that things haven't changed?"

But the game had a modestly entertaining side story playing out while the Leafs were getting their hats handed to them. Ponikarovsky, who had played for the Ukraine two long-ago Olympic cycles earlier, was announced as one of the pre-game scratches. As much angst as Ponikarovsky contributed to the collective mindset of Leafs fans over the years — he never fulfilled the potential hung on him for almost a decade — it was clear something was up. The trade deadline loomed a couple days hence and the big Ukrainian's pending free agent status after the season made him prime trade bait. A few fans in my section — 311 greens — were dutifully trolling the Internet on their hand-held devices to try to get a hint of any tangible action involving Ponikarovsky. It turned out the big lunk had been dealt to the Pittsburgh Penguins.

The return? A local kid named Luca Caputi.

Two days after watching the most thrilling Team Canada game of the modern era, talk suddenly switched to a trade involving a player who was a decade-long "what-if" as a Maple Leaf and a kid who, as it turned out, played just twenty-six games for them.

Only in Toronto.

7

CREATING MORE LEAFS FANS

MAKE BABIES OR WATCH THE HOCKEY GAME? CAN'T YOU DO BOTH?

No, this isn't some crude rehash of the old joke about a certain sexual position and still being able to watch *Hockey Night in Canada*. It involves having secured Leafs tickets on the same night your wife's meticulous charting tells her that she's likely ovulating.

Now that's a conflict.

Ask any couple who want to have children — it doesn't just involving snapping their fingers. The whole process can be a bit stressful. Ask the male half of that coupling just how stressful when it also involves planning around the Leafs, and, if his wife were within earshot, the answer may permanently impair his ability to produce children.

The night was February 20, 2007, and the Leafs were in a futile struggle to get into a playoff spot in the Eastern Conference. The Boston Bruins were in town and trailing the Leafs in the chase to get inside the top eight teams.

It was an important night not only at the Air Canada Centre but also at a nicely appointed semi-detached starter home in Toronto's west end, where the Robinsons hung their shingle at the time. Earlier that day, my frantic searching on the Internet had produced two tickets for the pending Leafs–Bruins tilt. A $160-something-plus-fees purchase was allayed by colleague and good friend Jason Logan, who was willing to pick up his share of the tab. Arrangements were made to meet on the Jane Station subway platform in time to get downtown for a few prime-the-pump pints and what was supposed to be a spirited tilt, a rarity for mid-week games.

The only pending obligation to that point was to walk my dad's dog, who was a house guest while my father was travelling. Aussie, the four-legged family member, was his usual accommodating self, bounding through our neighbourhood with that canine smile only yellow Labradors are capable of. He was just happy that someone was paying attention to him. To be honest, though, I wasn't really paying that much attention to him at all — I was distracted and just wanted to get downtown.

Heading back up the driveway, Aussie was pulling me along, knowing a treat waited at the other side of our side door. Little did I know that there was also something waiting for me on the other side of that door.

Now, Mrs. Robinson has endured a tremendous amount of impulsive activity on her husband's part since shortly after we met in the summer of 2000. (True story: we met at my family reunion — she was there as a guest of my cousin and *is not* an actual relative.)

Our first date a few days later included three table changes, ostensibly because the sun was in my eyes. In reality, I was so nervous, I needed to get out of the sun because I was paranoid that she would notice I was sweating (my sunglasses would have solved the sun issue but remained tucked nicely inside a pocket so as not to give away my ruse).

She didn't notice a thing. The date went well, as did subsequent ones. I think she even started to like me. Poor woman.

We were married in November 2003. The Leafs were in the midst of a western trip and tied the San Jose Sharks 2–2 on our wedding night. The marriage got off to a good start: she said all the right things about my wedding speech, in which I made reference to not having children until the Leafs win the Stanley Cup.

But it soon became obvious that if I didn't want to be an old, grey, angry Leafs fan with no offspring, I'd better reconsider. So, in the fall of 2006 I accepted that I should drop the precondition and get down to the brass tacks of procreation.

But some of that impulsive behaviour started to pop up: buying Leafs tickets. I had always been a fan and went to several games a year. Now I was going to dozens of them. Aside from the occasional raised eyebrow, my wife took it all in stride and was happy to offer the occasional shoulder to cry on when I came home slightly annoyed and slightly inebriated.

In spite of, or perhaps because of, my Leafs habit, the attempt-at-pregnancy thing wasn't quite as easy as slipping down to the Air Canada Centre. Trying was all good fun for the first few months, until we realized we didn't have the same biological makeup of teenagers on reality TV.

More substantial methods were undertaken. And that took some of the fun out of it, to be honest. Suddenly the normally enjoyable business of trying to create babies became more, well, robotic. Like math class without your clothes on. Charting, temperature-taking.

Mrs. Robinson spent increasing amounts of time with her nose in a massive book that reminded me of a university textbook I wouldn't dare think of reading, even in university. The book, and my wife's head stuck in it, became a ubiquitous presence around our house. She also took to visiting websites that made the whole business seem more like a chemistry project.

Things were starting to get a bit testy, and my normally easy-going better half suddenly had one rule: if it was *time*, it didn't matter what was going on, I had to drop everything I was doing and take action.

I distinctly recall adjusting my work schedule and, gasp, missing the occasional shinny skate to stick around the house waiting for *that* time. There were even times when I suggested a practice run but she waved me off in order not to spoil things when she entered the fertility red zone.

So, as the clock ticked just past five o'clock on the day in question, Mrs. Robinson suddenly struck *that* look just as Aussie pounced for a dog biscuit.

Talk about a dilemma.

On the one hand, Leafs tickets in my pocket, a ravenous animal tethered to my arm, and an oblivious friend on the verge of arriving on the subway platform several hundred metres up the road, and on the other, my wife before me, who never makes any unreasonable demands, with the temerity to demand sex. Right then.

The horror.

I took one look at Mrs. Robinson, another at Aussie, and I knew that I'd better be on my game.

And quick.

❦   ❦   ❦

I got to the subway about five minutes late.

Jason and I had worked together for many years at *SCOREGolf*, where he was that publication's managing editor. He's a fine wordsmith in the sense that he can polish others' work and he's pretty handy with his own pen. He doesn't suffer fools to the point that he can be a bit on the grumpy side with dunderhead colleagues and late friends. And I was often both.

This time, however, I managed to mutter something about being confused about where I was to meet him — the concourse of Jane Station or the actual platform — and he accepted the oversight. We caught the next train, and to this day he is unaware of the conundrum I faced a half-hour earlier. To him, it was just another trip down to the ACC.

That night, the Leafs buzzed all over the place, firing forty-four shots at the net occupied by Bruins goalie Tim Thomas, but not a single one got past the burly Michigander. The Bruins didn't have nearly as tough a task slipping the disc past their former teammate Andrew Raycroft, who is as bean-pole skinny as Thomas is squat.

It's amazing that Raycroft managed to accomplish three things during his two short seasons in Toronto. The first is that he won thirty-seven games his first season, which is technically a share of the team record with Ed Belfour. In reality, Raycroft won three games in shootouts, which weren't used as a method of breaking ties when Belfour was a Leaf.

Raycroft's second great accomplishment is that he still makes Leaf fans' ears burn at the thought of how he was handed the starting job in 2006–07 in order to validate the trading away of hotshot prospect Tuukka Rask. Completely incapable of stealing a win, or even standing firm in the crease in a key game, Raycroft was among the statistical minnows at his position. During his so-called record-tying season, most Leafs followers will tell you they have more memories of him looking forlornly over his shoulder at a puck that escaped his timely attention, or with his baseball cap affixed to his head, sitting on the bench, after being pulled.

The last great achievement of Raycroft is that he managed to make a folk hero out of a man named Jean-Sebastien Aubin. Aubin was a career journeyman who had put together an inexplicable 9–0–2 run when he took over the starter's job a season earlier when Belfour was hurt and Mikael Tellqvist wasn't up to the job. Aubin earned a contract extension but Raycroft was anointed the starter when he arrived in town without really earning it. Aubin was forced to sit and wait for opportunities such as the one he was about to get on this night.

With Raycroft playing against his old team, it was obvious the Bruins knew how to pick him apart, and by the start of the third period, his rear end was fastened as tightly to the Leafs bench as the customary cap was on his head.

The Leafs lost 3–0, even though they grossly outplayed the Bruins. They missed the playoffs that season by a single point, and the loss that night was one of a handful that could be identified as crucial setbacks.

But the Robinson household had something else to look forward to that spring, even if there was to be no playoff hockey. Baby number one was on its way. In due course the dizzying whirl that is life for young couples expecting for the first time confirmed that my balancing act on that February night really was a job well done. Even though the Leafs were shutout that night, I had managed to break one past the goalie.

❧   ❧   ❧

Throughout the spring and summer, Mrs. Robinson tastefully turned down all the Leafs and hockey references for baby names that

I put forward: Borje, Dougie, Wendel, Quinn, Lanny, and Darryl were complete non-starters as far as my wife was concerned, even as nominal middle names.

Now, the stretch run in any pregnancy can be a bit challenging. And it's a helluva lot more challenging when the expectant father has to constantly face up to the fact that no team with an Andrew Raycroft/Vesa Toskala goalie tandem is going to be winning many hockey games.

Leafs GM John Ferguson, knowing full well that Raycroft wasn't going to lead the team anywhere but to his own firing, had traded for Toskala that spring. The transaction saw the Leafs deal draft picks for the Finnish goaltender, as well as Mark Bell, who came with baggage all his own.

As the season started, I knew I had a narrow window to file down to the ACC as much as possible before Mrs. Robinson became too heavy with child. Like all Leafs fans, I ignored reality and hoped against all common sense that the team would be better that year.

C'mon, they missed the playoffs by a single point and have made some improvements in goal and elsewhere, what's not to love?

I was looking past reality a bit on the home front, as well, as thoughts of fatherhood were making my head spin. My wife seemed to think there was a race on to get the nursery done by the end of summer even though the baby wasn't due until November 30. I shamelessly went along with the plan, knowing that a finished baby's room meant more time watching the Leafs, both at home and at the ACC.

As she has done so many times, my wife surprised me with how easy-going she was about both her own situation and my Leafs habit. Included in that wonderful quality was her blessing on my trip to Montreal about a month before the baby was due, under what I realize now was a mistaken belief that the time to get back home from there was less than it would take the wee lad to come into the world if she unexpectedly went into labour while I was away. She didn't, but had she, my son would have been born when I was only about halfway home by car — that's how quick the little rip eventually came into the world.

The trip was wonderful. Liberal amounts of the wine and beer that always seems to taste just a bit better in Montreal were on offer. Most of all, the Leafs stole one at the Bell Centre when Matt Stajan scored on a third-period dribbler that Habs goalie Cristobal Huet should have had. The scene outside the arena that night and later on Rue St. Catherine was a festive one for all the fans in blue and white.

Back home, with a promise to limit my Leafs addiction to the television until our offspring arrived, it took me exactly one week to violate my pledge. I convinced my brother-in-law to bring my sister down from their suburban Toronto home to ours. Once they'd arrived, and just as Mrs. Robinson was giving a tour of the nursery, I mysteriously produced a pair of Leafs tickets. The boys took their leave while the girls stayed at home to do whatever it is that women do on Saturday nights when *Hockey Night and Canada* isn't mandated on the television.

And from that point onward, one of the most frustrating Leafs stretches followed. It started with an overtime loss to the New York Rangers, when for what seemed like the 11,246th time, a Toronto-born player came back home and scored the game-clinching goal. This time it was Brendan Shanahan, who ripped a shootout winner past Toskala. If that weren't bad enough, two other Toronto-area products played key roles: Steve Valiquette was in goal and super-pest Sean Avery scored once and added an assist.

Two incredibly annoying mid-week games against the Montreal Canadiens followed. I was fresh from gaining a dubious pass for the weekend game against the Rangers, and my wife was suddenly not bothered at all at the thought of me going to others, provided I kept my cell phone handy and my beer intake to a minimum. It was now mid-November and the baby was due at the end of the month.

The first game against the Habs on November 13 marked the beginning of the end for Bryan McCabe in Toronto. The Leafs defenceman, already the target of plenty of fan angst, tried to make an ill-advised pass to Nikolai Antropov in overtime. No less a plow horse than Mike Komisarek — who switched jerseys a couple of years later — intercepted the puck. In what seemed like an eternity,

Komisarek made his way to the Leafs' goal, scoring on a weak attempt that Raycroft should have easily stopped.

The next day after my own hockey game, a despondent group of physically exhausted rec league players tried to tackle the emotionally exhausting topic of the present state of the Leafs. To that point they had won seven of nineteen games and Ferguson's off-season acquisition of Toskala, Bell, and Jason Blake weren't looking so clever. Blake had been diagnosed with a form of leukemia in training camp but one that was, thankfully, treatable. Moreover, Jiri Tlusty, one of few decent young players the Leafs had in their system had just been identified as the naked person in a grainy image circulating around the dark recesses of the Internet. Just nineteen, Tlusty had sent the pic to a girlfriend the previous year, and the teenage indiscretion had come back to bite him.

Not to be outdone, Bell was making his return from a league-mandated suspension for being involved in an alcohol-related car crash the previous summer. Ferguson had gambled and lost that the NHL would not suspend Bell for long. That gamble went about as well as some of Ferguson's other rolls of the dice, and Bell was

Courtesy of Getty Images.

HAMPERED BY INJURIES THAT REQUIRED SURGERY, VESA TOSKALA NEVER QUITE FOUND HIS FORM IN TORONTO. THE 2007 TRADE THAT BROUGHT HIM TO TORONTO FROM SAN JOSE WAS ONE OF THE MOVES THAT COST JOHN FERGUSON JR. HIS JOB A YEAR LATER.

suspended for fifteen games and was clearly a step behind when he finally did return.

Aside from all the anguish of following a bad team, the Tlusty/ Bell/Blake situation put a depressing twist on the whole mess. One quick-witted shinny mate said, "The Habs have their slowest player score the winning goal," referring to Komisarek.

"What do we have?"

"A failed porn star, a criminal, and a cancer patient."

That statement, as crude as it sounded, pretty much summed up the Leafs season as it reached the quarter-pole.

Hoping for some good news as my son's arrival drew closer, I convinced my wife that a night out to watch a return engagement against the Canadiens two weeks later was just what I needed before the baby came. It was November 27, a Tuesday night, and the baby was due on Friday.

Saying something along the lines of "Enjoy it now because our lives are about to change," she agreed. I gave her a kiss on the cheek, a rub of the baby bump, and headed down to the ACC with a friend named Ian Lederer. A Habs fan, no less.

Now Mr. Lederer is a lovely fellow, but in addition to being a Habs fan, he can be a bit chatty at inopportune times. With the Leafs mired in a horrendous slump and having only won eight games to that point of the season, it may have been about the worst time on record to go to a Leafs–Habs game with a supporter of the enemy.

Despite an entertaining encounter in front of him, Ian thought it would be a good idea to remark on various banalities of the ACC and discuss my pending parenthood (he himself was the proud daddy of a little girl and later a son). When he pointed to the Leafs' thirteen Stanley Cup banners high up on one side of the ACC in order to frame a rhetorical question about what happened to the other side, I almost snapped.

"Easy, Leds," I barked, about to point out a fact that many Habs fans don't like to hear nor accept. "It hasn't been all shits and giggles for you guys since you were a little (but still annoying) Canadiens fan."

Ian left smiling. The Leafs played well, tying the game in the final seconds when Mats Sundin scored his 400th career goal as a Maple Leaf. But they eventually lost in a shootout that was delayed when the Zamboni failed to clean the ice properly.

The sheer annoyance was palpable. Knowing I couldn't down twelve beers to make it go away — moves like that tend not to go over well with a woman who is expecting the courtesy of a lift to the hospital before giving birth — I stewed all the way home.

But then, my life really *did* change forever.

My son had the good sense to arrive on a Wednesday, tucked in nicely between the Habs game the previous night and a road game in Atlanta against the Thrashers. As men, we all learn to appreciate the skill of, say, an Alex Ovechkin one-timer or the sheer all-round brilliance of Sidney Crosby. But bearing witness to the birth of your own child really does make you feel both amazed and a bit inadequate. No matter what certain athletes do that make our jaws drop, it's nothing like what women have gone through since the beginning of time.

When I glanced down and saw my son's head for the first time, time stood still; a living, breathing human being who kicks and cries and all that stuff. And he's mine. To that point, I thought my wife's most admirable quality (of many) was putting up with me.

For almost forty-eight hours I didn't even think about the Maple Leafs. The only way they entered my consciousness was when I was packing away my wife's stuff the next day and was taking special care to save a newspaper from the day my son was born. Sure enough, that edition of the *Globe and Mail* had an unflattering recount of the horror at the ACC the previous night. If, like many young boys and an increasing number of little girls, he goes on to be a Leafs fan, my son will soon have to accept the fact that the primary sports story the morning of his birth was a cutting loss to the Habs.

Later that same night, the Robinson clan got the green light to leave the hospital. The only thing left was a safety demonstration of how to put our new addition into his car seat. As we were waiting for the nurse, I must confess my mind started to wander because I knew the Leafs were playing in Atlanta that night.

Finally a friendly, outgoing nurse came into the hospital room. A lively conversation ensued between her and my wife about the joys of new motherhood. The nurse had just returned to work herself after her maternity leave, and the conversation soon became the first informal mommies activity my wife would take part in (that number is now well into the hundreds).

After several minutes, I was starting to get a tiny bit restless, but sure enough, just as I was about to make a strategic comment about the merits of getting home sometime in the next fortnight, the girls said their goodbyes and I went to retrieve the car. The first insertion of your new child into his car seat attachment really is a seminal moment, in much the same way as putting together your kid's first bike, as I found out a few years later. It's especially so if you have the tail end of the Leafs' radio broadcast on in the car and you're trying to decipher if the Leafs had won or lost that night in Dixie.

I distinctly remember the loosening, tightening, tugging, and pulling that went into fastening my son into the newfangled apparatus. I do it now without so much as a second thought, but that night it was like trying to assemble a Harley-Davidson in the dark.

I was multitasking, trying to get the baby into the seat while interpreting Alex Steen's faintly accented English as he was being interviewed post-game, which to my great relief was interrupted by Dennis Beyak's silky tones confirming that the Leafs had come out on top.

My son was undefeated as a Leafs fan.

Now, really, every parent, especially first-timers, thinks their child is the smartest, cutest, and all-round most talented kid since, well, creation. But seriously, it plays with your mind when the arrival of your child coincides with a horrendous hockey team suddenly peeling off four straight wins. My son, and it will take years for him to ever grasp this, if he ever does, was undefeated as a Leafs fan for ten whole days.

The win in Atlanta was one thing — the Thrashers weren't exactly the 1985 Edmonton Oilers — but a team that in many ways was the reincarnation of that fabled squad, Pittsburgh, came into Toronto two nights later and were soundly beaten by the Buds 4–2. Wins over the Rangers and Nashville Predators followed.

The latter victory was notable because I managed to earn a night pass when, like many new parents, we had realized that during the first few weeks babies really don't do much other than eat, sleep, and fill their diapers with oddly coloured discharges. That meant a night out down at 50 Bay Street with a friend who was visiting from Vancouver. Firmly entrenched in the belief that my son was the sole reason for the Leafs playing better, I watched in glee as Toskala absolutely stood on his head and stole a 3–1 game.

Freed from my pledge to keep the alcohol intake down, I poured back the overpriced pints in the dual celebration of becoming a father and bearing witness to a game the Leafs utterly did not deserve to win.

Heeding nature's call, I proudly announced to the couple of dozen men in the lavatory that my son, all of six days old, was now 4–0 as a Leafs fan. Anyone who has ever been in the washrooms after a Leafs win knows the feeling of elation even at the most modest Toronto victories. Wins over the California Golden Seals and Kansas Scouts, if those clubs still existed, would be hailed as Stanley Cup–style triumphs among men all united in the common cause of building up the Leafs while they empty their bladders.

In that atmosphere, my pronouncement was hailed as a declaration of a Stanley Cup spring until one smart aleck provided some levity: "Go buy him a Sidney Crosby jersey tomorrow so he can stay undefeated forever," said a guy using the urinal beside me.

For a brief moment I was offended, but then the man quickly explained that no young lad deserved the fate that awaited him as a Leafs fan. I completely forgot the incident until more than three years later.

Now three and a half and big brother to a baby girl, hockey entered my son's radar around the time of the Vancouver Winter Olympics. Interestingly, my son's hockey awareness came to light because he was confused at the difference between the two Maple Leafs — the blue and white and the one that adorned the Team Canada jersey.

Too young to understand the significance of the gold medal victory on February 28, 2010, my son was slowly coming around to watching hockey the following season. He began to understand the currency of being a good boy and staying put on the couch in order to watch the first period of Leafs television broadcasts.

It was a brilliant idea that any hockey fan could appreciate. Bribe your child with being able to stay up a bit later by making him sit still. When the first intermission arrived, the natural break roughly coincided with the amount of time it took to read a story and tuck him in. With kid conked out, Daddy extricates himself from his car-shaped bed — decorated with Maple Leafs bedding, of course — in order to repair back to the TV.

Mrs. Robinson looks on with amused approval — thinking that both the men in the household are a bit strange — and everyone is happy.

This routine went well for most of the second half of the 2010–11 season; so with a handful of games left on the schedule, I believed my son was almost ready to attend his first game.

Technically, it wouldn't be his first pro hockey game. That had come a season earlier when I had taken him to a Toronto Marlies tilt at the Ricoh Coliseum, and later he was at a junior contest at the Powerade Centre in Brampton. The junior game had gone well; the Marlies one did not. He mistook the concourse area that runs around the upper level of Ricoh as some sort of excuse to run for what seemed like days. It provided an amusing dilemma as my three-year-old son began dodging around arena patrons who included many scouts and other NHL team management types. John Ferguson Jr., the now former Leafs general manager, had my son dart around him as he was watching the game in this area of the rink. Ferguson was scouting the game in his new role with the San Jose Sharks. Rick Dudley, then with the Thrashers but soon to come to the Leafs as one of Brian Burke's twelve right-hand men, gave my son and me a knowing glance and a smile. How many kids can say they were scouted, sort of, before they turned four?

So it was that in the early afternoon of March 29, 2011, sitting at my office desk, I called home. Home was now Barrie, about forty-five minutes north of the city, where we had moved when baby number two arrived. My mother-in-law, firm in her dual role as nana and nanny, answered the phone and thought it was a rip-roaring idea — time for her grandson to attend a real, live Leafs game.

The problem was that the Leafs were playing some seriously good hockey, as was their post–All-Star Game custom to that point. They were still technically in the playoff race, though a loss three nights earlier in Detroit had seriously hurt those chances. On top of that, my son was now well past the age exemption at which kids weren't charged to enter the arena — if I was to take him, he would be a full-price charge.

With optimism in the air, the market for tickets was getting expensive and the Ticketmaster site was giving me no love trying to find a pair. Eventually, a trusted friend who dabbles a bit in selling tickets on the side promised he would give me a pair at the price he could secure them from a season ticket holder who was likely going to be calling him last-minute to sell.

I had to make one promise: if I wanted them, I had to commit right then and at the price he could secure without consulting me. I agreed, called my mother-in-law to have the boy ready, planning to boot up to Barrie and then swung back down to Toronto. The tickets were secured at the not-unreasonable price of $250 for a pair of greens, but just as I was about to leave, my mother-in-law called.

"He's sick," she said.

"What?" I asked.

"He's sick, he's running a fever and we had to go get him from preschool."

Yikes. No one wants to go anywhere but home when their little one is ill, so going to the game with someone else was not an option. My only way out was to honour my word to my friend and try to offload the tickets to someone, preferably in such a way that I could head straight home.

I posted an ad on Craigslist and was able to get a buyer for face value — about a $40 loss on what I had paid. The buyer was located, luckily for me, north of the city. A short detour on the way home and I managed to drop the tickets off, get paid, and head home.

When I got there my son was clearly under the weather but not seriously so. His Maple Leafs–blue eyes were offset by dark bags he had underneath them and he had a bit of a fever, but otherwise he was his normal self.

"You should have been here earlier," my mother-in-law remarked. "He threw up all over — like projectiles."

"Yeah, Daddy, I had throw-overs," he added, not quite getting the wording right but close enough that I knew what he meant.

When little ones are sick, it doesn't mean their brains don't function. The little fella still remembered our deal: stay up later if you promise to sit nicely on the couch for the first period.

We took to our usual position on the couch, and he faded in and out of sleep, watching the game.

"What do you think, bud?" I asked of the action on the screen in front of us.

"Daddy, the Leafs make me feel really sick," he replied.

I knew what he meant, but sometimes it takes a child to put things in perspective.

8

SCALPERS

IT TAKES ROUGHLY 325 STEPS FOR AN AVERAGE MALE TO COVER THE stretch that runs between York and Bay along Front. Front Street is the east–west artery in the heart of downtown Toronto that cuts across the face of Union Station, the transport hub that guards the Air Canada Centre a little farther south.

About three hundred steps takes you south down Bay to get to the east entrance of the Air Canada Centre; a similar stroll down York Street and a quick left turn on Bremner Boulevard takes you to the west-side entrance.

With the Gardiner Expressway and Lakeshore Boulevard limiting pedestrian traffic coming from the south, those are the two main outside pedestrian entry points for the entertainment complex that the Leafs have toiled in since early 1999.

Walking down the Bay Street side on March 14, 2011, I was angling to get a ticket for the Leafs. They were about to play their lone home game during the March Break school vacation — a rare opportunity for scalpers to get weekend prices on a Monday night. The Tampa Bay Lightning were in town, a team with a growing appeal because of hometown boy Steven Stamkos, of nearby Unionville.

But scalpers had obviously misread the market, as many were scrambling in the minutes before the game. It was one of the rare times where shrewd ticket buyers — with the Leafs in a protracted six-week stretch of playing well, many fans were still looking for seats — hold the upper hand. One seller, a young man in his early thirties who was surprisingly fit and trim for a scalper, tried to offload a single purple ticket, the cheapest seat in the house. Perhaps it was his relative youth and inexperience, but the scalper made a rookie mistake — he tried to show the price of a printed-off ticket from Ticketmaster with all the services charges included as the price he paid, asking for "face value" in the process. When someone buys a single from Ticketmaster's site and prints it off from their own computer, that single seat comes with almost the same fees as buying a pair, upping the price for a single purple seat to almost $70. By comparison, a pair of purples would have been about $130 because the fees are spread out across two tickets.

"I can get a single green for that price," I bargained against his $70 asking price.

"But you just want to get in to get to your friend's box," he countered, citing one angle scalpers often work to the Bay Street crowd who seek just a single ticket in order to then sneak into luxury suites by getting into the building but not holding an actual suite pass.

"Do I look like a Bay Streeter?" I asked. I was dressed in jeans and a casual shirt. "I need a ticket to watch the game, not to drink free booze."

"Well, what can you pay?" he asked.

At that moment I attempted to pull out my wallet to offer him $30, but instead grabbed an action figure I had left in my pocket from visiting McDonalds earlier in the day with my son. Expecting a wad of cash and a legit offer, the agitated scalper instead had a Happy Meal toy to contemplate.

"Well," I said, laughing at my own unintentional master-stroke. "I'll give you $30 and this action figure."

I did not elicit a happy response.

"Go fuck yourself," he shot back.

I couldn't help but laugh as I kept walking down Bay Street, and the aggrieved scalper scurried back to his group of fellow sellers, cursing me and my son's toy. But one of his confederates bided his time. He then followed me down the street and caught up to me when he was out of view of his buddies — it's a major no-no to undercut your fellow scalpers, but it routinely happens when the market dictates and they are confident they won't be found out.

To that point, I generally recognized most scalpers, but this wrinkled face was a new one. He nervously placed himself behind one of the massive concrete columns that help hold up the Union Station complex above so his fellow scalpers couldn't see him.

"Give me forty bucks," he said, fidgeting.

"Deal," I said, but reaching into my pocket I inexplicably grabbed the same Happy Meal toy again. "And, I can include the Happy Meal toy for that price!"

"Fuck off," he responded, half in jest, seemingly admiring my cheekiness. "Give me the forty bucks and go hang out with your buddies in their box."

I smiled, did the exchange, and made my way into Gate 2. But my satisfaction with outwitting a scalper waned soon after as the Leafs got hammered by the Lightning 6–2, leaving their resurgent playoff hopes in deep peril.

✿   ✿   ✿

Maple Leaf Sports and Entertainment uses the Air Canada Centre as a nerve centre from which to run its business. Hockey and basketball are the core draws, but concerts and other events also make up a tidy revenue stream and help keep the ACC humming all year long. The sheer amount of money that streams into the place for all those events is mind-numbing when broken down on both a micro and macro level.

Simple math dictates that the Leafs pull in a shade under $2 million a game by calculating the average ticket price and multiplying it by the seating capacity. Whatever the real total, it's a dizzying sum, especially when you consider that currently the Canadian dollar is essentially at or close to par with its American counterpart. Making up the deficit to the greenback used to be a significant disadvantage, even for the Leafs, but it is no longer an issue.

There is also a darker side to that type of revenue generation: scalpers.

The hockey team has a waiting list for season tickets thousands of names deep, so it's not surprising that the money to be made in the underground economy of ticket selling is itself no small industry.

It's a business that attracts its share of characters. The street grid already described is where the street hustlers operate in the main, with smaller pockets starting farther east and west along the parts of Front catering to the restaurant and bar crowds, or the subway passengers coming in from the north who disembark one stop before Union at St. Andrew or King Station.

The sidewalks directly in front of both Union Station and the Royal York Hotel across the street are surprisingly scalper-free for the most part due to local bylaws prohibiting selling on the property of the transport hub. As for the Royal York, it happily makes tickets available through its concierge desk. Resourceful doormen often help guests get tickets but have to be coy because they could pay with their jobs if caught taking a little something-something on the side.

The call for tickets stays fairly constant heading south down both Bay and York. It especially picks up in the "pit," the area immediately in front of the ACC's west entrance and where the rapidly growing Bremner[1] runs headlong into the west entrance of the ACC.

For years that area of Bremner was an unseemly eyesore where scalpers and desperate ticket buyers would park their cars among the scattering of construction trucks and material. The mess is gone now that MLSE's condo complex is completed and the Real Sports bar and e11even[2] restaurant are fully operational along with other commercial and retail space.

Operational, in the parlance of MLSE, means open and servicing the hungry/thirsty patrons anxious to prime the pump before shooting off next door for the game. For those who don't have a ticket but are willing to drop the same sort of dollars drowning their sorrows at Real Sports, MLSE is happy to oblige by providing them a venue in which to indulge.

It takes just a few trips down to the area to start to recognize faces. Your typical ACC scalper has one of two basic looks. There is the veteran: older, at least forty, unkempt but always appropriately dressed for the weather. As the hockey and basketball seasons generally run parallel to one another and in tune with the Canadian autumn, winter, and then early spring, the men selling tickets bring with them a grubby array of winter clothing. Ill-fitting oversized hats and toques and stained puffy jackets, the bulky pockets of which grow fatter with every cash-only transaction, are the basics of the wardrobe.

The younger ones are generally in their thirties. These men don't look quite as down at heel and their technique tends to be a little less aggressive and a bit more personable. Scalpers retain an enthusiasm for their job that wanes only as they get on in years. A younger scalper tends to work his cellphone more, networking with his brethren and the older veterans to try to pool their resources in selling product.[3]

Both young and older scalpers share one common trait: a casual relationship with speaking the truth. To sell tickets in a jurisdiction where hawking them over face value is technically illegal, a scalper has to have no shame in what he says and how he says it.

"I'm trying to make a living here," is almost always the first reply you'll get if you attempt to lower the first asking price. References to having to make child support payments, pay rent, or keep his boss happy will come later. Their blarney is almost always complete fiction, or half-true, a shtick refined to remove as much money from your wallet as they possibly can without ruining the sale.

One night in the hours before the Leafs' last home game of the year, on December 30, 2006, a scalper was briefly detained by the police and ticketed for selling on the property inside Union Station. He took the time to tell me his career story of scalping, first as a teenager. The money was so good he was walking around with thousands of dollars of pure profit in his pocket because of a special ability to hawk concert tickets. He was nineteen. Almost twenty years later, his past was catching up to him because he had pushed his luck with the police too many times, leading to more costly citations. Although he had no employment history or a real job record, he was musing aloud that his most recent brush with the police could be the impetus to give it all up. He claimed he was so bummed he would sell me a ticket for what he paid for it — $80 for a seat in the blues behind Toronto's net. I agreed. Once I got inside, however, I promptly learned from a Detroit family sitting beside me that he had actually paid them $20 for that ticket. The family was in Toronto for their son's minor hockey tournament but he couldn't attend the game because he had a looming early morning game. The family hadn't found anyone to take the boy's ticket, so they had agreed to sell it to the scalper for a fraction of the face value because they believed his sob story about not being able to get more than $25 for a stand-alone single.

By working both sides against the middle as he did, the scalper ended up making a tidy $55 profit selling to me while getting written up by Toronto's finest.

It was a similar sob story for the Leafs that night — despite outplaying the Ottawa Senators, they lost in overtime, crippling their playoff hopes with their fifth loss in six games as the calendar was about to turn to 2007.

There was also a crude side story playing out during inter-missions that night. Former Iraqi dictator Saddam Hussein was hurriedly hung earlier that day and the grim photos and video was slowly starting to leak onto the Internet. Many fans could be seen in their seats dialing up the gory scenes on their various hand-held devices during the game. Others were openly sharing the footage during the intermissions.

Now, I didn't have quite as bad of a time as Saddam had halfway across the world that day, but I was certainly pissed off about both the loss and being hoodwinked by the scalper after genuinely feeling sorry for him. I called the number he'd given me when I had suggested I would be happy to buy off him again in order to help him out and offset the huge fine that was awaiting him.

The number was out of service.

Scalpers are almost always in cahoots with one another. They get a sense of the landscape in the hours before the game and stick to a price scale that they've figured out among themselves not long after taking up their regular position on the street.

Prices vary widely from game to game and scalpers have taken a considerable beating as the Leafs have struggled on the ice during the period that the post-millennium economy slowed.

During the 2011–12 season, face value for upper-bowl seats ranged from $55 for purples and $95 for greens; lower-bowl seats typically went from $165 to $210, with a few select premium and rail seats trending all the way up to $600 or more. The fees if you go through Ticketmaster generally add about $15 per order once the final bill is added up.

From scalpers, tickets for seats in the upper bowl for mid-week games against modest, low-profile opposition can be bought for face value because of the Leafs' prolonged post-lockout swoon. (A scalper will always represent face value as the highest price possible, including fees, even if he never paid them.)

Even selling at face value, scalpers maintain a handsome profit margin for themselves because they drive an even harder bargain with the ticket holders they buy from than they do with the walk-up customers they sell to. Fear plays a role here. Season ticket holders — many of whom have had the tickets in the family for decades and can no longer afford the steep increases of recent years — wouldn't dare risk losing access to their tickets, which are perceived to be among the hardest to get across the entire North American sports landscape. Scalpers and ticket brokers swoop in and offer these ticket holders less than the list price; in return the ticket holder retains the tickets in their name.

Though they have no qualms about turning the screws on their suppliers, scalpers will never initially acknowledge or accept face value for upper-bowl tickets and will often wait until about fifteen minutes (or later) before game time before they even accept that price.

Lower-bowl seats for the same types of games against opponents with little appeal are more expensive but can often be bought for a steep discount on face value. Technically, it's a bigger bargain, but you're still paying more money to sit in a seat where sightlines are often no better (and occasionally worse) than the well-positioned upper-bowl seating.

The NHL has booked more high-profile opposition during mid-week games in recent years, even scheduling the rare Montreal Canadiens or Pittsburgh Penguins contest on a Tuesday night, for example. Because mid-week games don't hold anywhere near the same appeal to the wider fan base of both teams, this is the one time a fan could expect to pay only a small markup on tickets for a high-profile game. But you have to hold your nerve and be willing to haggle with scalpers to secure tickets at this price against decent teams.

All bets are off on the weekends, as that's when the scalpers rake it in. If the Leafs are playing a team with any sort of appeal — the Buffalo Sabres, the Capitals, or a good Western Conference opponent such as the San Jose Sharks or Los Angeles Kings — the minimum cost to get through the door is about $75 for nosebleeds. Lower purples — a bracket where the first few rows are not much different than sitting in higher greens — will be at least that price and often close to $100 per seat. Greens for games such as these are a bare minimum $125 and would take luck and/or untold amounts of back-and-forth with scalpers to get at that price.

The real money spinners are Canadian teams, the Penguins, Detroit Red Wings, or Chicago Blackhawks coming to town on the weekend. Even if the Leafs are in the midst of a skid, these games go from $100 (and that's often for just standing room) up to a few hundred dollars-plus per seat in the lower bowl.

A Montreal game is always the gold standard (as the Leafs are when they visit the Bell Centre). Buying tickets from scalpers for a Canadiens–Leafs weekend contest will depress you to no end and should be viewed as one of those once-in-a-decade splurges, or else you'll find yourself in the express lane to bankruptcy, divorce, or both. Even if you can afford the prices, it's not money well spent, especially when you consider that the Habs haven't exactly done their own glorious history proud since they last won the Stanley Cup in 1993. The minimum to get through the door for a weekend tilt between the two storied rivals is $150 and up to $1,000 for lower-bowl seats if the game could have any significant bearing on the standings.

The regular-season finale against Montreal in 2007 was the most expensive non-playoff game ever played at the ACC. Both the Leafs and Canadiens needed to win to keep their post-season hopes alive pending the result of the game between the New York Islanders and New Jersey Devils the next day. Tickets were going for as much as

$800 a pair for upper-level seats, and $1,000 or more for lower bowl, though the market was flooded and came down a bit after the puck drop. The scene around the entrances of the ACC that night was almost as funny as it was expensive for those looking for tickets. One scalper, a huge man who tipped the scale at around 350 pounds, wore a sandwich sign that was much too small, pronouncing his desire to buy tickets at "top dollars." The man's girth and signage made his attempts to run up and down what was then a massive, muddy construction site near the Bremner entrance that much tougher. Whatever the man added that night in profits, it likely didn't come close to the number of pounds he lost.

Though prices have dropped from the overheated market of 2006 and 2007, there were other high-priced examples from that time period aside from the Leafs–Habs game that closed out the schedule. A ticket to the Saturday night game on February 10, 2007, when Sidney Crosby and his mates rolled into town, commanded $700 for a pair of decent greens for a game that lived up to its billing. The Leafs erased a three-goal deficit, took two one-goal leads in the third period only to cough them up, then lost in overtime when the Penguins' Jordan Staal completed a hat trick.

A week later, the Leafs invited back members of their last Stanley Cup team from forty years earlier, including Dave Keon, the man whose self-imposed exile from the club has been well-documented. Tickets for that night were almost as high on the scalpers' market: $600 for a pair of good upper-bowl seats, $800 for two lower-levels — an amazing sum, given that they were playing one of the worst teams in the NHL, the Edmonton Oilers, and that most of their fan base has no living memory of the Stanley Cup triumph being honoured.

Scalpers are no longer the lone secondary source to secure tickets, of course. The mass appeal of the Internet roughly coincided with the opening of the ACC, and the ticket broker market has taken off since online selling made the exchange so much easier. As a general rule, tickets purchased through sites such as eBay, StubHub, and Craigslist can be had for slightly cheaper than on the street in front of the ACC, but there are risks in doing business that way.

It's one of the great ironies of buying tickets from scalpers that they are almost always legitimate. It's hard to imagine scalpers selling only valid tickets out of the goodness of their hearts — many would sell their mothers if the price was right — but it's bad for business and perhaps their own physical well-being if an on-the-street seller were to be hawking dodgy duckets. You never know when an aggrieved party might come back and confront you about being ripped off. Online, where money transfers usually substitute for face-to-face meetings, many possibilities exist to get ripped off with fake tickets. Unravelling the trail to the fraudster is virtually impossible, and though eBay and StubHub go to great lengths to ensure tickets sold on their sites are legit, there are never any guarantees.

If you regularly buy scalpers' tickets to get into the ACC, you learn to take the measure of the marketplace, the mood of the sellers, and the unseemly underbelly of those who do it. Some scalpers are likable rogues, others are merely doing it because it's all they've ever done, and some are hucksters who would make even men who sell 1987 Buicks for a living blush.

If you're aware of what you're getting yourself into and possess a modicum of common sense and backbone, dealing with scalpers can often be quite funny and memorable.

One of the most important things to remember is to recognize when the word "upgrade" comes out of a scalper's mouth; it's nothing more than an attempt to hoodwink you into taking some of his most unsellable tickets off his hands.

As described earlier, lower bowl seats have the least appeal to walk-up buyers and are the hardest to move because they are so expensive. A scalper will often try to "upgrade" someone holding upper bowl seats into the lower bowl with a small financial inducement — usually about $20 or $40 for a pair — in exchange for the more sellable upper bowl tickets. Consider the following example: about an hour before the Leafs–Atlanta Thrashers game on February 7, 2011, snow began to fall in and around the city, slowing traffic to a crawl on all the major arteries into the ACC.

Many ticketholders could be seen in the area around Gate 1 waiting impatiently for their seatmates to arrive, the feverish scramble to locate friends obvious by the sheer amount of anxious fans on the phone or tapping out text messages. As a result, large swathes of seats sat empty after the puck dropped, owing in part to the tepid appeal of the Thrashers, but mostly because of the difficulty getting to the arena.

Scalpers smelled blood.

I approached a scalper — a man with unkempt sideburns that looked as though they had grown out of his woolen cap — and offered a pair of green seats in the first row of the upper bowl for face value: $190. I was instead going to use lower-bowl seats offered to me by Norman Stewart, the father of the Thrashers' Anthony Stewart, whom I had known casually for years. Mr. Stewart's friend had no hope of getting to the arena anytime soon and he offered them to me for a cut-rate price.

The scalper, possessing a case of five o'clock shadow that would look like three-day growth on most men, rejected my $190 offer. Instead, he presented a "sweetheart" counter-offer: hand over both the greens *and* reds from Mr. Stewart in exchange for golds he had in his hands, slightly closer to the ice in the lower bowl.

It was sweet, all right, for the scalper. He was attempting to get rid of his most unsellable tickets without giving up any money in the exchange. In return, he would be able to sell the reds to cover the cost of his original gold pair, which was likely a fraction of the $210 per ticket face value price. The greens would be sold for pure profit. I told the scalper to beat it. The lone benefit to me as the seller would be to sit roughly ten rows closer to the ice, at an angle that most would consider a worse sightline to the play. Also, I wouldn't be able to sit beside Mr. Stewart, who would have been rightly annoyed that I sold-on his original tickets.

This is not to suggest there aren't legitimate deals to be had. One afternoon in December 2006, I was just starting to get the hang of buying tickets off scalpers and beginning to notice signs of a flooded marketplace. I saw an ad posted on Craigslist by a seller who clearly knew that he was stuck with too much inventory and likely too lazy to spend the hours that afternoon fighting Christmas crowds to get rid of his excess supply. The man posted his phone number in an ad — exposing himself as a known ticket broker — saying he was feeling particularly charitable, in the spirit of the season, and was willing to let his first-row greens in front of the Maple Leafs alumni box go for face value (which was then about $80 per seat). There was a catch — you had to drive to Richmond Hill to get them. The suburban community is not an easy drive to get to whether you're coming to or going from Toronto proper. After an hour's drive, I arrived. It was obvious why "Howard" was selling his tickets for face value: his car was broken down. Greeting me with a nice smile that almost made you not notice the mustard spread all over his left cheek, Howard handed over the tickets, took the $160-and-change, and thanked me.

It was a good deal for both sides. Howard knew full well that he couldn't make much more than that and likely would have to get downtown to scoop perhaps an extra $20. In the end it was worth it for Howard to keep stuffing his face and save the time and bother. From the buyer's perspective, the Leafs did their part in making the drive to and from Richmond Hill worth it. The team hammered the Rangers, who were in the midst of a post-lockout roster overhaul that saw them eventually dump the likes of Darius Kasparitis and Michael Nylander, plus a few others who played that night.

The 9–2 final score was also the high-water mark for Leafs waterbug Kyle Wellwood. A surprise out of training camp the previous season, the former junior star was tabbed as a career minor-leaguer when the Leafs drafted him in 2001, but he was benefitting from the season-plus crackdown on post-lockout clutching and grabbing. He scored a hat trick and added another two assists that night, setting off the obligatory speculation among fans and media that he was a future star. Wellwood never became a star, of course, either in Toronto or elsewhere. He got bought out at the end of the next season but he was always there to see when you tried to buy tickets on Ticketmaster's site because his photo ran along that of Mats Sundin and Tomas Kaberle's as your ticket request was being processed.

The Rangers were in town again on December 29, 2007, and were starting to hit their stride after the changes of a season earlier. The Leafs, on the other hand, had settled into their customary win one, lose one, drop another in overtime or shootout mode that gave false hope they could be considered a .500 team if they could beat the Rangers that night.[4] There was also a conflict on the sporting calendar in a city that is normally Leafs first, second, and third on virtually all nights they tee it up. The New England Patriots were playing the New York Giants in an attempt to finish the regular season with a perfect 16–0 record. The ticket market that night was a little slow as the city was also stuck between Christmas celebrations and New Year's, which lurked two nights hence. Throw in the football game and getting a ticket wasn't quite as painful as the usual song-and-dance a Saturday night against an Original Six opponent would be.

An optimistic reading of the tea leaves suggested a trip down on the subway could lead to a decent deal. Soon after, a scalper claimed he wanted to do a good deal for both sides because he was a big Giants fan and wanted to get off the street and in front of a TV. I'm not sure I believed him, but I succumbed to his blarney because I, too, was a Giants fan and had planned to nip off and watch the football game if I couldn't secure a decent price. After some haggling, the princely sum of $160 was struck and he surrendered a ticket in the reds of section 113 behind the net.

It afforded a nice sightline for lots of goals, indeed, as the Rangers popped in three in a little more than seven minutes in the middle frame on their way to a 6–1 thrashing of the Leafs, a score that actually flattered the Leafs.

With the score 5–0 after two periods, half the building was off in search of the score of the Pats–Giants game. Like the Rangers, the Patriots also won handily, but the Giants got the ultimate revenge a month later in the Super Bowl.

I left the building annoyed at myself for spending my hard-earned cash watching a bunch of stiffs, a feeling common among Leafs fans exiting on nights like this; it's almost as if thousands of perfect strangers can nod to one another to acknowledge their shared feelings of disgust without even speaking. To top it off, I was also nursing the sting of the Giants losing. Looking for a diversion and seeing one available in the movie listings of a newspaper I found on the subway, I stopped on the way home to catch a late flick: *Atonement*.

Like the book, it was an excellent film and a title any Leafs fan could relate to.

9

SCRAMBLE FOR TICKETS

THE PERFECT SNAPSHOT OF LEAFS NATION STARTS AT THE AIR Canada Centre about twelve hours before each Saturday night home game. Around 7:00 a.m. you'll find the crowds starting to gather just outside the Ticketmaster outlet near Gate 1. People arrive there because late, returned, or rare unsold tickets are made available for that night's game. Once those tickets are gone, those still in line who missed out on getting a ticket are given a wristband and told to come back to see if their number comes up for any that may be available later in the day, usually around 5:00 p.m.

People from all walks of life come out in the early-morning hours, compelling evidence of the hockey team's appeal to all segments of Toronto's population. Hopeful ticket-seekers run the gamut. One is a woman originally from Northern Ontario whose family came to Canada from Barbados. She got hooked on the Leafs when a customer in her hair salon told her about the Saturday morning ticket line. She showed up one morning, got tickets, brought her son to the game that night, and kept coming back.

Another is a man who worked for Canada Post and who grew up in one of Toronto's northern suburbs, making weekly treks down to Maple Leaf Gardens. A man of modest means, he openly admitted that virtually every cent of his disposable income is spent on Leafs tickets, most of which he acquires on Saturday mornings. "I don't know what it is, but I prefer to watch games here, not on TV," he told me one morning. Those words have stuck with me because I've used them to justify my own ticket expenses, but also because I'm not completely sure I know what *it* is either.

Others there at the crack of dawn include tourists, one-off visitors, and those who show up when their favourite team is in town.

The first arrivals generally turn up about 6:00 a.m., but by 7:00 the crowd slowly grows. With nothing to do but to kill time, people mingle with one another; people who otherwise wouldn't know each other from a bar of soap. There is nothing else to do and you can't leave or you lose your hard-fought-for spot in line, so it becomes much easier to talk to perfect strangers. After a couple of weeks of showing up, you get to know one another a little too well. Though not intentionally, I would often divulge information that even some of my good friends didn't know to people I had just met or recognized from previous visits. One morning, after somehow ending up deep into a discussion about my wife's pension, I realized that perhaps I should take a bit more care about what I revealed to people whom I likely wouldn't recognize if I ran into them anywhere but while in line for tickets. And so I learned the art of speaking without really saying anything after being stuck in a few conversations that I couldn't escape from.

Others never find their internal editing switch. I once helped a woman plan her husband's fiftieth birthday party and another woman's trip to Southeast Asia. The intimate details I learned about both women's marriages made me feel a bit like a relationship counsellor.

The most sober interaction I had over the perhaps twenty-five Saturday morning visits occurred when a man who, after knowing me for less than an hour, told me he was there that morning to try to get tickets for his son who was struggling with substance abuse.

On occasion, passersby would attempt to converse with one of us, even try to impart some advice and talk some sense into people who, from their perspective, clearly needed some guidance. The best of these interactions came when the Maple Leaf Square site was still under construction. Workers would report to work around the same time as fans were lining up in earnest for tickets. It's not lost on me now that we were indirectly funding the costly wages of tradesmen toiling on weekends, no doubt at time-and-a-half, or even double-time. One man, whom I later found out was named Kofi and was originally from Ghana, couldn't help taking pity on us.

"People, look at you," he said in formally accented English. "You need something else in your lives ... the Lord, people, the Lord can fill the void."

Kofi, sir, this is our religion.

It's quite rare but public figures and players sometimes pass by the line. One morning early in 2007, Jay Triano, then an assistant coach of the Toronto Raptors, came down to the ACC just before 8:00 a.m. He glanced to his right as he was about to go through the doors of Gate 1, shook his head, and kept going. A few weeks later, on February 17, 2007, the Leafs were set to play the Edmonton Oilers. A Canadian team on a Saturday night is a huge draw, especially with the Leafs planning to honour their 1967 Stanley Cup championship squad on its 40th anniversary. Two Oilers players, goaltender Dwayne Roloson and forward Ryan Smyth, came in through the same doors near the construction site. It remains the lone time I saw players while queuing up for tickets. Roloson and Smyth didn't say anything, but the look on their faces said it all. It was clear that even they were surprised that almost a hundred people would come out that early in the morning for tickets — and it's not as though playing in Edmonton they were from a virgin market.

For me, waking from my Saturday morning slumber wasn't a question of insanity. I played hockey on Friday afternoons, which, with the aid of a few post-skate pints, generally meant I was ten-toes-up a little earlier than other nights of the week. Early to bed, early to rise, so I would often wake between 4:00 and 5:00 a.m. the next day without the aid of an alarm clock, so the trip was easy for me to justify. Honestly.

Later, after my son was born and proceeded to wake the Robinson household every morning before 6:00 a.m., I even thought the previous year of heading down to the ACC most Saturday mornings had served as a nice dry run to the routine of new parenthood. It was parenthood, by the way, that eventually put the kibosh on regular Saturday morning forays down to the ACC.

Saturday mornings are one thing. It's the constant effort to find, pay for, and then attempt to find the time to enjoy *all* Leafs games that becomes a grind — the team plays forty-one regular season home games a year and at least four home exhibition games. Though they're a faint memory, playoff games could be on top of that, as can other events such as team skills competitions. In all, the Leafs are in action about forty-five nights a year.

The Leafs season ticket subscriber base is full and, as is widely known, the waiting list is decades-long. If you are like the vast majority of Leafs fans and don't have season tickets, there are generally three ways to secure them.

The first is to be connected in your business or personal life to someone who has season tickets or who is a decision-maker at a company or corporation who holds some. As a general rule, most leading corporations with a Toronto presence have at least one pair of Leafs tickets and often many more. It wouldn't be the worst idea to make friends with a few high-level marketing, lawyer, or banker types. It's people of this ilk, their families and friends, who populate large swathes of the Air Canada Centre every night. As a note, people who dole out those tickets to clients and others tend to greatly appreciate it if you don't pester and bug them. If you offer to pay for the tickets, you'll almost certainly move way ahead of others in the imaginary queue that person has formed in their mind.

I hate to offend, but if you are not willing to pay, you shouldn't ask anyone for tickets. Requesting free tickets is annoying to the person in charge of them and it's exactly that sense of entitlement on a mass scale that has made the ACC a dead zone for fan excitement. It's one thing to accept free tickets without asking, it's entirely another one to be searching them out without an expectation of paying. My single biggest surprise in close to a decade of sourcing Leafs tickets for myself and friends is the expectation some people have of not having to open their wallets.

The second way to get tickets is to attempt to operate on the margins of the market and buy or trade with scalpers. The one upside to dealing with scalpers and ticket brokers is that if you decide you want to go to a game at the last minute, you can make an impulse buy. As long as you are willing to pay the premium that comes with such a purchase and possess a reasonable amount of nerve to deal with people who aren't exactly saints, you'll be fine.

The third way is to try to buy through the limited ticket-buying channels available to the general public, almost all of which go through Ticketmaster. As the scene on Saturday mornings shows, finding tickets on game day or during their lead-up is where things can be incredibly time-consuming. Make that life-consuming. Once Ticketmaster opens at 9:30 a.m., which almost always ends up being about 9:40, you are likely to be greeted by a twenty-something at the ticket window who looks as though he or she is the walking embodiment of Generation Y cool. Getting a helpful and on-the-ball ticket agent who can quickly walk you through what tickets are available for that night's game is a bit of a hit and miss proposition. Even the astute agents have challenges turning their microphone on, a problem because the window glass is very thick and impossible to hear through. You learn to get used to the people ahead of you saying "What?" or "Pardon?" or "Turn your damn microphone on!"

Well, things don't normally get that testy, but you get the point.

It's tough to pin down exactly what it is that determines game-day availability, but through experience and interpreting the corporate-speak of Ticketmaster, it goes something like this: Unsold wheelchair-accessible seating — usually just called accessible seating — is made available to able-bodied patrons on the day of the game. To a first-time buyer this seems odd and can often lead you to question the ticket agent — "Hey, is this guy so asleep he thinks I'm in a wheelchair?" — and decline the purchase. That would be a massive mistake. Accessible seating is the best value in the ACC and in many ways is like sitting in a corporate box. You have quicker access to the washroom, infinitely more leg room, and generally a much more agreeable space to sit in. It's one of the great unspoken truths about ticket buying at the ACC that special needs spaces mandated by local bylaws and building codes are rarely sold out to people who actually need them. Maple Leaf Sports and Entertainment wouldn't dare advertise this fact publicly — it would be a tad unseemly — but they would never pass on the tidy revenue stream, either.

Bottom line: if these types of seats are available, buy them.

Beyond that, most games have a pair or two of upper-bowl tickets that somehow came available. This option is next-best in terms of cost, and if you're serious about going to the game that night, these tickets should be snapped up at the first opportunity because it's very likely the person in line behind you has his or her eyes on them. You have to be near the front of the line to get access to these types of tickets if they are available at all.

There are generally a few lower-bowl pairs on offer on game days, as well, but they are more expensive and generally take a bit longer to be sold. In other words, you can actually take a few minutes to ponder whether it's the best idea to be dropping close to $400 for a pair (and often more if they are golds or platinums).

Going online adds many different wrinkles to the equation. Ticketmaster has done a better job in recent years of cleaning up its functionality in ordering tickets online but it can still be a mind-numbing, frustrating experience. Securing a pair of tickets this way comes down to one thing: dumb luck. If you happen to go online when a pair becomes available, you can snap them up, but it's rare that two are available for sale.

In a half-dozen years of having my finger on the Ticketmaster trigger, and several more before that being casually engaged, I've noticed there seems to be a spike in availability on game days when certain teams are in town. Pinning down why is tough to figure, but there seems to be some logic in the argument that these NHL clubs have fewer visiting players with ticket requests. NHL players get two free tickets per game in the lower bowl and have options available to purchase more. If you glance at the roster of a visiting team and notice that they have few players from Ontario, or Canadians in general, this suggests that those teams return tickets on game days because there are fewer family and friends connected to the team in the local Toronto area. That excess supply then finds its way to Ticketmaster. Or it least that's the theory.

Over time, I've discovered that the New Jersey Devils, New York Rangers, and Washington Capitals fit into this category. The New

York Islanders and Minnesota Wild do, as well, but their visits to the ACC likely mean more ticket availability simply because both teams have much less appeal outside their own markets.

It's not surprising that the grind to find face-value tickets is enough to make you question your own mental health. Surely, if you were told ahead of time that searching for tickets would take hours and hours, often with little return on your time, you wouldn't do it, right? And surely, knowing that the reward for finding tickets is the privilege of tacking hundreds of dollars onto a credit card would scare all right-minded individuals away, right?

In the interest of not having medical professionals clad in white arrive at my door some day inquiring about my state of mind, I won't answer those two questions. Let's instead look at some rather entertaining stories about acquiring and then finding use for Leafs tickets. And some of the best take place when, as hard as they are to find, you actually have *too many* tickets and can't find anyone to bring along or to sell to. Seasoned ticket buyers know this dilemma. It occurs when tickets become available on game day and your searching not only finds you a pair but you managed to land four. Ticketmaster gives you a few minutes to decide before they are electronically yanked back. It's just the right amount of time to do either of the following: scramble to grab your credit card, or call a friend to see if he's in and can find someone else as well. They never give you enough time to do both; the folks that run Ticketmaster are not stupid.

One such occasion took place when my frantic online searching landed me four tickets in November during the 2008–09 season. The Leafs were off to a good start with Ron Wilson in charge for the first time and there was some hope that perhaps things weren't going to be quite as grim as was forecast a few weeks earlier. My problem stemmed from the fact that I had managed to find four tickets a couple of hours earlier. I bit hard, choosing the "TicketFast" method to print them off at my own computer. But soon after that, my friend called and told me that unless I wanted him sleeping on my couch for at least a week, he couldn't make it. His wife apparently did not want to spend a rare Saturday night out together watching hockey. It would have created a marital emergency had he still elected to go to the game. I accepted his explanation, knowing I had been swept up in the euphoria of being able to get four tickets together. I had the added trouble of having printed the tickets at home. These are particularly vulnerable to fraud, meaning most shrewd ticket buyers won't purchase them. Scalpers, if they are willing at all, will pay only a pittance of their cost.

In a panic, I posted an ad on Craigslist stating that I had bought four tickets for a game that night against the New York Rangers and I needed someone to take the extra pair off my hands.

My inbox and cellphone had modest traffic. Almost all responders were scalpers looking to give me a fraction of what I had paid for a pair of greens a few rows up from the balcony, roughly in line with centre ice. I was discouraged, but mildly amused by one scalper who was emailing me from three different email addresses and leaving two different phone numbers, pretending to be a different person each time.

My phone rang one last time just after 6:00 p.m. and just before my wife was about to strangle me. Even understanding spouses lose their patience at an already $200 night doubling with little in return except for extra leg room.

"Hello," I said.

"Are you selling hockey *ticket*?" came the reply, in an unmistakable French Canadian accent.

"Yes," was my hopeful response.

"I can't believe this, but we want to go watch the worst hockey team in the world," he said.

I took the insult in stride, knowing the voice on the other end was coming out of the mouth of a Montreal Canadiens fan. We soon agreed on a deal. Marc would pay me $140 for the $208 pair (including fees) and he and his friend, both Montrealers in town on business, would sit beside my wife and me for the upcoming tilt. I put one condition on the sale: that Marc would not tell my wife how much he paid me. I'm not one to lie to Mrs. Robinson, but if she didn't ask, she wouldn't know that I took a $68 bath, plus the cost of our own tickets.

Marc, his friendly mate (whose name I never did get), my wife, and I met a few minutes later just outside St. Andrew Subway Station on University Avenue, about a kilometre from the ACC. We did the exchange and said we'd see each other later in the rink.

At the game, Marc and his friend were perfectly fine fellows. I endured the predictable Leafs jokes and have to give Marc credit; he correctly predicted that his favourite team would some day regret giving up on Mikhail Grabovski, who was then early in his first season with the Leafs.

"But he's one of the only good ones you got," said Marc.

We know, we know.

Marc bought me a beer late in the second period and then got a text message from a business colleague sitting in the lower bowl informing him that two seats were open beside them. He nudged his friend, I thanked him for the beer, we shook hands, and off they went to the better seats.

"Ah, nice guys," my wife said, not long after he gave her that two-cheek peck that French Canadians always seem to pull off better than everyone else in Canada.

"Sweetheart, he's a Habs fan."

Mrs. Robinson completely missed the joke; just like she was unaware we had partially subsidized Marc and his friend's night out at the ACC.

The Leafs won that night 5–2 and, all things considered, it was a pretty impressive win, coming back late from two goals down. The financial hit I absorbed in off-loading my extra tickets didn't sting nearly as much as it could have.

But that night was nothing like what took place on February 10, 2007. The game that night marked one of the more entertaining post-lockout tilts down at the ACC. On this night the Pittsburgh Penguins were in town and just starting to become the marquee team that they soon would be known as. Then, as now, the Penguins' appeal was keyed by Sidney Crosby, but unlike in recent years, he was healthy, riding high, and this was only Crosby's third career appearance in Toronto. On game day, I was up by 4:30 a.m., was on the Gardiner Expressway downtown by shortly after five, and managed to get the third spot in line at the Ticketmaster booth at the ACC.

Hours later, when I was called to the window, there were no tickets available in any of the other cheaper categories of the upper bowl — the last pair had been snapped up by the aforementioned woman from Barbados. But two tickets in accessible seating in the cheapest area of the lower bowl — then about $275 for a pair — were available.

My credit card was swiped through the old metal machine — as of this writing Ticketmaster still uses the old-fashioned method of charging cards through a tabletop, hand-powered swiping machine — and I was back home shortly after 10:00 a.m. A short nap followed — oh, the lost joys of pre-children mid-morning, mid-afternoon naps — but I was awakened by a phone call. Someone whom I had offered to buy tickets from in a pinch for that game was trying to sell. But it wasn't just anyone; it was the owner of the company I do considerable work for. I didn't want to go back on my word and possibly leave him in the lurch, so I agreed to buy them. Within minutes I had put up a posting on Craigslist in an effort to sell my original tickets.

With Crosby and Co. in town and many months before the economic malaise that began in late 2008, my inbox lit up like a Christmas tree. I received literally dozens of emails offering all manner of sums, most of which sounded as though they were from people who couldn't be trusted — such as the guy who claimed to be "Rocky Brando." Another particularly persistent fellow came through my inbox as "Cheap Watches" and signed his email missives with a couple of different names.

I had been in this position a few times before and was never comfortable playing the role of ticket broker. Generally, if I had an extra pair to sell, I would charge about $20 extra per seat in order to cover the costs associated with selling them, such as driving around the city and parking. On this particular night, I justified selling my $275 red seats for $350 because the $75 profit was roughly the extra cost of buying the new seats in the gold section. Also, I had been down at the ACC ticket window before the crack of dawn — I deserved a little love. The lucky buyer was a woman whose online persona made her sound like an innocent babe in the woods who was taking her husband to a game for the first time. In reality, when she arrived at my house to pick up the tickets, she came across as a pushy A-type personality seriously put out with having to pay so much to go see a hockey game. She was completely unaware that scalpers were selling the same seats for double the price she got hers for.

I bit my tongue, but as fate would have it, I should have told her to go find an alternative way to chip away at her husband's patience than spending it at a Leafs–Penguins game. That's because flush with the $350 I got from her and the slightly higher amount that was already in my wallet in order to pay for our new pair of tickets, my wife and I set off to meet a couple of her friends for drinks before the game.

I can't say for certain whether it was the getting up at 4:00 a.m., the interrupted nap, dealing with a dragon lady, the few casual drinks, or a combination of all those factors, but while taking the short cab ride down to the ACC after our meet-up, I became distracted when my cell phone rang. It was one of my best friends, Tim, calling. He works in Alberta's oil patch, and had no way of knowing that it was near game time in Ontario. With the phone to my ear and my brain evidently switched off, I exited the cab without my wallet and the several hundred dollars it had in it.

What was to be a roughly $350 night just became a $1,000 one, plus a few gift certificates that still lingered in my wallet from the Christmas season six weeks earlier.

I can't say it was a great game for me personally, for obvious reasons, but it definitely lived up to its billing. After a so-so start, the Penguins caught the Leafs taking an early break before the end of the period and scored. They then raced out to a 3–0 lead in the second before Toronto goaltender Andrew Raycroft realized that he was supposed to be playing in a hockey game that night. With their goalie finally able to stop the occasional puck, the Leafs came roaring back and tied it at three. Delirious with excitement; and maybe a bit from the vodkas I was liberally downing to try to drown the pain, I proudly announced to Mrs. Robinson that I felt confident my wallet would be returned and equally sure the Leafs were going to win an epic encounter. She patted me on the head and smiled, in much the same way you would with the family pet.

This time it was Pens goalie Marc-André Fleury who lost his way. The Leafs scored two more goals, but each time Raycroft matched Fleury in the incompetence department and allowed Pittsburgh to tie it. The game went into overtime tied at five before Penguins rookie Jordan Staal scored his third goal right in front of us, with Raycroft sprawled out looking as though he had dove to find my wallet. The Leafs lost 6–5 and to describe my mood as sour as we left the ACC would be a little bit like saying losing several hundred dollars is dispiriting.

It wasn't Raycroft who found my wallet, by the way. A few days later, I got a call from a woman asking me if I had lost my wallet downtown the previous Saturday night.

"I'm sorry, there is no money in it but I managed to find your number through the address on the ID," she said when I sheepishly asked what was in it. "Do you want to meet me or do you want me to send it to you?"

For whatever reason, I thought meeting her would be a better option, so we set a time for the next day at a Tim Hortons.

At the appointed hour, in came a slightly disheveled but otherwise completely normal and pleasant-looking woman of around fifty, short, about 5'3" and 150 pounds. At the same time, I felt something wasn't quite right about her. Although she looked as if she took decent care of herself, she wasn't wearing the makeup, nail polish, or jewellery that women typically wear in public. With salt-and-pepper hair and a general appearance that could be described as not down-at-heel but working class, I began to wonder if she was homeless.

We sat down and she handed me the wallet. Indeed the cash was long gone, but unbelievably the gift cards were still in it, as were all my identification and credit cards. She told me she had found it not far from the ACC on the side of the road near the GO bus terminal. It sounded as though the cab driver had grabbed it when he saw that I had dropped it, emptied it of its cash, then chucked it out the window, likely before I even realized it was missing.

Whatever the case, the fact that the gift cards were still in it was a sure sign it wasn't this woman who had stolen the cash. I voiced my appreciation at recovering the roughly $150 in various gift cards, but especially that all the ID and credit cards were there, saving me infinitely more time and hassle in cancelling and replacing them.

The woman wouldn't take any money from of me as a reward but allowed me to buy her lunch. I did so, bought her an extra twenty-dollars-worth of Tims gift certificates and returned to our table.

"Okay, thank you, I can treat myself," she said of the gift, first not wanting to even take it.

What followed was an incredibly rewarding and enlightening conversation over lunch. To that point I really had no opinion on the plight of the homeless or Toronto's downtrodden. Of course, I was aware that some people were incredibly down on their luck and there are others who have simply lived that type of life for various sociological reasons. Since meeting this woman, I'm still not sure I have a more informed opinion on the wider issue of homelessness, or its causes. But I do now know this: that woman was absolutely lovely. Not only was she honest and kind enough to get my wallet back to me. She was, frankly, very interesting to chat with.

She had lived in Toronto most of her life and had overcome a number of abusive relationships, which she spoke openly about, and she had also dealt with what sounded like some substance issues, but she was a bit more vague on the details about that. She was living an existence that could probably be described as not exactly homeless but of no fixed address. She told me she had a room to stay in and it seemed like she was somewhat on her way to getting back on her feet. She was still spending large amounts of time visiting friends from that world in Toronto that doesn't make the tourist brochures. It was on one of those nights that she found my wallet.

"Sorry," she said. "I don't have access to the Internet very often, so it took me a few days to find you."

A serious conversation followed — I can't remember everything we discussed but I remember one conversation starter was our shared love of carrot muffins.

After about twenty minutes, the conversation migrated to, what else, hockey. "My dad was a Montreal Canadiens fan," she said. "I remember that because he used to say that Foster Hewitt looked like a pig. I dunno, I never really liked hockey, and when I was young, girls never really played like they do now."

I laughed because my own father had often made the same comment about Hewitt, and his father, my grandfather, who died before I was born, apparently used to say the same thing.

I explained that I loved hockey, both playing it and watching it, and that I spent too much money on the Leafs, that they were driving me crazy, not least because they lost games like the one on the previous Saturday night, which was made far worse by me losing all that money.

"Sorry about that," she said, before asking a bunch of questions about the Leafs, how to get tickets, and why I had so much money on me at the time. Her mouth literally dropped open when I started explaining the sums involved to get inside the ACC.

"Why would anyone spend their money like that?" she asked.

It's always the simple question that is so profound, isn't it?

We said our goodbyes. I don't even know if I really meant it, but I told her to stay in touch and that perhaps I could take her to a game some time when I had an extra ticket. She said she would and went out into the February cold on King Street, not far from the ACC.

I proceeded to the counter and got a coffee to take away. When I got back to my car, I fumbled around for my keys and spilt some of my coffee on the notepad on which I had copied down her name, meeting place, and time. I distinctly remember it because the hot coffee splashed onto my skin in the winter chill.

Months later, during the next hockey season, I *did* have an extra Leafs ticket and thought of her. I racked my brain to try to remember her name and whether I even still had her contact details. I finally remembered and retrieved my notepad, but the spilt coffee had rendered her name and details completely illegible. To this day, I can't remember her name, and I've never heard from nor seen her.

10

BURKE'S GREAT GAMBLE

EVEN IF THE MOVE HANGS LIKE A PALL OVER THE FRANCHISE, calling out Maple Leafs general manager Brian Burke for acquiring Phil Kessel in September 2009 is only plausible given the benefit of hindsight. The Leafs had shown signs in training camp of being a much better team than the year before and an honest-to-goodness young star player could have pushed them well into the mix in the NHL's Eastern Conference.

Trading two first-round picks and a second-rounder to the Boston Bruins for Kessel is a deal likely any other GM in Burke's position would have done. Perhaps the Leaf GM bit the poison chalice common among so many of his brethren, especially those who formerly held his position, but Burke deserves credit for trying to make a splash. He had also put his stamp on the club by signing defencemen Francois Beauchemin and Mike Komisarek as free agents and had successfully lured Swedish goaltender Jonas Gustavsson to Toronto. Those moves took place over the summer, but the real blockbuster occurred during training camp when the Kessel deal was made, and it gave everyone a sense that the Leafs were now back in business after four seasons of missing the playoffs.

Kessel, coming off a thirty-six-goal season with the Bruins, was the type of player the Leafs had been sorely lacking for much of the previous four seasons since the NHL work stoppage ended. And though Kessel was slated to miss the first several weeks of the season recovering from surgery, his acquisition was real cause for optimism, especially considering the Leafs won six of nine exhibition games without him.

But the Kessel deal also represented a gamble, even if most hockey fans weren't familiar with the exact details at the time. That's because in Windsor, Ontario, and just across the Canada–U.S. border in Plymouth, Michigan, two electric young talents were playing junior hockey with the Windsor Spitfires and Plymouth Whalers respectively. Both young men even had similar names, Taylor and Tyler, giving headline writers infinite possibilities leading up to the 2010 NHL Entry Draft the following summer.

Taylor Hall and Tyler Seguin could become the NHL's next Alex Ovechkin and Sidney Crosby double act. Even if they don't ascend that high, both players have the ability to achieve a level just below the two most marketable stars in the world. Both Hall and Seguin were that good, and whatever teams ended up earning the number one or number two pick in the 2010 selection process was guaranteed to have one of them to build their team around for the next decade or so.

Burke and his scouting staff would have been aware of Hall and Seguin when the Kessel deal was struck. But, flush with the optimism of the off-season signings, it didn't matter, right? There was no way the Leafs were going to be one of the worst teams in the NHL and then have the draft lottery ball bounce in such a way that they would have a number one or number two pick. Right?

No, seriously. Some nineteen years after the Leafs traded for defenceman Tom Kurvers and gave back the first-round draft selection that the New Jersey Devils would eventually turn into future Hall of Famer Scott Niedermayer, history was about to repeat itself.

❦　❦　❦

The Air Canada Centre is an impressive place. Really, even if you hate the Leafs, you can't deny how nice their home is. Even if you, like virtually all Leafs fans who can remember going, wished they still played at the Gardens, the ACC is not exactly a poor fall-back.

Forever mindful of the opportunities to increase revenues under the guise of improving the "fan experience," in 2009, Maple Leaf Sports and Entertainment expanded the west end bar — called the Ice Box — to give it a bigger and more hip feel.

It worked. The Ice Box is now a sprawling space, complete with dozens of high-definition screens and a seating area that looks an awful lot like what Arthur C. Clarke might have pictured in *2001: A Space Odyssey*.

The work was completed in time for the 2009–10 campaign and it completely changed the feel of the west side of the entertainment complex for the better. The west entrance and the new bar area above it are connected by an escalator and wide staircase. The masses file in and out here every game.

Courtesy of Getty Images.

PHIL KESSEL'S TRADE TO TORONTO WILL BE A TALKING POINT FOR YEARS TO COME.

On the ground level, Leafs TV is filmed on a set erected just inside the west doors, right at the foot of the escalators and stairs that fans with upper-level seats use to get to their assigned positions. This area is also used by folks seeking a bit less bustle to mingle between periods. You can repair to the relative quiet of the escalator and stairwells to make a phone call, though a cynic could easily be excused for thinking the atmosphere in pretty much every seating area is sufficiently quiet to gab away all you want.

A game on October 10, 2009, against Pittsburgh was the third home tilt of the regular season but the first Saturday night contest since the new bar opened. It was obvious that many fans were impressed with the futuristic new facilities and its feel of a chic nightclub.

This was the setting that I encountered as I attended my first game of the season. The Leafs had lost the first three contests to start the schedule but there was still some optimism in the air. The presence of Sidney Crosby and rest of the defending Stanley Cup champions likely had a lot to do with the anticipation. But I digress.

Two mulleted Leafs fans were coming down the escalator after leaving the new bar area. Well lubricated and each holding a half-finished beer, the telltale cigarette tucked behind the ear of one of the fans was a sure sign they were heading to the smoking area just outside the west entrance.

"There are 20,000 people in here and only two of us are partying," yelled out one of the inebriated duo, his tight Leafs jersey a reminder of the 1980s, but also of the effect of too many beverages and fast food restaurant visits enjoyed in the interim.

"Come on, people, let's get 'er going," he called out as he scrambled to balance his beer and the cigarette that wouldn't quite behave behind his ear while the stairs moved beneath his feet.

Now, to be fair, Saturday night crowds tend to be a bit more enthusiastic. As discouraging as the 0 and 3 start may have been, having the defending Stanley Cup champions in the building, not to mention the best player in the world, created a buzz. Everyone, myself included, still maintained hope that this season really would be different from the previous four.

Perhaps because of that tepid anticipation, a few patrons took up the drunk duo's call, hoisting their $14.50 (tip not included) beers in the air in a show of solidarity. For about thirty seconds there were some whoops and yelps and catcalls, as people were slowly making their way to their seats.

The puck dropped and the atmosphere was somewhat energetic — for two hundred seconds. That's the point at which Penguins pest Matt Cooke[1] scored, giving his team a lead they didn't relinquish, highlighting the yawning talent gap between the two clubs.

After the Pens went into the first intermission with a 2–0 lead, Leafs plugger Jay Rosehill gave the home team's fans some brief hope as he scored his first career goal early in the second period. But while they were announcing Rosehill's goal, Crosby scored. Just like that, the atmosphere went as flat as the overpriced beer.

Eventually the Pens won 5–2 in one of those masterly efforts good teams always seem to manage on the road against poor opponents. And that's what this game represented; the demarcation point where the Leafs, despite the pending arrival of Kessel and whatever changes had taken place, clearly showed themselves to be a bad team.

A loss on opening night in overtime to the Montreal Canadiens was, in retrospect, a killer. The Leafs deserved to win that game and by the time the ninth contest rolled around, the Leafs had managed just a single point, notched in that opening-night setback. The loss against the Habs had set in motion one of those domino-like trends that can happen to teams thin on talent but heavy on hope.

If you attend many games at the ACC, it is contests such as the Penguins tilt that lead you to glance forlornly around the building. Once the Leafs fall behind, there's almost nothing worth watching on the ice — unless you enjoy seeing a Leafs opponent protect a lead with little bother from the home side — so you become interested in some of the most inane objects that dot the various areas of the building.

On this night a handful of empty suites were visible from my seat in section 312, an increasingly common sight at the time. To my immediate left was our loyal usher, Gene. He's a frequent presence at that end of the building, clad in his blue uniform and wearing his trademark sterling silver rings on what remains of his hands.(Having lost fingers decades earlier, Gene wears a whack of silver ring-wear that, I'm not sure he realizes, only seems to draw more attention to his missing digits.)

If you accept the premise that seemingly ordinary people have remarkable stories to tell, Gene is the type of guy who will leave you transfixed for hours. Short, pushing sixty, and with a few distinguishable physical characteristics such as his salt-and-pepper hair, tattoos, and the aforementioned preference for wearing lots of silver on his surviving fingers, Gene's true calling in life was to produce children at an alarming rate. He's the father of nine of them with several different women; a few decades ago Gene helped bring two kids into the world, born days apart to two different women in the same hospital.

Who said the Leafs haven't produced a champion since 1967?

Many of Gene's kids have inherited his fertile gene — or at least some of it — and he's now a proud grandpa to fifteen grandchildren. As his life story and basic description perhaps detail, Gene is one of those men that you can tell was one tough hombre in his day. Any hard edge is long gone, and aside from the faded tattoos, there is little evidence of anything but the kind, generous, and likable man he is.

And he shows the warm paternal instinct to everyone in his section. Almost always perched in one of the Ice Box sections — 312 through 315 — behind the net the Leafs shoot twice on, he's as recognizable back there as Armani suits are down below.

Female season ticket holders are routinely hugged — Gene's softness for the fairer sex is never far from the surface — and men greeted with a firm handshake. He possesses an encyclopedic memory of what a handful of his best customers take in their Tim Hortons coffee.

And his generosity shows itself in other ways.

On this night, for example, our seats are directly below an air-conditioning duct. A cold breeze was blowing down the back of my wife's light sweater vest — it could have been a metaphor for the chill that was already taking hold of the Leafs' playoff hopes after just four games. With goose bumps forming on my wife's partially exposed arms, she was giving off the unmistakable signs that women are especially adept at when they're cold.

Gene flew to the rescue. A fleece blanket — left over from an earlier credit card promotion — was retrieved; problem solved, with two white Leafs toques thrown in for good measure. It wasn't *that* cold in the ACC; he intended the hats for my two nephews — he remembered me bringing them to a game ten months earlier.

"Mean Gene," as he's affectionately come to be known by regular Leafs and Raptors fans in his section, is an interesting character, to be sure. But here I was attending my first game of what was supposed to be the season the Leafs finally broke through after the lockout and the most notable thing to talk about was our loyal usher. And the silence was deafening; I could almost hear the clock ticking until Kessel's return to see if he could make things better.

Sitting with Mrs. Robinson beside me, clutching $95 tickets, $15 beers, and $6 hot dogs, in a facility that holds the population of a small town, I felt like we were in the reading room of a senior citizens complex. Even discounting the fact the Leafs were getting beat, it was as if the fans on this night, as they are on so many others, were *trying* to be quiet.

For all its glory — as mentioned, the Air Canada Centre is a first-class entertainment facility — the arena can be one of the most soul-destroying places in all of sports if the Leafs aren't playing well. Sorry, make that the second-most soul-destroying — no place is more depressing than a half-empty Rogers Centre with the roof closed.

Pockets of the ACC can show life on most nights — all are in the upper bowl — but most of the vast acreage of seats are populated by people who could pass for cast members of *The Truman Show*.

The loss to the Penguins that night was part of one of the most discouraging stretches in modern Leafs history. Burke's first full season in charge, and he was watching this game up high in the Leafs management box. No other executives were in sight, but the unmistakable shock of ginger-grey hair was clearly visible. A younger man sat immediately to Burke's left and seemed to be enjoying himself, but he also looked as if he was wondering why the Leafs GM was tapping out so many messages on his BlackBerry.

The in-house video feed later confirmed the young buck beside Burke was crooner Michael Bublé. Bublé, an ardent hockey fan and passionate Vancouver Canucks supporter, presumably has been friends with Burke since the latter's days on the West Coast.[2]

The Leafs game operations staff did their level best to try to pump some atmosphere back into the building with many new features on display for that first Saturday night game versus the Penguins. The 2009–10 season also marked the debut of the new Leafs anthem, "Free to Be," a sappy but strangely addictive song by Glass Tiger front man Alan Frew. The opening of the revamped Ice Box complex added some élan on the west end of the building to go along with the giant HD screen atop that entrance.

But it was all for naught, with the low point coming on back-to-back home games on October 13 and 17. On the first night, the Colorado Avalanche rolled into town. A team searching for identity after the retirement of Joe Sakic the previous spring, the Avs had two then eighteen-year-olds — Matt Duchene and Ryan O'Reilly — in their lineup. Both players had strong connections to the Toronto area, with O'Reilly having grown up in Mississauga. Duchene played junior hockey in Brampton and was from Haliburton, about two hours north of the city. In other words, they were two bright young talents who would have looked awfully good in Maple Leafs uniforms.

Both youngsters had made the team after being drafted by the Avs a few months earlier. Watching Duchene and O'Reilly play for the other team was bad enough; imagine if it had been known at that point that the Leafs had just dealt away the rights to either Taylor Hall or Tyler Seguin.

Watching former Leaf Darcy Tucker almost single-handedly beat the Leafs on this night was quite another thing altogether. Tucker, playing in what ended up being his last NHL season, scored once and had an assist as the Leafs fell 4–1. The worst part? Tucker was in the midst of a $6-million buyout that the Leafs were paying him to get out of the disastrous $12-million contract he had signed three years earlier.[3]

Tucker was in typical Sideshow Bob mode as he made his return to the ACC. A video tribute was played on the scoreboard, and Tucker seemed genuinely moved by the warm reception he received from the crowd. To that point, Tucker's welcoming back was the most intense sign of emotion a Leafs crowd had shown since opening night two weeks earlier. Tucker scored in the second period and then showed his appreciation to the Leafs faithful by striking his classic bug-eyed face. Many fans had become familiar with that look over the years; it was equal parts Jack Nicholson and a man looking intense because he knew the television cameras were on him.

With the loss to Colorado, the Leafs were now 0 and 6 on the season and already effectively dead ducks. But the miserable stretch that killed the season before it had barely started had two more losses to come as the New York Rangers rolled into town four nights later.

Before the game, the Leafs welcomed back several players from the 1990s — an era when the club was a competent hockey team, and a very good one, at that, during several of those seasons.

In a classic case of the Leafs brain trust meaning well but not necessarily understanding the full message they were sending, the team chose a game against the Rangers to honour players such as Felix Potvin and Bill Berg. Both men played vital roles in two runs to the conference finals in 1993 and 1994 — those teams still serve as a high-water mark, especially the 1992–93 club that came within a single game of the Stanley Cup final.

Here's the rub: the Rangers actually won the Stanley Cup during one of those two seasons; in 1994, they defeated the Vancouver Canucks in seven games to take the trophy.

That triumph ended a fifty-year run of Stanley Cup futility by the Rangers and left the Chicago Black Hawks[4] and the Leafs holding the records for the longest Stanley Cup droughts.

So, in a ceremony that was modestly entertaining, Leafs fans were also subjected to the painful reality of what it means to be a staunch supporter: even when you try to celebrate some of the rare achievements of recent years, it often illustrates some of the bigger failures.

The game itself was a replay of the Avalanche contest, with one added feature: the goaltending struggles of Vesa Toskala. Playing against Rangers netminder Henrik Lundqvist, one of the best in the world, Toskala was hopelessly outmatched.

Toskala had played injured the previous season and was being given a second chance by both Leafs management and fans in the hope he would be better after off-season surgery. But he came back worse after getting his torn labrum fixed.

It was not long after the Leafs fell two goals behind the Rangers in the first period that it became another case, just as it had been a week earlier against the Penguins, of looking for something else to watch other than the hockey game.

On this particular night, a young man sitting in front of me was going to great lengths to get on either the big screen or the CBC broadcast on *Hockey Night*. The twenty-something had the look of a university student who had scored his dad's company tickets. He managed to strike a nice balance between having fun and being loud, waving a small flag that was vaguely familiar. He was loud but not annoying or intrusive.

It became obvious later, given his reaction to the "Luke's Troops" honouree that he was a member of the Canadian Forces who had just returned from Afghanistan. The small flag turned out to be his regimental colours and he spent most of the night waving it about while trying to prevent it from slipping into his beer. All the while, he was trying to get the attention of his buddies sitting in an adjacent section and waving the same colours.

Luke's Troops is a promotion that the Leafs defenceman started in his rookie year in 2008–09 that is designed to honour a serving member of the military.

The man honoured was a career navy man in his forties who had just returned from a deployment off the coast of Somalia. The much younger military man in front of me suddenly became incensed.

"A navy guy!" he shouted out to his buddies a section over to his right. "We dodge bullets for months and this guy gets free tickets for driving around in a boat and getting a sun tan? "Fucking unacceptable!"

In his anger at a navy man being honoured, the young army veteran didn't realize that his disgust was misplaced. It should have been directed at the Leafs. He had probably spent a good deal of his own money — even if his tickets were free, it was obvious by his increasingly inebriated state that he had spent at least $100 on beer and food.

The Rangers poured in four third-period goals to dust the Leafs 7–2. The crowd was incensed in one of those faux-Toronto ways. Boos rained down, roughly on par with those earlier that week against the Avalanche.

It was like the crowd felt it *should* be angry and therefore made a nominal effort at looking the part. Angry, but not angry enough to seriously consider not coming back.

The night ended with a horde of fans gathered around the huge screen outside the west entrance. The HD signal beamed out *Hockey Night* over Maple Leaf Square. Don Cherry, no fan of then Leafs head coach Ron Wilson, could be heard delivering a sermon in his post-game wrap-up with Ron MacLean; Cherry was defending both Wilson and the Leafs.

Cherry has often been accused, or complimented, depending on your perspective, of using his perch on "Coach's Corner" as a bully pulpit. That description was especially appropriate in this case because the massive screen is perched high above the ground and stretches the length of the vast entranceway. The hundreds of fans standing outside listening to Cherry on this mild late-October night looked as though they were seeking guidance from on high. Their faces were bathed in the blue hue from the projected colours of the HNIC set. More bizarre were the nods of agreement by the Leafs faithful as Cherry bellowed on about the Leafs righting the ship. If you believed in such things, it was almost as if Maple Leaf Square was some sort of hockey Lourdes with Cherry serving as the giver of miracles, the healer of the hockey sick.

And the Leafs would need a miracle now. In the space of less than three weeks, they had frittered away the optimistic outlook going into the season and started 0–6–1,[5] killing any realistic hope of making the playoffs with seventy-five games left on the schedule.

Leafs crowds don't need any reason to be indifferent; they are perfectly capable of that without cause. Now, there were thirty-six more home games of mundane atmosphere, with expensive food and drink, tepid crowds, tangible disappointment, and the utter lack of hope.

Any chance the faithful had of ever seeing Taylor Hall or Tyler Seguin in a Leafs uniform was gone, as well — traded away for a player who had yet to play a game before the team had essentially blown its chance to even make the post-season.

Seguin went to the Bruins the following spring at the Entry Draft with the number two overall pick secured in the Kessel trade. After some rookie uncertainty, he cracked Boston's lineup as an eighteen-year-old and played well in the playoffs, helping the Bruins win the

Courtesy Aaron Bell/CHL Images.

TYLER SEGUIN, SEEN HERE WITH DON CHERRY, BECAME THE PLAYER THAT BOSTON PICKED WITH THE FIRST DRAFT CHOICE IN THE PHIL KESSEL TRADE. SEGUIN WON THE STANLEY CUP A LITTLE MORE THAN A YEAR AFTER THIS PICTURE WAS TAKEN.

Stanley Cup. When it came time to spend his day with the Cup during the summer of 2011, Seguin brought the trophy to his condo near Maple Leaf Square and very near where the crowd had gathered less than two years earlier to listen to Cherry's sermon. A stark reminder of how bad the trade had gone.

Now *that* is unacceptable.

IN DEFENCE OF TORONTO

CANADA TENDS TO LOSE ITS COLLECTIVE MIND OVER HOCKEY. WHAT other nation on earth can say that the national broadcaster cancels and/or pre-empts its regular programming for two full months a year as the CBC does in order to accommodate the Stanley Cup playoffs?

We are lunatics about our national game. And with that passion there is plenty to like from all seven Canadian NHL cities. I will confess an admiration for Vancouver fans and their dedication that I now suspect outstrips the Leafs' support in Toronto. Aside from being jealous that the Oilers and Flames have won a hell of a lot more Stanley Cups than the Leafs have in the time I've walked this earth, I can't think of one harsh thing to say about Albertans. Besides, many people from that province give off the impression that in the event of things getting unruly they can handle themselves in less time than it would take for their massive Grade AAA steak dinners to get cold.

Winnipeg is everyone's second-favourite team because the fine folks in that city should never have lost the Jets in the first place. Ottawa almost lost the Senators, but it's to the capital city's great credit that they've hung in there because going to their Kanata-based arena could be confused for a day-trip to the middle of nowhere. It takes an hour just to get out of the parking lot. It's a tribute to Senators fans that they make that harrowing trek as often as they do. And don't even get me started on what it must have been like to put up with Bruce Firestone *and* Rod Bryden, both former team owners.

Montreal? This is the only time you'll hear me say something nice about the Canadiens, but you simply can't argue with the legacy and culture that the team represents. Frankly, I think it's cool, even if I wish the Habs would take their silly Montreal Expos mascot and go play in the East Coast League.

What rankles is how all the other six Canadian teams have a segment of their fan base who seem to think people from Toronto run the gamut of unlikable human qualities. Take your pick: arrogant, rude, even boring and dirty (the city, not its people). The arguments used to support their beliefs are often supported on out-of-context facts, hubris, and illogical brain cramps.

Okay, I submit — read on to the next chapter — that there are times when the scorn is earned. But the lack of common sense among most Toronto-haters makes me despair at their sheer stupidity; to wit, my experience on an overnight flight from Vancouver to Toronto one July evening in 2011.

I was on my way home from a seventeen-day work assignment in Western Canada, and I was grateful to have experienced what is surely the most beautiful scenery on earth. My time had been spent travelling between Banff, Kelowna, and Vancouver, and pretty much all parts in between. I'd encountered mountains, lakes, wildlife, and friendly, welcoming folks at every turn. I felt blessed to have the type of professional gig that allowed me to travel to such locales and, frankly, quite proud that our country has such tremendous places to visit.

I had been out West to cover the Canadian Open golf tournament, and write a couple of travel stories about areas such as Kelowna and the B.C. interior. As much fun as I had, though, I missed the wife and kiddies and that underrated feeling of sleeping in one's own bed.

I took my seat on the WestJet flight and, perhaps a bit too giddy about going home, I extended my hand to the woman beside me, something I almost never do.

"Hello," I said in introducing myself. "Going home or on holiday?"

She looked at me as though I had invited her to a swingers' convention.

"Ahmmm," she said, scrambling for words, "ah … holiday."

It turned out she was travelling through Toronto on the way to Newfoundland with her boyfriend, who was seated on the other side of her and who had nodded at me when I shook his girlfriend's hand.

Perhaps it was because I was about ten years older and didn't have my nose pierced in as many spots as she had, or the fact that

I have only one small tattoo that paled in comparison to the ink almost completely covering her exposed arms and shoulders, but this woman clearly had no interest in conversation.

The truth is, neither did I; I was just being polite (and a bit giddy). I grabbed a book and was out cold not long after takeoff. A few hours later, seatbelt warnings woke me up. Toronto was getting pelted with an overnight thunderstorm that was shifting the plane left and right.

Just as day broke, we were within sight of Toronto, the telltale sign of suburban sprawl, a dozen or so golf courses visible to the naked eye and the CN Tower off in the distance along the shore of Lake Ontario.

It wasn't exactly as dramatic as flying in to, say, Vancouver or Kelowna, but the scenes we saw from the airplane were still easy on the eyes. We began our descent with rain lashing down and were just about to touch down when the plane inexplicably lurched upward and took off again.

It was jarring and I was scared, but not nearly as much as some people; two women across the aisle from me were clutching rosary beads and openly praying. My seatmate had other concerns.

"Toronto is such an ugly city." She said this in a tone and volume that made it clear she wanted others to hear. "Look at the smog, like, gross. Is this Bangkok?"

Huh?

To be fair, it wasn't Toronto at its best because of the rain. We were landing in the midst of severe weather that laid a grey film across the horizon everywhere we looked. We were enduring some of the worst turbulence I've ever experienced flying, and spent almost an hour out over Lake Ontario waiting for permission to land after the first aborted attempt.

I spent the time silently contemplating what had given rise to my seatmate's condemnation. It was a cool midsummer Monday morning below — the pilot had confirmed temps in the mid-teens while he was explaining our delayed landing. Further, to the extent that Toronto is still home to factories, manufacturing plants, and other smog-producing industry, they were extremely unlikely to be operating overnight on a Sunday into Monday in the middle of the summer. The woman was confusing Toronto's grey veneer that morning to it being a smog-covered morass.

In other words, she was basically clueless, merely firing out a stock comment that she had picked up about Toronto and its so-called ugliness. The Bangkok comment only proved she had never been there.

I took the high road — though I was dying to say something to her — but a man immediately in front of me and to her right didn't.

"Relax … too bad we're on seatbelt lockdown here or you could order a granola bar," he snapped at her, peering back and over his seat with a look that gave the impression her tattoos were making him squint.

Given his harsh retort, I was glad I hadn't responded; he more than did the job of pointing out the folly of her comments.

Later, in the terminal, I ran into her boyfriend as he was washing his hands in a lavatory. He immediately recognized me in the mirror as I walked up to do the same.

"I know what you're going to say, mate," he said in a faint Aussie accent that I hadn't detected on the plane. "She doesn't have a high opinion of this place and I can't understand why — I've always enjoyed Toronto when I've been here."

His semi-apology was a nice gesture, and he was clearly embarrassed by the tiff on the plane. But that confrontation was symbolic of sentiment that I've encountered dozens of times when travelling across Canada — people carving up Toronto despite not having so much as visited the city. Travel the country and the strikingly dumb reasons why people voice their displeasure with Toronto and its residents would be funny if the attitude wasn't so ingrained. Often these Toronto-haters will admit, if asked, that they haven't spent any significant time in the city.

"Why would I go there?" is the general response.

So you hate a place you've never really visited?

Of course there are some exceptions. A good many Canadians actually like visiting Toronto and have a grand time while there.

They even cheer for the Blue Jays as Canada's lone Major League Baseball team. And, admittedly, Torontonians can be a tad different, or at least they are viewed differently than people from other parts of the country.

But when this frustration boils over, it's often the Leafs that are the focus, even when the conversation is not even meant to be about hockey. That Leafs-specific anger stems from the fact that Toronto-haters, no matter where they live, feel as if they can't escape Leafs coverage. Too often, everywhere they turn, the most benign Leafs item tops the newscasts, or so the argument goes.

If you hate Toronto, imagine how grating it is to be living in Brandon or Fredericton and tune in to Sportsnet and TSN, then have to wait through a five-minute report about Luke Schenn sitting out as a healthy scratch, or Nazem Kadri's latest call-up or demotion, before you can hope to hear about anything else.

I agree. It's annoying, but it's annoying even for many Leafs fans. It's also a simple fact, even if some in other parts of Canada don't like to acknowledge it, that there is no shortage of benign news reported about the Vancouver Canucks, Montreal Canadiens, and the four other Canadian NHL teams. For example, the game between the Canucks and Boston Bruins played on January 9, 2012, the first since both teams met in the Stanley Cup Final six months earlier, was hugely significant. The Canucks won, and Bruins weasel Brad Marchand laid out Canucks defenceman Sami Salo with a dirty hit. But did this incident really merit the coverage it got for days after? Or what about the over-the-top coverage by all types of media of the Montreal Canadiens and their various ham-fisted moves involving the coaching staff and playing personnel during the 2011–12 season? Randy Cunneyworth got more press, all of it negative, over a few weeks for not being able to speak French than he ever received during his 866-game NHL career that spanned almost two decades. Mike Cammalleri's modestly testy remarks about a "losing mentality" — which appeared testy only because of the complications of English-to-French-back-to-English translation — were followed by his subsequent trade to the Calgary Flames. L'Affair Cammalleri was the single biggest hockey news items reported at the time, knocking back the announcement of All-Star Game participants and a Leafs' four-game winning streak at the time. And we need to go over the Zdeno Chara/Max Pacioretty incident how much? (A season earlier the former had violently run the latter into an unprotected stanchion in Montreal's Bell Centre, causing a concussion and broken vertebrae. The replay was telecast over and over, so much it was enough to give non-Habs fans a broken neck recoiling from being forced to watch it so many times.)

As for the argument that *Hockey Night in Canada* is Leafs first, second, and third, well, the CBC goes to great lengths to also include Saturday games broadcast to local areas in Ottawa and Montreal. Also, since the emergence of the double-header on Saturday nights, there is almost always a second home game from Western Canada.

So what's the problem?

The central issue determining which teams are broadcast across the CBC's main network is cold, hard cash. Ask any television executive or magazine publisher what draws the most eyeballs to their product in Canada — almost always it's a Toronto-themed tease, either on the cover of a magazine or backdrop to a television program.

Toronto sells. And as hard as it may be for the rest of the country to understand and accept that, it's the chief reason the Maple Leafs get so much airtime. Don Cherry, for all his quirks, makes no mistake about his affection for the Leafs, and it's not because it comes from the man's heart. During a "Coach's Corner" segment that eventually went viral on YouTube with hilarious musical cues, Cherry made no secret why he focuses so much on the Leafs: ratings.

The Leafs win, more people tune in. It's a pretty simple metric. If the Leafs win a lot — look at the four times in the past two decades they have fashioned long playoff runs to the conference semi-finals — the city and wider area goes bananas.

Cherry acknowledged as much in the "Coach's Corner" segment in question. "Let's be honest," he said. "If they ever got in the playoffs, our ratings would go whacko."

No matter what you may think of the man, at least he's being honest — and *Hockey Night* is in business to make money. Many

IN DEFENCE OF TORONTO

of the people who bitch and complain about Leafs overexposure are precisely the same folks who call out the CBC for its reliance on public funds. The Mother Corp creates a property that actually makes money — gobs of it, if even the most modest reports are true — and suddenly it's wrong because it offends the sensibilities of non-Toronto types? Get over it, people, and remember, your team is available on secondary feeds.

But perhaps the most frustrating element to the Toronto-haters is their inability to turn even a modicum of their own judgment on themselves. As mentioned, there is no shortage of completely irrelevant or marginally interesting coverage of Canada's other six NHL teams. How much, for example, has the status of Jarome Iginla been bandied about in the national media since it became obvious that the Calgary Flamers weren't nearly good enough to return to the Stanley Cup final as they had done in 2004? Anyone force themselves to watch both seasons of *Changing Oil*? Sure, you can completely understand why Edmonton Oilers fans would want to watch it, in much the same way Leafs followers would surely do if there was a similar show on the Buds. But a second season, shown nationally on TSN, with the same overdramatic narration about a team that will be good some day but right now is certainly not?

Winnipeg, God love their long-suffering fans, have established a reputation early on that the MTS Centre is a tough place to play and full of crowds that are loud and emotional. Understandably, Jets fans were annoyed when noted space-cadet Ilya Bryzgalov told the media that he wouldn't consider moving with the Phoenix Coyotes, his then-team, when it looked as if the struggling NHL club could end up in Manitoba. It was a dumb thing to say. The resulting anger led to a mealy-mouthed apology from Bryzgalov when his new team, the Philadelphia Flyers, rolled into town for the first time.

Fine.

But Shane Doan? Hating the God-fearing Coyote from Alberta is, to borrow a simile from the comedian/talk show host Jon Stewart about Canadians, like hating toast. Jets fans found a way, though. Doan had been quoted as saying he wouldn't want to return to

Winnipeg — where he played as a nineteen-year-old rookie — simply because he had spent the overwhelming majority of his career and adult life in Phoenix, raising his family there. What did the good folks of Winnipeg do? They booed Doan mercilessly — the only original Jet still playing in the NHL.

You can only imagine what Jets fans think of the Leafs.

Brian Burke and the rest of the Leafs organization from the get-go had said all the right things about Winnipeg returning to the NHL. What's more, it was a genuine sentiment. When it finally happened, Burke cited a concern that everyone has or should have: what happens when the U.S. economy comes around and the Canadian dollars dips, two things that many people eventually expect to happen? Winnipeggers went whacko-angry and took it out on everything resembling the Leafs until the team eventually visited for the first time on New Year's Eve, 2011. Then they really went nuts hating the Leafs. Okay, given what that city had been through, it is understandable that Winnipeggers lost their judgmental compass, forgetting things such as the Leafs warmly embracing Jets fans the first time the team visited the ACC on October 19, 2011, reacting with a standing ovation when a scoreboard tribute was played welcoming Winnipeg back to the NHL. Manitobans get a pass.

In fact, fans overreacting anywhere is fine. It's part of the central meaning of supporting a team: you love your own more than what makes sense and hate others way more than you should. This disproportion helps the sporting world retain one of its central characteristics. In Canada, there is one notable exception where it has gone too far: Vancouver.

If Leafs fans are ignorant, sore losers, and all-around arrogant big-city blowhards, what does that make Canucks fans and a hockey team that is talented to be sure, but one that can be annoying and petty as well? Ed Willes, the fine Vancouver-based commentator, wrote an excellent column that appeared in the *National Post* on January 13, 2012, asking why the Canucks had such a poor reputation around the NHL. In a well-written piece, Willes pointed out that the Canucks had perhaps a few more agitators in their lineup than your average club, but that it was also chockfull of skilled, clean players who were upstanding members of their communities. The Canucks certainly have plenty of those wonderful qualities but it was what Willes *didn't* write about that could have answered the wider question.

Where to start? Well, let's see. Does anyone recall an incident that took place at GM Place in 2004 involving a Canucks player named Todd Bertuzzi? I dunno, something about a guy, a player named Steve Moore, who hailed from Toronto, no less, getting clobbered and never playing again? And the ugly aftermath when Canucks fans and players implied and often explicitly suggested that the whole incident was at least helped along in part by the Moore family and their superiority complex — all three brothers were Toronto-raised and Harvard-educated, after all.

Or what about the fact that many visitors to what is undeniably a gorgeous city have become increasingly alarmed with the hard edge of Canucks fans? To wit, what does it say about a city's fan base when a native son tries to bring home the Stanley Cup, as has been the tradition for decades, but for the sake of public safety has to have a private function to show it off? That's exactly what happened to the Bruins' Milan Lucic, and even though he isn't everyone's cup of tea, his treatment in his home city raised eyebrows. The ugliness got even worse when a church the Lucic family attends in Vancouver was defaced.

Most of all, no comment about Vancouver and its hockey team can go without mention of the unseemly and monumentally sad events of June 15, 2011.

We all know what happened. The Canucks lost Game 7 of the Stanley Cup final to the Bruins; soon after, Canucks owner Francesco Aquilini went on a profanity-laced tirade that very few media in the city even chose to report, but which was bravely detailed the next day by *Vancouver Sun* columnist Cam Cole. Around the same time that Aquilini was throwing his toys out of the crib, the club's fans tore out the heart of the city's downtown core. It was the worst case of hockey violence since the so-called Richard Riots in Montreal in 1955. In fact, the Vancouver riots could be seen as worse because the events in Montreal more than half a century earlier had clear political undertones given the time, place, and soon-to-be not-so-Quiet Revolution. What happened in Vancouver that night was the convergence of a number of different factors. Poor police planning, unfortunate timing — being played early in the west to accommodate east television views, the game was over while it was still daylight — and the complete wanton disregard for their fine city by some Canucks fans. It was an embarrassment for the city, for the country, and for hockey.

So, what happens in the aftermath? There was a rush to brand those involved as "not true fans." And what of all those idiots standing around watching and taking photos on their phones, often doing it clad in Canucks jerseys?

Why does Vancouver come in for such harsh words in this narrative? Simply, they are the best Canadian hockey team, and with success comes closer scrutiny. I would argue that what is happening now with Vancouver is about the same as what Toronto went through ten years ago when the Leafs were the best Canadian NHL team. It's not necessarily fair, because part of being a fan is granting yourself licence to act a little nutty provided you don't cross the line. The line in Vancouver was crossed.

Branding a hockey team's fans all with the same brush is especially unfortunate for Canucks supporters when you consider that Vancouver and its people put on the stunningly successful Winter Olympic Games. It was the biggest reason why — the athletes aside — Canada enjoyed what seemed like seventeen consecutive days of Nirvana. I would argue that all of Canada owes Vancouver a debt of gratitude for hosting the Olympics. But the degree to which Vancouver hockey fans will point the finger at others in order to explain some injustice that only they can see is a head-scratching part of what is otherwise a passionate sports culture.

So, please, if you're going to point the finger at Leafs fans, you have to also look at yourself. Too often (and right now Vancouver is the worst example), hockey fans from elsewhere in Canada cite the Leafs as the source of all things bad.

"*SportsCentre* covers the Leafs too much." — "*Hockey Night in Canada* is obsessed with the Leafs." — "Their fans are a bunch or arrogant fools who follow a terrible team." And on and on and on. It might even be true. But be careful what you wish for. If you turned the same intense spotlight on yourselves and your own team, you could be a bit surprised to find what it shows.

12

TORONTO FANS

"Before, we had to put up with the Leafs being shoved down our throats," said the voice on the other end of the line. "Now, they are going to be shoved up our rectum."

The call came from a trusted Vancouver-based colleague and was made after the announcement that Rogers Communications and Bell Media had agreed to join forces to buy the Ontario Teachers' Pension Plan's share in the hockey team. That, along with a small bump in minority owner Larry Tanenbaum's existing share, ensured that the two massive media companies would put their intense business rivalry aside, all in the name of good business.

The fact he's asked to remain anonymous because it could hurt his business with Toronto-based colleagues, is not unreasonable, even if his description sounds a bit painful. And *pain* is the best word to describe the effect the Leafs give off to large parts of Canada.

Painful to watch, painful to listen to, and painful to digest in what seems like a never-ending 24-7 news loop.

And the Leafs are just part of it.

Among die-hard CFL fans, there is a story that perfectly sums up the rest of Canada's angst with the residents of Toronto. It took place during the 1992 Grey Cup that was played in Toronto at the SkyDome, as the Rogers Centre was then known. Torontonian sensibilities — others could call it pretentiousness — got in the way of a tradition almost as old as handing out the trophy itself when Calgary and Winnipeg fans descended on the city to cheer on their beloved Stampeders and Blue Bombers.

The Calgary faithful, clad in full Western regalia — cowboy hats, boots — and all showing the effects of liberal amounts of alcohol, arrived at the doors of Toronto's Royal York Hotel looking to do what they had always done: parade through the lobby with the team's mascot leading the way. One problem: the team's mascot is a horse.

They were met by a befuddled hotel manager who couldn't conceive that people would want to do that. Even if they did, they weren't doing it at the ritzy Royal York. Something about new carpets was cited as an excuse, and the Calgary fans, four-legged one included, were sent on their way.[1] It was likely the only time since the tradition started that Calgary fans haven't been led into their hotel by their mascot during Grey Cup week.

Tradition? To some in Toronto the Calgary custom is something the heathens from the countryside, from places like Calgary, or Saskatchewan, or Winnipeg, would do. You see, Toronto is a *world-class* city and stuff like riding in on a horse is so *provincial*.

We're Toronto, we're world class. New York, London, Tokyo … Toronto, don't you know.

It drives people from other parts of the country to distraction, white-hot anger in many cases. The self-styled centre of the universe has that effect, and the Leafs are the biggest example of what gets under the skin of the rest of the country. At least to those who follow hockey, which covers a sizable portion of Canada's population.

The other six Canadian teams are hit-and-miss propositions to have a home game on Saturday night's *Hockey Night in Canada* broadcast. The Leafs are about as dead-certain to have that slot as they are not to be playing hockey in May.

There may be a perfectly reasonable explanation why Canada's sports media seems so Toronto-centric, but it's also equally understandable why the rest of the country gets its back up about it.

It comes down to simple logistics, really, because so many decisions are made in Toronto, the voice of the so-called national media has a Toronto-bias. Many Torontonians, if they even care, don't accept that premise, but it's undeniably true, and if you take the time to travel around the country it's painfully obvious.

One of the most frustrating parts, even for people who live in Toronto, is that some of the city is hopelessly out of touch with NHL hockey. Trying to assess why likely depends on where you're from. Toronto defenders often cite its virtually limitless entertainment options to explain why this swath of its citizenry doesn't always grasp the nuances of hockey the way other Canadian cities do.

While it's true that there are many things to distract a typical Torontonian's attention, Calgary, Montreal, and Vancouver also have an awful lot on offer for its residents, but the hockey fans in those cities don't seem as utterly out to lunch as some in Toronto.

That lack of knowledge is audible everywhere at the Air Canada Centre (more on that in a moment), but there is no better place to gauge the hockey IQ of Toronto than a visit to the local arena.

❖ ❖ ❖

Trying to beat back the aging process a bit after celebrating my thirtieth birthday a few years before, I took up the game again in 2005. The ebb and flow of Toronto's recreational hockey scene has many levels and elements, but one common theme if you play in the city is the Maple Leafs.

Go out to a rec hockey session, and if you're playing with ten others, you'll likely find eleven opinions about the state of the Leafs. Dressing rooms from Woodbridge to Whitby are filled with half-baked theories of what should be done to fix the team.

It was around the same time as my return to playing rec hockey that blogs and fan sites, and later Twitter and other social media, began to reshape the media landscape. The various forms of new media have added a lively edge to Leafs coverage because it tends to be a more accurate reflection of the joy (yes, there still is some joy), pain, and sorrow Leafs fans go through, rather than a conventional journalist's interpretation of it all. In other words, blogs and Twitter are merely a reflection of the various zingers that fly around hockey dressing rooms. And, boy, are there some dunderhead comments.

Assess the plausibility of this nugget from one Leafs fan: when then-Leaf forward Nik Antropov was coming to the end of his contract in February 2009, one guy I encountered regularly while playing hockey honestly believed it would be possible to trade the inconsistent Kazakh forward for Sidney Crosby, straight up.

"Have you lost your mind?" was my response.

"No," said my surprisingly confident friend. "Think about it. Crosby will want to come here because it's Toronto so you won't have to give up as much as other teams would. But Antropov can be a really good player if he wasn't surrounded by all the pressure of playing in Toronto."

Whew, how an otherwise high-functioning human being could come up with that logic is anyone's guess. At the time, Crosby was in the midst of a season that would later culminate in his first Stanley Cup triumph with the Penguins. He had already re-signed with the Penguins and there was nothing indicating he was unhappy in Pittsburgh and would want to move.

The Cole Harbour, Nova Scotia–raised superstar also grew up a Montreal Canadiens fan and has never, not once, given any indication of any sort of allegiance to the Leafs, aside from torching them most times when he visits as a member of the Penguins.

When all these facts were pointed out to my out-of-touch hockey mate, he was adamant that it could happen, but had clearly been unaware of Crosby's background, including that he grew up near Halifax a die-hard Canadiens fan.

From the wider view, if you accept that hockey know-how is tied in to success, Toronto's lack of it makes sense in an odd sort of way. A team that hasn't won the Stanley Cup since 1967 is not likely to have as knowledgeable a fan base as Calgary or Montreal. There also is an argument to be made (and it has been made) that dim-witted fans can't necessarily put the pressure on the team's management to produce a winner the way an astute base of supporters can. *They don't know what they're talking about,* any sensible general manager could say under his breath, *so why should I listen to them? If I do, I'll soon be sitting with them.*

If John Ferguson Jr., Cliff Fletcher, and Brian Burke — the team's last three GMs — actually ignored the sentiments of fans during their time at the helm, they never have said it publicly. In fact, all three men have said that it's difficult to construct an extensive blueprint and follow it to the letter because so much of the dedicated fan base demands a winner immediately.

Well, they've been waiting since 1967 for a Cup and since 2004 for a playoff appearance, so perhaps Maple Leafs fans have a little more patience than they are given credit for.

Patience aside, a little digging among the faithful reveals a stunning lack of knowledge of even the most basic facts of other teams, even the most successful ones.

Terry Koshan is a reporter for the *Toronto Sun* who has covered the Leafs for several seasons. He is fond of telling a story about the time when Ferguson was fired and the long search had begun for his replacement, a search that eventually ended with Burke installed as the new man in charge.

In early spring 2008, Koshan was playing hockey at his regular Sunday skate in Brampton, just north of the city, while the ongoing process of hiring a new general manager was still playing out. Fletcher was temporarily holding down the job. Just as it was across the entire Greater Toronto Area, conversation was flying about the dressing room as to what the Leafs should do. After the room mostly cleared, one particular lively conversationalist asked Koshan his thoughts, given his unique position of having covered the team.

"They should go after Kenny Holland," Koshan suggested, naming the man who is largely credited with putting together the Detroit Red Wings juggernaut over the past two decades. It was the type of response that many media people get used to giving when asked their thoughts on the Leafs — you eventually get beaten down by how many times you're asked so you trot out a well-used and obvious answer.

Koshan's comment was met with stunned silence and then this meagre retort:

"Who's Kenny Holland?"

Now, most people in Canada who still play or follow hockey as adults would at least be aware of the man who has been the most successful hockey executive of his generation. But if you spend any amount of time around Toronto's rinks, conversations like the one Koshan had are not rare.

Media members are not immune, either. Some of the missives written in newspapers, on websites, and on blogs can drive a sensible Leafs fan to tears and make non-Leafs fans laugh out loud.

Consider the following: While preparing to take an overnight flight to Italy for the 2006 Winter Olympics in Turin, Team Canada assembled for its lone practice at Mississauga's Iceland complex near Toronto's Pearson Airport. With most of the national media personalities already in Turin, only a few regular hockey stragglers from the Fourth Estate were on hand to file and write the obligatory reports before Wayne Gretzky's men headed to Italy.[2]

With a collection of some of the world's best hockey players on the ice before them — and just a single Leaf, Bryan McCabe — one respected reporter mused aloud about the ability of then-Florida Panther Jay Bouwmeester.

"He sucks," said the scribe.

"What? Look at the guy, he's the best skater in the NHL," I replied.

"He sucks," repeated the scribe.

While he hasn't lived up to the expectations first thrust upon him, the idea that Bouwmeester — a player who in 2003 had been voted the best defenceman at the World Championship before his twentieth birthday — could be dismissed by a Toronto hockey reporter was surprising. Was the then-twenty-two-year-old Bouwmeester not as good, as, say, current Leafs Andy Wozniewski, or Ken Klee, or McCabe?

"He sucks," came the mantra one last time.

Another conversation was particularly revealing. It came from a colleague who is, to be honest, a good guy, possessing that lovely human fault of sometimes blurting out what he thinks before considering the true effect of his words. He's a Leafs fan, in other words.

My colleague once produced a piece on Kyle Turris at the 2007 NHL Entry Draft, the player eventually picked third overall by the Phoenix Coyotes.

"He sucks," was his verdict, sharing the enlightened opinion and prose of his ink-stained brethren above. "He also had really small hands," in reference to the impression Turris had apparently left on him while shaking hands.

Almost in the same breath, the same individual sang the praises of Greg McKegg, an eighteen-year-old Leafs prospect with whom he had crossed paths while covering junior hockey.

To put his contrasting opinions in perspective, Turris is a former number three overall draft pick. Despite having an uneven start to his NHL career that saw him traded to the Ottawa Senators, Turris is on a path, if not to stardom necessarily, to a career all-too-rare for Leafs prospects. In fact, once in the nation's capital, Turris has been credited as being one of the reasons why the Senators exceeded expectations after the club's disappointing 2010–11 season.

McKegg, on the other hand, is a third-rounder (sixty-second overall) draft pick from 2010 and is projected to be a role player at best (if he even makes it) in the NHL. Though a very good junior player, McKegg was not once even invited to Canada's world junior selection camp, whereas Turris a few years earlier was one of Team Canada's leading players. Now, at least my friend was able to acknowledge the schism between Turris and McKegg's pedigrees and he had some deprecating fun at his own expense when I pointed out the difference. Many Leafs fans can be similarly very good-natured when you call them out on their cluttered logic — the banter has made late-night radio in Toronto fun to listen to for the past twenty years.

There are times when the ignorance by the media and fans runs almost in perfect symmetry to one another. For example, not long after the start of training camp to kick off the 2010–11 season, utility forward Tim Brent began making a strong case for a full-time gig with the Maple Leafs.

Brent, then twenty-six, was a career minor-leaguer who had been drafted twice by Anaheim and played in nineteen NHL games with four NHL teams. On that basis, he was a surprise and frankly a heartwarming story because he was a true underdog and a genuinely nice human being.

But that only told part of the story. Brent, in fact, should have been no stranger to Toronto hockey fans and media because he played for the Toronto St. Michael's Majors of the Ontario Hockey League as a junior. St. Mike's was a very solid, if completely unappreciated team in its market. Brent was the squad's best player and led the team on a long playoff push in each of the four years he played there. He also made the Canadian World Junior team over Christmas in 2003. That edition of Team Canada lost a heartbreaking final game to the U.S. when goalie Marc-André Fleury, now of the Pittsburgh Penguins, banked a clearing attempt off his own defenceman's rear end and into his own net for the Americans' winning goal.

So, you would think that a player who earned the status as one of Canada's best teenage hockey players while toiling at a midtown arena at Bathurst and St. Clair would at least resonate with Leafs fans and media alike?

Not a chance. Brent's emergence during training camp was treated as though he was an alien who had descended from the outer cosmos to make the team. There was also little mention of the fact that Brent had been injured during the previous season's training camp, robbing him of a chance to make the team. When Brent returned from that injury he was likely the Toronto Marlies' best player, earning a call-up for the final regular season game against the Canadiens in Montreal.

Had fans and Toronto's hockey media been following properly, they ought to have known that Brent's arrival as a full-time player was only a mild surprise.

Media speculation and dressing room scuttlebutt are just two perspectives. Going to a game and attempting to have a thoughtful conversation about the sport and the team with your fellow Leafs fans can take thoughtless banter to a whole new level.

Among the twenty thousand or so that stream into the ACC every game, the conversation that takes place can show a lack of depth of even basic knowledge of what's going on in front of them.

On February 8, 2010, the Leafs were playing their final home game before the Olympic break. The San Jose Sharks were in town and riding high with four Canadian Olympians on their roster, plus a few others from different countries.

As I took my seat in section 315, two young men sat down directly behind me. It was soon obvious that it was going to be a long night of hearing snippets of conversation between two people whose interest in the game was roughly that of your average person's familiarity with Latvian politics.

"C'mon, Manny," called out one of the two men. It suggested he may have had a fleeting connection with the Sharks' Manny Malhotra. But Malhotra would have had an awfully difficult time hearing the encouragement — he wasn't playing. He wasn't even in the building.

"Hey, bud," I said, trying to get his attention while performing the always-difficult turn-around to speak with someone directly behind you. "You realize Malhotra's hurt and not playing tonight, right?"

The look was priceless, like a man who had packed up the family car and drove to the campground only to forget the gas stove back in the garage.

"Russ, did you know that?" he asked his mate sitting beside him.

"Why would I know that?" Russ answered back.

Well, you're sitting in almost $200 worth of seats, have already bought $50 in food and drink, and made the effort to get to the arena, so the small detail of checking if your alleged friend was playing may have been worthwhile.

Something was muttered about how he and Malhotra had gone to high school together in Mississauga and had a few mutual friends, and how they had, therefore, jumped through hoops to get tickets to the Sharks–Leafs game for that reason.

It was all for naught. With Malhotra not playing, it only gave Russ and his friend more of an excuse to natter back and forth. It was like listening to two schoolboys trying to talk over the teacher. One of the topics discussed: how much money each had saved to buy a condo. Apparently, they were in a feverish competition to see who could come up with a down payment first, but both were dismayed at spending too much money on clothes and in nightclubs. Just once did these two late-twenties/early-thirties men make reference to the hockey game taking place in front of them, even as the Leafs were about to lose to the Sharks 3–2.

"Too bad Manny wasn't here," the one not named Russ said, in a tone that sounded as though he could have been referring to baseball player Manny Ramirez rather than the player he claimed to know.

"Gentlemen," I wanted to say, "You've got tickets to watch the Leafs play one of the best teams in the NHL (the Sharks, at the time) and you're having a conversation that sounds like it could be taking place at Tim Hortons."

It's not just conversation during games that Leafs fans engage in. Their routine before the game can leaving your scratching your head, as well.

About ninety minutes before an October 18, 2007, game against the Florida Panthers, one Leafs fan was picking up his son, aged around five. His wife had dropped the boy off in the lobby of one of the tall office buildings immediately to the north of the Air Canada Centre. Dad gave Mom a peck on the cheek and turned his attention to the lad.

"Are you ready, son?" asked Dad, clad in a new Leafs jersey, one that had the look of having been hung on his office door and worn once or twice a year when father and son headed off to a game.

"Daddy, I want to eat," was the young boy's reply.

Not an unreasonable or unexpected response from a child. The father and son pre-game meal could be just as enjoyable as the game itself for both of them. But Dad's choice of restaurant was very Toronto; the pair meandered through the crowded warren of streets in front of the ACC until Dad found his sweet spot: Take Sushi restaurant on Front Street, just down from the Hockey Hall of Fame. Apparently the traditional pub/restaurant fare of burgers/hot dogs and beer/pop — standard grub to most hockey fans — wasn't quite the same as feeding your young son raw fish before watching his beloved Buds.

The game itself, given that it was taking place in one of those hollow patches in the schedule, had a reasonable atmosphere on this night. But that didn't prevent a few howlers being made from the section around me.

Courtesy of Graig Abel.

FANS AT THE ACC HAVE THEIR MOMENTS, BUT THE BUILDING HAS BEEN CHARACTERIZED BY A STALE ATMO-
SPHERE VIRTUALLY FROM ITS OPENING, BUT ESPECIALLY SINCE 2005.

"Why are those side men doing that?" came one notable question from a woman who made the astute observation while momentarily looking up from her BlackBerry. I still distinctly recall her screensaver was a photo of her fashionable handbag she never took off her arm all game. She was asking why the Leafs' wingers hung around the Panthers defencemen when the puck was in Toronto's zone.

"No wonder the Leafs never win — their players just stand there."

I was sitting in the 600 section; normally a bank of accessible seating that is made available on game days to able-bodied patrons. The roomy sections tend to promote a bit more casual conversation between fans in their seats and ACC staff.

To that end, one of the youngsters who was standing behind her heard this woman's question. The polite young fellow, standing in that spot as a reward for helping sell 50/50 tickets, took the time to explain that the wingers go there because they have defensive responsibility to cover the opposing teams' defencemen and to try to create a quick puck transition up-ice.

"I know that," the youngster whispered back to me, with just a hint of a Caribbean accent creeping through, "and I've had skates on [my feet] twice in my life."

"Oh," was all she could muster in reply.

The game was taking place on a Thursday night, a surprisingly rare slot on the schedule for the Leafs. Thursday nights downtown around the ACC can have a fairly robust feel to them and it's not uncommon for restaurants and bars to be doing a roaring trade.

With a long work week almost over, you could almost feel that many in the ACC had thoughts of going out on the town after, a happy side benefit not usually in effect for the regular Tuesday night home games.

And with the jolly mood, one mantra that all Leafs fans know well was audible many times; it's the one word Leafs fans pick up at birth and never lose: "Shoot." Or more accurately, "Shoooooot," with a drawn-out cadence that is unmistakable to anyone who has taken in a game at 50 Bay Street.

On this night, the Leafs were locked into a defensive struggle with the Panthers, with the visitors taking an early lead before getting into some penalty trouble in the second period. The resulting Leafs power plays were greeted by that never-ending crescendo every time a Leafs player, especially a defenceman from the point, had possession of the puck.

"Shoooooot," echoed everywhere.

"I don't know about you, but I think that if a guy is an NHL defenceman, he knows when to shoot the puck," said the same kid with a shake of his head.

McCabe, the Leafs defenceman, was able to take advantage on one of those power plays in the second period, scoring to help erase a 2–0 deficit and tie the game. In the end, Antropov, still a Leaf for another two seasons before he left for New York in exchange for a second-round pick (not Crosby), scored from a scramble in front of the net to seal a 3–2 win in the final minute. All the Leafs fans left happy, walking out into an unseasonably warm autumn night. I left giggling, enjoying the fact so many ACC patrons are weak on hockey knowledge but also finding it oddly endearing.

13

BARREN SPORTS LANDSCAPE

THE OFFER CAME VIA EMAIL FROM A GOOD FRIEND, AND THOUGH just a short missive, it said all you need to know about the sporting scene in Toronto:

> I'm back in North America. I realized the other night that I didn't return the favour on the Leafs game from earlier this season. My bad. But I'll offer you these choices:
>
> +A Jays game — before they are mathematically eliminated from the playoffs
>
> +A Toronto FC game — after they are mathematically eliminated from the playoffs (which is from today on)
>
> +An Argos game
>
> Or, of course, you can wait until next season.
> Let me know.
> Jim

The message was sent April 14, 2011, a critical time in the sporting calendar, especially for cities with multiple teams to follow, such as Toronto.

The Leafs, when their fans dream their dreams, would be just starting the playoffs. The Blue Jays are just getting into the cut and thrust of their schedule. The Raptors, well, see the point about the Leafs. And Toronto FC is a few games into their season.

Even the Rock, economic minnows but nicely ensconced in their lacrosse niche, are gearing up for their own playoff push at this time of year.

Aside from the Argos, who are six weeks from opening training camp, every one of Toronto's professional sports teams, big and small, should be in action. Three of five teams could be in the playoffs and the other two flush with the hope of a new campaign.

Indeed, most major league sports cities are full of anticipation at this time of year. In Toronto's case, with winter having released its icy grip, spring should especially be the season where hope springs eternal.

But you'd have to have a long memory to see it that way. Even assuming that mid-April hasn't yet brought despair to the Jays' fortunes — a leap of faith since they last won the World Series in 1993 — you would have to stretch back to 2002 to find a season where there was anything resembling multi-sport anticipation in the early spring.

Peel back the onion a few extra layers, and there's even a bit of hidden meaning in Jim's message. He was emailing because I had taken him to the October 18, 2010, game against the New York Islanders.

The Leafs had done the unthinkable and won four consecutive games out of the gate, with two looming home games against both New York teams. The hockey club was looking at the distinct possibility of going 6–0 to start the season because both the Islanders and Rangers represented easy-beats.

The plan was for Jim to return the favour post-Christmas, preferably after the February trade deadline, with the Leafs hopefully in playoff contention.

What seemed a distinct possibility took on a more ominous tone as the Leafs dropped both games, first against the Islanders in overtime[1] and then a particularly horrendous effort versus the Rangers four nights later. Both were dreary 2–1 results.

A 4–0–0 record and almost breathless optimism soon read 4–1–1 with doubt suddenly creeping into the picture.

Jim's crushing travel schedule soon became an issue. It didn't help that the Leafs managed to completely throw away the good start and were essentially out of the playoff picture by Christmas. That's an incredibly difficult thing to do after starting 4–0 and gaining nine of a possible twelve points through the first six games.

Out of the country for weeks on end and perhaps subconsciously not relishing the thought of spending a few hundred bucks on one of the handful of meaningless games he was around Toronto for, Jim understandably forgot that it was his turn.

There are many other things Toronto sports fans would love to forget about in the past decade.

Let's see. The Leafs missed the playoffs the first seven seasons (and counting) after the lockout that ended in 2005. The only bright spot being the decent season of 2006–07 where the team posted a 40–31–11 record, the only thing resembling a legitimate post-season push (two other close brushes don't count because they were the result of piling up wins once the pressure was off).

The Toronto Argos brought the city four Grey Cup championships since 1991 but those titles combined would be hard-pressed to move the needle as much as a single Leafs playoff run. Besides, when the Argos field a decent squad, they tend to be very good. When they are bad, well, this being Toronto, they are spectacularly bad. In a city that has been largely indifferent to CFL football for two generations, the four championships mean little in the big picture, as much as I and other Argo fans may enjoy it when the team plays well.

When Toronto was announced as host of the Grey Cup again in 2012, its hundredth anniversary, the team's hard-core supporters looked toward that date with equal parts anticipation and utter horror because of the Argos' penchant for laying an egg when it's most important.

The Blue Jays, stuck in a division that ensures they have to play the powerhouse New York Yankees, Boston Red Sox, and Tampa Bay Rays a combined fifty-four times a season, have been equally stuck in neutral for almost two decades.

With the Jays, there have been positive strides during Alex Anthopoulos's reign, but their place in the city's sporting landscape is a bit tricky because of damage done by the man who used to run the show before Anthopoulos.

That man is J.P. Ricciardi. During his time in Toronto, Ricciardi always had the appearance of being the smartest guy in the room. Apparently nonplussed with the city, Ricciardi continued to raise his family in Boston, seemingly unaware of the message it sent to both Torontonians and, by extension, the many Blue Jays fans across Canada.

If Ricciardi didn't deem it important to spend all but a minimal amount of time here, how convincing could he be to players he attempted to sign and keep in the city?

Ricciardi spent most of his management/coaching career in Oakland before coming to Toronto in 2001. The experience he presumably gained there was said to influence the decision to hire him because he had supposedly learned how to field a competitive team while spending less. How a team owned by Rogers, a massive media conglomerate, would want to spend less is a source of much frustration for Jays fans. That Rogers later bought into the Leafs could provide an interesting parallel for hockey fans.

Ricciardi's reign was marked by a never-ending carousel of players coming and going, most being trumpeted as being a key piece of the "plan." It was all done with a tone of a man addicted to describing his own genius.

In the end, it was eight seasons of mostly failure, marked by the grace and excellence of Carlos Delgado early on and Roy Halladay throughout; those two men's remarkable talent and personal loyalty to Toronto was sadly spoiled by the numerous bad contracts given out by Ricciardi. Despite joining the Jays, many of those players signed by Ricciardi had an air of "just visiting" during their time in Toronto. A little like the man himself.

Ricciardi even attempted to woo pitcher Gil Meche to the Jays by taking him to a Leafs game versus the Boston Bruins on November 28, 2006. Meche and Ricciardi's mugs were flashed on the big screen during the Leafs' 4–1 loss and each had the look of a man not exactly enjoying the attention. The courtship didn't end well: Meche signed with the Kansas City Royals, Ricciardi questioned Meche's value, and the whole thing made the Jays GM look petty and completely in over his head.

Most of all, there were hundreds of annoying sound bites from a guy who reminded many Canadians of that yappy tourist you get stuck beside at dinner while on holiday in Mexico or the Caribbean. Those people usually last a week in your life, but Ricciardi's stay was eight full years, and the mere mention of his name still burns the eardrums of any self-respecting Toronto sports fan.

I distinctly recall the moment I got the feeling that something wasn't right with Ricciardi. It was not long after he was hired, in that uncertain time in the immediate aftermath of September 11, 2001. There was a malaise on people's outlook in general. It was also a time when newspapers still put out big editions, with the *National Post* running an informative feature that asked an interview subject twenty questions. Doing a feature on Ricciardi made perfect sense. He was new in the job and people wanted to know more about his outlook for the Blue Jays and about the man himself. Given the time frame, it was inevitable that Ricciardi would be asked about the horrible events of about six weeks earlier and the increasingly militant tone from the neo-conservatives in the U.S.

Ricciardi's response was telling. He said that he supported whatever it was that the then-president George W. Bush would do and that as an American he inherently stood for all things good and free. And that his ancestors had come from Italy, much like so many others had done from places such as Germany and Ireland, to the land of the free and home of the brave.

No reasonable person would begrudge an American for being patriotic in the face of the worst terrorist attack on American soil. The point was that Ricciardi was completely unaware of the fact that virtually every Canadian — the fan base of the new baseball team he was now running — had a similar story. That we, too, were a new nation filled with immigrants that had come here for a better life. In fact, Canada's borders remain much more open than those of the U.S. The man simply didn't get it and had, at best, a loose understanding to the sensibilities of his market. And it was a market that knew its stuff when it came to baseball, even if Ricciardi didn't think Torontonians could tell a baseball from a bowling ball. Torontonians in 2001 still had very fond memories of the Blue Jays and what Pat Gillick, Paul Beeston, and Cito Gaston had done in building teams that first contended in the 1980s, and then won two World Series titles in 1992 and 1993. It's not an exaggeration to say that those three great men even cut significantly into the appeal of the Maple Leafs in the timeframe between, say, 1985 to 1995.

As a city, province, and indeed country, and given the fact that the Blue Jays retained a significant appeal across Canada, we didn't need some yappy Yank preaching to us as though we couldn't possibly understand the nuances of a sport that wasn't in our blood.

Listen, you little twerp, I grew up with this game and have watched great teams play and win here, don't preach to me about anything, just shut up and show me what you can do.

How many times a Blue Jays fan, myself included, yelled at the television with Ricciardi on it with words to that effect would number in the millions. Ricciardi's routine was no different than a Canadian hockey executive going into a place such as New York, or Boston, or Minneapolis, and preaching to fans that they couldn't possibly understand the in-and-outs of the sport the way he could.

Understand the parallel?

Ricciardi's decision to treat Toronto as a hotel — nice place to visit, wouldn't want to live there — also ran counter to what Beeston, Gillick, and Gaston had done during their time in charge. Beeston was a Toronto native and remains in the city during his second go-around with the Jays. Gillick and Gaston were both Americans who took an immediate shine to the city and country, both of which loved them back unconditionally. Both men immediately moved to Toronto and Gaston has remained for decades, with Gillick raising his family here and retaining ties long after he left the Jays.

Though now a situation that could be heading for an ugly divorce if things don't improve on the ice, when Brian Burke was hired as the Leafs general manager, he very much took the tact of Gillick and Gaston in embracing the local community.

If Ricciardi wasn't enough, along came Mo Johnston, brought in to run the MLS franchise awarded to MLSE for the 2007 season. Toronto sports fans had the joy of having both of them in the city at the same time for two full seasons.

Toronto FC was a curious and interesting case because it was easy to draw parallels with it and the Maple Leafs and Raptors given that they had the same corporate masters. It was easy to assume that the brain trust behind the soccer team had many of the decision-making policies in place. This is to say curious ones, at least.

The lead-up to the soccer team's debut was not particularly successful and it wasn't just Johnston's hiring that later proved to be such a bad move. The casual sports fan showed only tepid interest, and it was tough to gauge whether the city's immigrant communities would translate their long-held fascination with the European soccer leagues into bums in seats at BMO Field.

One night during the early-season Leafs schedule in the fall of 2006, the big screen in Air Canada Centre carried a picture of a young man who appeared slightly sheepish, with just a hint of anticipation as he waited to see whether the crowd could figure out who he was. He was fashionably dressed, with a haircut that looked as if it had been imported direct from a chic European salon a few months ahead of the curve in North America.

Jim Brennan was the first TFC player to sign in the fall of 2006 and a few months later was brought to the Leafs game in a nominal promotion effort. A local lad who grew up in nearby Newmarket, he had toiled with some success in the English leagues and was now coming home.

Brennan proved to be a decent player, but TFC was otherwise an unmitigated on-field disaster through the club's dance with Mo Johnston. The damage wrought by his regime was felt through the first five seasons. In retrospect, it's a miracle that Brennan's good-looking mug didn't dissolve on-screen that night — that's how bad things have gone.

Even the stadium, its building, and its operation had a classic Maple Leaf Sports and Entertainment unseemliness to it. Built not far from the waterfront on the grounds of the Canadian National Exhibition where the old Exhibition Stadium used to stand before it was demolished, BMO Field was erected as a soccer-only facility and MLSE managed to get all three levels of government to kick in vast sums of money to pay for the majority of the project and its twenty-thousand-plus seats. In return for its own relatively modest investment, MLSE got to own the building and sell the naming rights.

It was a sweetheart deal by any definition, no matter where you stand on the question of public funds being used to help already-profitable private companies. The only obvious concession that MLSE made in exchange for the government funds was a pledge to make the field available to the public. In order to fulfill that commitment, artificial turf was installed so it could be used year-round.

Disaster number one.

MLSE had managed to undercut its own team even before it played a game. Even by the standards of MLSE, this broke new ground in stupidity. Installing artificial turf in the twenty-first century is the sporting equivalent of showing up to a black-tie party in a hair shirt.

In the world of professional soccer, which never took to the then-newfangled technology even back in the 1970s and 80s, you might as well have placed a sign on BMO Field's marquee telling prospective signees: Don't Play Here. And that's effectively what happened: high-profile free agents from both North America and overseas gave Toronto a pass because playing on turf was a complete non-starter. Though natural grass was later installed in 2010, the damage was done.

If the turf was a looming disaster, the hiring of Johnston was an immediate one. He was a very good player in his day, but a simple Google search would have revealed Johnston's sparse managerial and coaching acumen. He came to Toronto after a modestly successful run in New York as an assistant. Promoted to the top job in the Big

Apple, he won just two of twelve games before being dismissed. Fresh off the doomed Raptors tenure of GM Rob Babcock, who had extensively more basketball managerial experience than Johnston did in soccer, it was a stunningly bad hire by MLSE upper management. The results showed quickly, despite a massively warm embrace from the local community. Fans streamed into BMO field and the team had to cap season ticket sales. A number of passionate supporter organizations formed and TFC fans are still generally regarded to be the best in the MLS. Players such as Brennan and Danny Dichio became fan favourites, and the developments off the pitch could not have been better.

It was, and still is, a windfall that MLSE couldn't have possibly imagined when it first awarded the expansion team. Or perhaps the MLSE suits did know how well it was going to turn out at the turnstiles and yet still managed to get it so wrong in the front office.

The fans have been repaid for their support with a managerial and coaching gong show that has made the club the expansion stepchild of the league even as players from other teams respect the club's supporters. And this is where Johnston's incompetence comes in. Aside from the drafting of a handful of decent players, highlighted by Maurice Edu with the first pick in the MLS draft, Johnston failed to make another selection or signing that stayed long enough to have a positive impact.

Brennan's time in Toronto was reasonably successful but signing a hometown boy whose career was coming to a natural end in Europe is hardly the result of yeoman's work on the part of management.

Dichio, though English-born, was right at the end of his career in his own country and gutted out an admirable three-year, fifty-nine-game showing for TFC in his new home. Whether Johnston is due credit for Dichio's presence in Toronto is debatable, because the player's contribution to the club was more in providing an emotional identity common with expansion teams in all sports.

What is not a matter of debate is Johnston's penchant for the trading and cutting of players, many of whom went on to vastly more successful careers once they left Toronto.

The parallels to certain ex-Leafs who left Toronto and fared much better in their new home is too obvious to ignore and painful to digest.

Dozens of players came and went and you'd need to have a MENSA-level memory to keep track of them all. But a few moves by Mo stand out and scream Titanic-esque disaster.

The first was the trading of Conor Casey. Deemed an excess part by Johnston, he was moved to Colorado, his home-town club, shortly after Toronto picked him up in the 2007 league expansion draft. Johnston got back a player named Riley O'Neil and what are referred to as "allocations" in MLS parlance — basically salary-cap money. O'Neil never played a game for TFC.

Casey? Well, he's scored more than forty goals for the Rapids. He's played numerous times for the United States and was almost single-handedly responsible for the Americans' win over Honduras in 2009, which booked their spot in the 2010 World Cup in South Africa. To top it off, Casey was selected MVP of the 2010 MLS Cup, leading his team to a league championship at the neutral venue of, I'm not making this up, BMO Field in Toronto.

So what did the MLSE suits do with Johnston after his first year, a season where TFC was out of contention by the time summer rolled around and the club netted the inglorious distinction of going the longest stretch in league history without scoring?

Why, they promoted him, of course. Now, MLSE would never say it was a promotion, especially given how things eventually ended. The company line was that he was moved upstairs to concentrate on his managerial duties and away from the touchline where he was even more out of his depth, apparently.

In came John Carver, a likable soccer lifer from the northeast of England, an area where people are known as Geordies for their hardscrabble loyalty to community and their love of the game. Comparisons to Canadians' love of hockey were not without merit when assessing the vibe Carver gave off regarding his passion for soccer, or football as Carver would surely prefer.

Perhaps because of those admirable traits, Carver quit when MLSE officials threw him under the bus for his criticism of the refereeing in a match, which resulted in a small fine. Annoyed more at the principle of not being backed by his bosses rather than the financial penalty, Carver packed his bags and left.

But not before he left his mark in subtle ways. Not one to suffer fools, Carver had some rather unusual ways of calling out players during his little more than a season in charge. Without realizing it — or perhaps aware of the fact but smart enough to make it look otherwise — Carver was calling out Johnston.

One of several players who drove Carver and the TFC faithful to distraction was Jeff Cunningham. A gifted scorer and not one afraid to tell the world about it — his number ninety-six in Toronto was selected to symbolize how many goals he had scored to that point in his career — Cunningham got the Toronto flu when Johnston acquired him for Alecko Eskandarian.

Eskandarian was a solid MLS player who seemed happy in Toronto. Cunningham, though not exactly a petulant brat, seemed a soccer version of one of those Blue Jays or Raptors players who fancied themselves a bit too good for Toronto. Whatever the case, his contributions to TFC were modest compared to what he did before and after his time in the city. Mo's kind of guy, in other words.

Carver openly mocked Cunningham's ability to score goals when he missed a "sitter" during the 2008 season, wondering aloud how such a plodder could have scored almost one hundred goals as a professional player.[2]

After Carver took his leave, the circus clowns rolled in for real. Carver was replaced on an interim basis by Chris Cummins. Just thirty-seven, also English, but from the south of that country, Cummins was a sort of yin to Carver's yang. But he, too, possessed an underrated sense of humour and seemed to realize that he was playing a supporting role in a sort of soccer version of the theatre of the absurd.

Having not coached or managed at any sort of significant pro level before — again, another curious example of MLSE's criteria for installing important personnel, even if he was just an interim hire — Cummins threw caution to the wind.

The team played well at times and bagged its first title with him at the helm. TFC poured in six goals against the Montreal Impact to overtake the Vancouver Whitecaps and win the 2009 Canadian championship on the final day of the competition.

A championship is a championship, but this one was contested separately from the regular MLS schedule. Winning a cup competition in Europe is big business but the Canadian version was a little like winning the crown as the best mother-in-law at a family reunion. It certainly wasn't what the great masses of fans had imagined when the 2007 inaugural season started with such a positive vibe. In fact, TFC's failings on the pitch that continue as of this writing have been allayed by the club's consistent efforts at winning the Canadian championship even if contending for the MLS crown remains a pipe dream.

The second most notable accomplishment of Cummins's stint in charge came when he told the media he was going to get "leathered" after a particularly stressful game. It's tough to imagine in this age of professional sports a coach or manager being so candid — even if completely truthful — but Cummins's youthful bluntness and levity provided glimpses of comic relief needed in the context of Mo's House of Horrors.

Of course, this being Toronto, it didn't end well even for Cummins. After compiling a decent record of around .500 in limited time with Cummins in charge, Toronto needed to win its final game of the season in New York against the Red Bulls to have any sort of hope to make the playoffs for the first time in its three-year history.

Final score: Red Bulls 5, TFC 0: an utter train wreck for a team that had been headed off the rails from the moment a ball was first struck in anger.

Cummins, muttering something about being annoyed his wife couldn't get a Canadian work visa, was on the first plane back to England, his contract not renewed.

But there was a fitting symbolism to the night TFC's 2009 season came crashing down. It was taking place at precisely the same time as the Leafs got beat 3–1 by the Vancouver Canucks on the West Coast.[3]

The setback ran the Leafs record to 0–7–1 to start the season.

In the final analysis, October 24, 2009, was a sort of Night of the Long Knives, with one game officially killing Toronto's chances in soccer, the other unofficially ensuring that the hockey season would go down in flames without a playoff appearance for the fifth straight year.

Perhaps deluded into thinking that men with only one name are a sure-fire way to success, Johnston's hiring of Preki (given name Predrag Radosavljević) as coach for the 2010 season was his last card to play.

Brazil gave the world sublime soccer and the maestros that play it with one name. Neither Brazilian, nor a maestro on the touchline, Preki fell on his face not long after his hiring. He and Mo walked the plank together in September that year, just as another lost season was about to be finished off.

The graceful Aron Winter, brought in to succeed Johnston, was a respected international soccer figure stemming from his playing days in Europe and for the Dutch national team. He, too, failed miserably despite leading TFC to a pair of Canadian crowns. That a man of Winter's background could also not get it right during his time in charge of TFC strongly suggests a complete institutional failure on the part of MLSE.

Again, the parallels to basketball and hockey can't be denied.

Discounting the hockey men formerly in charge who, surprisingly, have for the most part retained their professional reputation and dignity after leaving the Leafs, Mo Johnston is the most glaring example of former executives that left the city in sporting disgrace in recent years.

J.P. Ricciardi, Rob Babcock, Mo Johnston. Three men who were hopelessly unqualified to run a major sports franchise. And two were hired by MLSE, the results as predictable as their resumés should have indicated when they took the job.

The trio's time in Toronto was nicely summed up before a Leafs game in the fall of 2010. Nursing a pint in Jack Astor's on Front Street in Toronto while waiting for a friend, I turned to my left and nodded to acknowledge a TFC supporter who pulled up the stool beside me.

Wearing a TFC cap and Lycra sports pullover, he clearly was going to have an opinion on the state of the club. Johnston had been sacked about a month earlier, so I thought it would be wise to regale the thirty-something man with the one Mo Johnston story I had gleaned by often priming the pump in Jack Astor's before and after Leafs games.

"You know where you're sitting?" I asked the man.

"No," he replied.

"Where Mo Johnston would before and after Leafs games," I told him. In truth, it was on only two occasions I had seen Johnston in that pub and sitting at or near where we were now.

"Yeah?" he snorted, before taking a slight pause to deliver his response. "Well, tell me … what do you get if J.P. Ricciardi and Rob Babcock ever had a love child?"

"I dunno," I answered.

"Mo Johnston."

That biological impossibility is all too real for Toronto sports fans.

14

TRAGIC HEROES

THE 2007–08 SEASON WAS RIFE WITH STORIES, INCLUDING THE FIRING of general manager John Ferguson — big news by any definition but not the biggest event for the Maple Leafs. That revolved around Mats Sundin and his eventual decision to not waive his no-trade clause as his contract was about to expire. Sundin, of course, wouldn't consent to a move and that decision pretty much ensured that his legacy in Toronto would remain mixed, though he perhaps helped throw a bit of mud in the picture himself when he wound up in Vancouver the following season.

In the past forty-plus years, Sundin's end in Toronto was a different tune of the sad song that always concludes the same: star players' careers go down either in flames, or with a whimper. The Leafs have not been blessed with a long roll call of players who could legitimately be considered stars. But the relative few the team has had in that span have left a sour taste in everyone's mouth as they made their way out of town.

Dave Keon: banished by Harold Ballard and then happy to remain in exile.

Lanny McDonald: traded to isolate Darryl Sittler.

Sittler: dealt himself, but not before having to stew as his formerly solid team was dismantled around him.

Wendel Clark: moved to Quebec, but never quite the same when he did come back.

Doug Gilmour: to New Jersey, only to have it end so sadly upon his return.

Curtis Joseph: gone for nothing, even if the Leafs did manage to sign Ed Belfour to replace him.

Are you picking up on a trend here?

Even Borje Salming, the lone Leaf star who spent his entire career where it started, in Toronto — that odd Detroit sojourn aside — had most of his prime years wasted by the self-immolation of the Ballard years.

Bloody hell, even Blaine Stoughton departed without fanfare to the WHA only to come back and score fifty goals twice for the Hartford Whalers, of all teams. Stoughton wasn't the same level of player as the others and so his name doesn't exactly fit on the same list. But having Stoughton around in the late 1970s before Punch Imlach came back to tear down the team Jim Gregory had built could have been what the Leafs needed to get them over the hump.

Sundin, the key piece that came the other way when Clark was traded, was forced to endure a prolonged death march in much the same way Salming was, even if there wasn't quite the circus atmosphere his idol and fellow Swede had to put up with. With that case history of all the departed stars behind him, it's amazing that Sundin's final few seasons as a Leaf were as relatively controversy-free as they were.

The final story came with some confusion of a different kind.

On the evening of October 11, 2007, Toronto was hosting the New York Islanders. The Leafs were coming off a 7–1 hammering by the Carolina Hurricanes two nights earlier. That night, boos had rained down all over the ACC as Carolina had made the Buds look foolish on home ice. Early in that game — despite the final score, the Leafs scored first — Sundin had assisted on a power-play goal by Bryan McCabe. It gave him 916 career points as a Maple Leaf, tying him with another captain and all-time great, Sittler. Given how the game had turned out against the Hurricanes, it would have been a shame for Sundin to register another point that night and break the club record while getting beat so badly. Imagine, as diabolically fitting as it may have been in certain ways, Sundin scoring a goal to make it 7–2 for the Hurricanes, breaking a long-standing record as the Leafs were taking a home-ice haircut.

Now, on October 11, the big Swede, God love him, would get his chance. And sure enough, in the second period an announcement

Courtesy of Graig Abel.

SUNDIN NEVER WARMED THE HEARTS OF CERTAIN LEAFS FANS, PERHAPS BECAUSE OF HIS DISTANT AND SLIGHTLY AWKWARD APPEARANCE WHEN HE FIRST ARRIVED FROM QUEBEC AS A HIGHLY TOUTED SWEDISH STAR.

was made that he had got an assist on a goal by Tomas Kaberle that made the score 3–1 for the Leafs. Sundin had broken the record, or so everyone thought. A tribute on the video screen showed Sundin scoring various goals over the years. The goals had started not long after his arrival as a fresh-faced, Jofa-wearing man-child who seemed, well, gangly — a little like a Swedish Bambi but slightly more sure of himself. Sundin's remarkably consistent performance throughout his decade-plus in Toronto was relayed in vivid detail, potting picture-perfect goals and parking his large Nordic posterior down low and muscling pucks into opponents' nets. The faces surrounding Sundin on the video screen changed so much over the years it was impossible to keep track of them all, but one thing always held true: they never matched his remarkable physical gifts.

The ACC crowd reacted a little slowly to the images on the screen, but eventually warmed to the occasion. His teammates on the bench were clearly moved by the video being played above their head. It's always the great ones' teammates who know better than anyone else how good these stars are.

I was sitting in the golds that night thanks to tickets provided to me last-minute at a steep discount by a colleague named Eric Barlow, who couldn't go to the game. My friend Jason was beside me. I have to confess that I had forgotten that Sundin was so close to breaking Sittler's record. Given the way things were turning out, I was grateful to have a chance to witness Sundin create Leafs history.

Jason and I, like everyone else in the building, were standing saluting Number 13. From my vantage point, I had a perfect view of the Islanders bench and it was clear even a few of them were impressed. There was one huge problem: Sundin didn't look like someone who had just broken a record, nor was he exhibiting his usually sheepish, humble grin. In fact, he looked a bit embarrassed at all the fuss, and when he lifted his stick to acknowledge the crowd, Sundin looked as though he was trying to hide behind the twig.

There was a perfectly good reason why he was acting that way — he knew that he hadn't touched the puck and shouldn't have been credited with the assist. Sure enough, several minutes later it was announced that there was "an official scoring change on the Maple Leafs third goal." The assist was taken away from Sundin and the Leafs captain was back to 916 career points, tied with Sittler.

It's hard to describe how typical such a mistake is for the Toronto Maple Leafs. It was no one's fault — mislaid scoring points are a frequent occurrence and unavoidable in a game that moves as fast as NHL hockey does — but there was something so appropriate that Sundin would become the all-time scoring leader of the Leafs and then all of sudden be back to being tied. The tease was a microcosm of what it's been like to follow the team for much of the past forty years.

Sundin, who never got nearly the credit he so richly deserved in Toronto, put things right. With the Leafs firmly in control and sticking it to the Islanders in much the same way they'd had it done to them two nights earlier by Carolina, Sundin scored halfway through the third period. It wasn't a classic, nor did he will the puck across the line by battling as hard as he always did around the net. The record-breaker actually went in off an Islander defenceman's skate. It didn't matter. The record was now certainly Sundin's, set by him scoring a goal, which seemed much more fitting as the Leafs eventually hammered the Isles 8–1.

The reaction around the building to Sundin's goal, knowing there was no way it was being taken back, was almost comic relief. The man himself was clearly much more comfortable in the spotlight this time, and he was made the first, second, and third star of the game. It being a Thursday night, with a small hint of weekend revelry in the air, the crowd was much more ready to celebrate than is sadly the case some nights down at the ACC.

Sundin played out the rest of that season, was straight in saying that he was staying as per his no movement clause, but eventually left to sign with and play a half-season the following year with the Canucks. The drawn-out, mild melodrama of "will-he-stay-or-will-he-go" that season ensured yet another ending that happens too often in Toronto: Sundin became the most recent example of an excellent player, the type that is all too rare in Toronto, whose career in the blue and white ended on questionable terms.

Courtesy of Graig Abel.

THE MIXED LEGACY THAT MATS SUNDIN HAS LEFT IN TORONTO IS TOUGH TO FIGURE OUT GIVEN HIS SPLENDID TALENT AND REMARKABLY CONSISTENT PERFORMANCE OVER THIRTEEN SEASONS.

Not every player, even all-time greats, can win the Stanley Cup. Only a minuscule portion of the great ones go out by hoisting the Cup in their final season. But great players deserve at the very least a soft landing, to be able to dictate the terms of how they finish up. Aside from Clark, every single elite star Leaf has had an unseemly end in Toronto. Stretching back to Keon, and including virtually every player of top-rank quality that wore the Maple Leaf up to Sundin, it generally ended badly, or at very least not the way it should have (many believe that the trend started with Frank Mahovlich, but I have no memory of the Big M playing).

Now Sundin didn't have to endure the complete mess that McDonald and Sittler had to go through, or the utter tragedy of what happened to Gilmour. McDonald's departure to Colorado and Sittler's being left in the lurch back in Toronto was schoolboy pettiness played out in the front office of an NHL hockey team only a decade removed from its glorious past.

Gilmour's injury the first game back is about as unfortunate as it gets in the hard-knocks world of professional sports.

There was another different yet no less dramatic element to Sundin's time in Toronto: the players he had to play with, including many of his regular linemates, were so far from the level you would expect an elite player to be grouped with, it was like a collection of lounge singers landing a gig with the Beatles.

Using the night when he eventually broke the Leafs scoring record, consider this fact: Sundin notched Toronto's seventh goal of the game, sandwiched around ones by Andy Wozniewski and Simon Gamanche. Those two players scored six others between them in a combined 127 career NHL games; Sundin had 563 career goals, 419 as a Leaf. Even if you accept that example as a statistical quirk — and though symbolic, it is — consider some of the players Sundin regularly played with on a forward line or worked the Leafs power play beside: Derek King, Todd Warriner, Sergei Berezin, Mike Johnson, Jonas Hoglund, Freddy Modin, Darcy Tucker, Alex Steen, Alexei Ponikarovsky, Nikolai Antropov, and Jason Blake. All of those players have had their moments in the NHL, but they came long before arriving in Toronto, after leaving, or simply because they had the good fortune to play with Sundin.

None of them landed in the proverbial pot of butter more than Hoglund. In the three seasons he split between Calgary and Montreal before coming to Toronto, Hoglund notched thirty-nine goals. He was unceremoniously dumped by both teams, who were also-rans at the time. In his first season as a Leaf, Hoglund scored twenty-nine times, then followed that effort with twenty-three more the next year, both seasons playing mostly on Sundin's line.

In fact, in Sundin's thirteen seasons as a Leaf, and discounting the brief period he played with Gilmour at the very beginning, only Alex Mogilny and Gary Roberts, and perhaps Steve Thomas, could be cited as the type of players who had the necessary tools to complement Sundin's talent. Combined, Mogilny, Roberts, and Thomas played just ten seasons in Toronto while Sundin was there, and all of those came when they were past their own primes.

In the final analysis, Sundin ascended to a level where he was among a handful of top forwards in the game despite never really having a regular linemate of complementary talent. He was let down by Leafs management, who had a thoroughbred in their stable and ended up pairing him with a bunch of standardbreds. It's not the lesser players' fault — what were they supposed to do? — but it was only when Sundin left that we truly began to appreciate what a special player he was.

Gilmour's departure, through a 1997 trade with New Jersey, was probably, in retrospect, the best thing given that it afforded him an opportunity to play for a contender, and the return was good with Steve Sullivan, Alyn McCauley, and Jason Smith coming back. No harm, no foul, and I even quietly hoped that Gilmour would do well with the Devils and later with the Chicago Blackhawks when he signed there as a free agent. But one of the oddest images in modern Leafs history was captured when Gilmour, clad in a Blackhawks jersey, watched the closing of Maple Leaf Gardens as the two teams played the final game in that building. Seeing Gilmour watching the ceremony clad in another team's colours was a bit like inviting an old girlfriend to your wedding even though you secretly wished you were marrying her.

Gilmour continued to be a solid NHL player in Buffalo, arriving there in a trade from Chicago, then later in Montreal, slowly morphing into a veteran role player who could still contribute offensively in fits and starts. These moves set the stage for his return to Toronto in 2003, with Gilmour looking ideal for a similar role with the Leafs that he had played in Montreal.

He returned, all right, for two shifts. Gilmour, having joined the Leafs on the road in Calgary in a trade deadline pickup, collided with Flames forward Dave Lowry on just his second shift of the game. And like that, Gilmour's return to the Leafs, and ultimately his career, was over. The sight of Gilmour in clear physical distress on the Saddledome ice caused a pain to shoot through the heart of every Leafs fan. Gilmour was denied a chance to play in front of the home crowd, who were also denied a chance to welcome their hero back.

Most accounts of what happened to Gilmour detail what happened — he tore his knee and was done for the year — not its possible effect. That year the Leafs had loaded up and were among the most talented squads ever assembled in the post-Ballard era. Hopes were running high for at least a return to the conference final. But the team fizzled after Gilmour was hurt, though not necessarily because he was missing — we'll never know what he could have provided, or if the downturn was caused by something else entirely. There was perhaps an indicator that things weren't right when Shayne Corson left the team during the playoffs. Whatever the underlying issues, the end came with a dispiriting 6–1 Game 7 loss to Philadelphia in the first playoff round.

The Gilmour trade and his immediate injury wasn't the only thing that left a bitter taste. Moves to bring in Owen Nolan (who also suffered a serious leg injury), Glen Wesley, and Phil Housley never really panned out, with two rare young talents — Brad Boyes and Alyn McCauley — and draft picks spent to acquire the veterans. Moves such as these went a long way to hamstring the Leafs a few years later when the post-lockout reality set in.

Leafs GM/coach Pat Quinn — he would relinquish the first title after the season ended — was correct in trying to stock his roster and certainly couldn't have known what the world was going to look like eighteen months down the road when the NHL locked out its players. When the labour stoppage ended, the NHL was a different place. Players such as Boyes and McCauley were desperately needed; Boyes topped the forty-goal mark soon after becoming a regular NHLer and though McCauley's career was ended prematurely because of injury, many felt that he could have been a future captain. As far as the draft picks that were moved — another case of not knowing what could have been.

♣ ♣ ♣

Wendel Clark's time in Toronto ended in 2000, not necessarily with a whimper but too damn quietly. There is a special significance in Clark and Sundin essentially being traded for one another (though other players were involved). Sundin had to fight the perception for close to a decade that he wasn't a winner, a false belief strengthened because his acquisition meant Clark leaving. I would argue that they both had to endure precisely the same thing in Toronto because Clark was forced to do too much, with a largely incapable supporting cast around him until Cliff Fletcher came to town and started to build a workable hockey club.

The sight of Clark, barreling around the ice with little regard for his body and even less for that of his opponents, is what made him a fan favourite from the second that beautiful goateed mug landed in Toronto in 1985. Though he was a beast on skates, he could also score and play the game in other ways. But that energy also had another result: his body wore down. The thought of a teenager — who wasn't even six feet tall — having to fight, score, dish out body checks, and be a team leader — seems insane nowadays. Is it any wonder that his body soon failed him?

Though not easy to do, you could accept that Clark had to go in 1994 simply because the Leafs got Sundin in return — Toronto

Courtesy of Graig Abel.

A RARITY: A STAR PLAYER UNIVERSALLY LOVED AND RESPECTED. WENDEL CLARK BATTLED INJURIES, BAD TEAMS, AND THE LAST VESTIGES OF THE HAROLD BALLARD REGIME, BUT IT HAS NOT TARNISHED HIS LEGACY ONE IOTA. HE ALMOST SINGLE-HANDEDLY KEPT LEAFS FANS ENGAGED IN THE LATE 1980S AND EARLY 1990S.

gained a younger, more talented, former number one overall pick, after all. But the fact that Clark bounced around, spending short spells on teams such as the Quebec Nordiques, New York Islanders, and Tampa Bay Lightning while battling injuries throughout just seemed so utterly wrong. When Clark came back in 1996, he was just a sliver off, but he remained the folk hero he had been in the previous years in Toronto. But, tragic hero that he was, his best years during the second go-around happened to fall when the Leafs were clearly in a decline and in need of a rebuild. He was all but a spent force when he returned for a third time in 2000. For a guy who was on his last NHL legs, he did just fine going on emotional fumes. He was one of the best players through the first few games of an eventual seven-game loss to the Devils in the conference semifinal that spring. He retired not long after.

Aside from his splendid talent and the physical gifts that he willed out of such a small frame, Clark's enduring appeal is that he looked every bit the Prairie farm boy he was. Ask any Leafs fan, say between the age of thirty and fifty-five, and they will almost assuredly recognize the words "Kelvington, Saskatchewan" as Clark's hometown. They may even feel like they know it, even if they've never been to the village of fewer than one thousand residents.

Another more nuanced by equally significant legacy around Toronto: The sweater number that is always — and I mean always — one of the first picked on men's recreational teams. In fact, it's not unusual to see 71 on the backs' of many weekend warriors in rinks from Oakville to Orillia (in hockey tradition, if you want a number already taken, you always go for its inverse numeral as a second choice). In and around Canada's biggest city, 17 is as popular as 9, the one worn by so many all-time greats.

Clark's number while playing for the Leafs: 17.

Off the ice, Clark looked no different in street clothes — unless he was sporting one of his many cuts or black eyes — than a guy you'd run into at your local pub or the hardware store. Hell, seeing him now, he looks every bit the nondescript hockey dad he is. But throw skates on him, and it's a different story. I'm not sure I can imagine someone tugging at my heartstrings like that again, just as much as he scared the living shit out of me at the same time (and surely did to his opponents as well).

Like Clarke, Salming's career as a Leaf petered out more than ended in disappointment. The Swede was denied a chance of winning a Stanley Cup because he showed a loyalty to the Leafs and stayed despite all the unseemly events around him that virtually ensured he wouldn't get his just rewards.

When the International Ice Hockey Federation announced its all-century team in 2000, Salming was one of two defencemen on it. The fact a Leafs player was cited as one of the six best in IIHF history was telling, considering that his immense contributions in Toronto over sixteen seasons amounted to little team success.

♣　　♣　　♣

Dave Keon has continually resisted efforts to bring him back into the Leafs fold. His bitterness at his treatment by Ballard is completely understandable. But his insistence at not making peace long after Ballard's death now seems excessive. Frankly, it's hard to feel sorry for Keon simply because his continual coldness seems misplaced. The result: most fans under the age of fifty have zero memory of Keon and wouldn't know him if he sat down beside them.

There is a certain symbolism in that sad reality, especially given that many Leafs fans over fifty consider him to be the best Leaf of all; the Leafs best player, the greatest to ever wear the blue and white, essentially an anonymous figure to a large segment of fans.

It was obvious on February 10, 2007, as well. Keon was there with the rest of his 1967 Stanley Cup teammates for a ceremony to commemorate the fortieth anniversary of their victory. All the big names were called out to centre ice — Johnny Bower, Frank Mahovlich, George Armstrong — and even a few who were perhaps less well-known — Milan Marcetta and Larry Jeffrey, for example.

When Keon came out, there was a strange feeling in the air. It was like everyone wanted to give him his dues, but something

HOPE AND HEARTBREAK IN TORONTO

wasn't quite right. The whole ceremony was pleasant and Keon's presence in it was nice, but it was also a reminder of the sheer agony of what had taken place since the Leafs had last won the Stanley Cup. The applause lingered for a while, even grew loud for a bit. Then all the past champions left the ice, the game against the Edmonton Oilers started, and by the middle of the first period, all was pretty much forgotten. Keon even told the media after that he was there for his teammates, not for the organization.

Having watched it unfold, I couldn't quite work out what it was that rankled about the commemoration. There was a disjointed feeling about the whole exercise. But with Keon's gentle but clear clarification, it only seemed to cement the undeniable feeling that the Maple Leafs have trouble loving the truly great ones.

15

OWNERSHIP/MANAGEMENT

THE MEDIA MADE NO MENTION OF A DODGY SMELL WHEN THEY reported on the opening of a homemade copper box on January 26, 2012, but there was a distinct familiarity to the odour. The box had been buried near the cornerstone of Maple Leaf Gardens and discovered by workers about a year before. Inside, among other things, were a Gardens stock prospectus and a collection of newspapers all dating from September 21, 1931, the day the box was sunk into the ground in a civic ceremony.

The newspapers were full of how Britain had suspended the gold standard and its stock market the previous day. The tone of the stories was very similar to how Canada would react today if the U.S. were to undertake such harsh economic measures, not surprising given the strong ties that a pre–Second World War Canada still had with the mother country.

That wasn't the really smelly part. The familiar stench came from the prospectus. It said that the new building expected to generate $500,000 in revenue against expenses of just $235,000. Then, as now, and even in the midst of the most crippling economic depression in modern human history, the Leafs were making money hand over fist. But the broadsheets and the prospectus told drastically different stories.

Two years after that box was buried at the Gardens, though no one could have known it at the time, there was another harsh harbinger of the Leafs future. In 1933, an amateur club team from Toronto represented Canada at the world championship in Prague and lost in overtime to the U.S. The coach? A twenty-nine-year-old Torontonian named Harold Ballard. The Toronto National Sea Fleas had won the 1932 Allan Cup and were coached by Harry Watson, a decorated First World War fighter pilot. Watson had returned home after the conflict to resume his playing career, eventually winning an Olympic gold medal and election to the Hockey Hall of Fame as a player. He briefly took up coaching the Sea Fleas, but soon gave it up, creating a vacancy that Ballard filled.

The hockey club had the rather awkward nickname because it had been sponsored by the National Yacht Club and a sea flea was a fashionable racer of the day.

Little record of Ballard's athletic accomplishments survive aside from almost drowning as a twenty-something in a sea flea accident, but as the son of a prominent businessman, young Harold landed a few coaching gigs, probably through his fledgling industry connections. He was an assistant on Canada's 1928 Olympic championship squad at St. Moritz, but things didn't go nearly as well on his European adventure five years later. The Sea Fleas' loss in Prague was the first setback for Canada at the world championship and concluded a season that was rife with chaos for the club. Ballard was even said to have got into a number of altercations as the team toured around Europe.

It may be generations ago, but Ballard in the 1920s and 1930s doesn't sound much different than today's offspring of wealthy businessmen. He puttered in sports administration, apparently looking for an expensive toy. Given that he had such trouble when the water wasn't frozen, it made perfect sense to gravitate to a game played on ice. And so he dabbled in coaching, migrating to junior hockey not long after the 1933 debacle in Europe and around the time he took over his father's manufacturing business after the senior Ballard retired and, soon after, died.

During his junior days Ballard managed to catch the attention of the Maple Leafs organization and was listed as being part of the management structure of both the West Toronto Nationals and the Toronto Marlboros when those teams captured the Memorial Cup (in 1935–36 and 1955 respectively).[1] Over the decades, and with some incredibly lucky breaks, Ballard ended up with a partial stake in the Maple Leafs when original owner Conn Smythe divested himself of his shares.

Between the early 1930s and 1969 Ballard went from being a poor little rich kid during the Depression to a cantankerous old fart. An old fart who, along the way, managed, with his Gardens partners Stafford Smythe and John Bassett, to harness the massive changes taking place in society. By hosting various concerts and other events such as conventions, the hockey arena brought in huge sums of money. It didn't matter that both Ballard and Smythe were essentially stealing

Courtesy of Graig Abel.

HAROLD BALLARD DESTROYED HIS PRIZED POSSESSION, AND IT TOOK THE TORONTO MAPLE LEAFS YEARS TO RECOVER FROM IT AFTER BALLARD'S DEATH IN 1990.

from the company. Smythe died before going to trial — Ballard bought Smythe's shares from his estate — but Ballard went down hard, going to jail on theft charges.[2] He may have been a dyed-in-the-wool conservative fossil for much of his later years, but he benefited enormously from Canada's rather liberal corrections laws. Despite being convicted on a string of charges in the fall of 1972, he was out by the start of the hockey season the next year, having served only a year. Ballard then enjoyed an almost two-decade run at the helm of the Gardens and the Maple Leafs, its chief tenant. From that point on, Ballard drove the team on the express lane to virtual oblivion.

Unless you're a Leafs fan who's pushing seventy, your memories of Ballard are likely primarily that of an old man who would occasionally stick his head out of his bunker at the Gardens. His old, greying head, which was always well groomed, was almost always accompanied by the aging pate of King Clancy, the Hall of Fame player and referee. The two men watched games together until Clancy died in 1986. Shown together on television, Ballard and Clancy looked so much like the two old men from the Muppets you would swear that creator Jim Henson had been a Leafs fan.

If Ballard was a questionable coach in the 1930s, imagine how out of touch he became by the post-expansion era when he took over as the controlling owner. His tinkering and interference with the Leafs is, aside from the club's thirteen Stanley Cup triumphs, the one enduring legacy the hockey team has left from its otherwise glorious past. In fact, so chaotic were the Ballard years, especially once the 1970s gave way to the 1980s, it could be argued their effects are what underpins the team's undying support now.

Back then, some fans became so fed up with the Leafs that, if not necessarily abandoning them, they kept them at an emotional arm's length. Once Ballard was gone, though, and the Leafs had, superficially at least, a more competent body running the show, the team started to garner the undying loyalty from the masses that it enjoys today.

Ballard's cheapskate ways, which stood out, especially considering the tidy revenue sums, were made worse by the petty disputes that he created with leading players. The turmoil could not have come at a worse time because, for the first time in the history of the NHL, players had employment options when the World Hockey Association sprang up in 1972.

The departure of Dave Keon to that league, and later the Darryl Sittler and Lanny McDonald trades, were killers, driving a stake through the heart of a team that had rightly earned a reputation of as one of the NHL's best young clubs in the late 1970s. To put the club's decline into perspective, the Maple Leafs beat the New York Islanders in the 1978 quarter-finals, with McDonald scoring the overtime winning goal in Game 7. Though the Leafs were swept in the next round by the Montreal Canadiens, it's telling, the divergent path that Toronto and New York travelled from that point forward.

In 1980, the Islanders won the first of four consecutive Stanley Cups and are regarded as one of the true dynasties in the post-expansion era. The Leafs? They won a mini best-of-three set in 1979 versus the Atlanta Flames but didn't capture another post-season series victory until 1986, when they downed the Chicago Black Hawks. Fuelled by the energy provided by Wendel Clark in the late 1980s, the team managed to win a few playoff series, but otherwise the entire decade was a writeoff after the last one ended with such promise.

To put that decline in perspective, compare it to what is regarded as an inexcusable drought now experienced by the Leafs. The current team has missed the playoffs for seven consecutive seasons. It is, frankly, an embarrassment, a sad slide for a hockey team that had some fairly solid clubs in the post-Ballard years between 1990–91 and the last NHL season before the lockout in 2004–05. But at least the reason for it is somewhat clearer now. Everyone knew, or ought to have known, that the Leafs' moves to try to win the Stanley Cup during the Pat Quinn years, 1998 to 2004, would hurt the team immeasurably once the new reality of post-lockout NHL took hold. Having dealt away so many high draft picks and relying on signing veteran free agents left the cupboard pretty bare when the NHL started back up again in 2005. And so the pain felt now may have lasted much longer than necessary, but it's at least explainable.

Back in the late 1970s, the Leafs had three of the very best players in all of hockey in McDonald, Salming, and Sittler, plus a solid supporting cast that included goalie Mike Palmateer and Dave "Tiger" Williams, one of the best tough guys in hockey history, playing in an era when that mattered. With passionate fans, a strong core, and the two dynasties of the day — Philadelphia and Montreal — fading, the Leafs should have been right there with the Islanders as one of the preeminent teams in the NHL, or at the very least a club that couldn't be taken lightly. However, it went entirely the other way with former GM Punch Imlach brought in to perform Ballard's hatchet work.

Ballard was, at best, a meddler and a bad influence; at worst, he was an erratic creep whose political views and attitude toward women likely would have forced him to sell his team had he came along after society's sensibilities had changed. Ballard

JIM GREGORY (LEFT) PUT TOGETHER SOME GOOD LEAFS TEAMS IN THE 1970S BUT EVENTUALLY LEFT TO WORK FOR THE NHL. HE'S NOW IN THE HOCKEY HALL OF FAME AND IS SEEN HERE WELCOMING FORMER LEAF JOE NIEUWENDYK UPON HIS ENSHRINEMENT IN THE HALL.

was essentially a slightly less volatile and male version of Marge Schott, the late lunatic owner of baseball's Cincinnati Reds. His interference with the team saw all the players mentioned above and others leave, along with GM Jim Gregory. Gregory, a graceful and dignified man who has been inducted into the Hall of Fame, is distinguishable by his head of snow-white hair. One can only imagine how much of it turned that way during his decade working for Ballard as Leafs GM.

Since Ballard died in 1990, the team has been better run and more competent on the ice, even if Leafs fans still endure an odd combination of Ballard-esque pursuit of the bottom line and strange organizational structure in the managerial and ownership setup.

Now, as bad as the team has been after the stoppage, it's never been quite as bad as what was routine in the 1980s, but the petty dealings and minor scandals were still with us. First, Steve Stavro's wheeling and dealing somehow managed to install him as the controlling shareowner, brought the Leafs and Raptors together as one corporate entity (and later the Toronto Marlies and Toronto FC after Stavo left), and built the Air Canada Centre. Stavro, by all accounts a good man on a personal level who inspired loyalty to those who knew him, struggled to come up with the financing to build Air Canada Centre.

During Stavro's reign there were some awkward management combinations and personality clashes. Ken Dryden, Anders Hedberg, and Mike Smith seemed a completely unworkable trio right from the start, though for the most part they did retain their collective composure. All three men's hockey acumen was beyond dispute. Smith in particular brought with him a deft hand that led to key signings such as Curtis Joseph and to Pat Quinn coming on board as coach. The Joseph/Quinn addition, which came at the expense of Mike Murphy, who didn't have much to work with in his two years behind the bench, led to a dramatic turnaround in the NHL standings. The Leafs also played an upbeat style that was the exception rather than the norm at the time, as the NHL was firmly migrating toward what is now known as the "dead-puck" era.

An unwieldy management structure pretty much ensured there would be issues and it didn't take long for some to emerge. Dryden eventually fired Smith, but left before his personality conflicts with Quinn completely fractured the management of the hockey team. It also emerged that Dryden, for all his intellect and polished literary skills, had a clumsy side. He frequently lectured the media about this and that, demonstrating a tin ear to the sensibilities of both Leafs fans and the accepted norms of the NHL. When it emerged that he had fired Smith over the phone while Smith was taking his wife to cancer treatment, Dryden's public reputation took a knock. Dryden left the Leafs' fold to run for the federal Liberal party. His time in politics was not unlike his time with the Leafs — it never quite lived up to its billing.

Quinn endured after the departure of his two former colleagues and he essentially became the face of the team even after John Ferguson Jr. was hired and became his boss. Though the Leafs were relatively successful on the ice around this time, the team's

PAT QUINN WAS THE FACE OF THE MAPLE LEAFS TEAMS FROM 1998 TO 2006 AND WAS GENERALLY REGARDED AS ONE OF THE NHL'S TOP COACHES DURING THAT TIME. HIS GENERAL MANAGER TENURE HAD MORE MIXED RESULTS.

management structure never seemed to pass muster and the whole arrangement simply didn't make any organizational sense. When Ferguson arrived in 2003, he was considered a bright young executive, but his relationship with Quinn had the feel of a young pup trying to teach an old dog new tricks.

With the team now playing out of the Air Canada Centre, the faceless and utterly staid Teachers' Pension Plan and its stewardship of the team was in full swing. The Teachers' Pension Plan, the fund that manages the retirement savings of Ontario's school teachers, acquired a majority stake in the entire operation now known as Maple Leaf Sports and Entertainment. There is some dark humour here, as many Ontario teachers began to joke that they "own" a hockey team, despite earning an income that makes it incredibly difficult to even buy tickets for all but the least expensive seats in the ACC. The percentage of people who pay for their own tickets is painfully low. But it's a virtual guarantee that few teachers could ever afford to walk through the ACC doors on their own dime.

The pension plan has now sold its stake, but its legacy will be that it dumbed down the on-ice product, raised prices to excessive levels, and subjected Leafs Nation to the hidden charms of Richard Peddie. And if there is one man who came to represent the corporate largesse of Maple Leaf Sports and Entertainment, it is Richard A. Peddie, president and CEO of the organization. Peddie would never see it that way. If he said it once, he said it a million times during his thirteen-year run as the head of MLSE: he grew the business and made shareholders very happy. That's what presidents and CEOs are supposed to do. Measured by that yardstick, Peddie was a complete success — MLSE had a threefold revenue growth from when he left compared to when he started. But Peddie was the head of a company whose core business was sports teams, where winning should be the yardstick on which success is measured. By that measure, he was a spectacular failure.

Peddie always defended the Leafs' and Raptors' lack of silverware by saying that only one team can win a championship each season. That was a bit disingenuous. Peddie's comments made it sound as if achievement was reached by luck, rather like drawing a number out of a hat. The winning number goes home happy, the others are the losers. But even moderate sports fans know that half the fun is the journey to get there. In fact, the Leafs' no-Cup-since-1967 walk in the wilderness is especially painful because the team has failed to take part in any playoff games for almost a decade.

Peddie's explanation for not winning was all part of the slick mantra that he developed while in charge. First off, he simply didn't address why (aside from the Leafs in 2002) none of the three major-league clubs under the aegis of MLSE came anywhere close to winning a championship. Toronto routinely ranked among the lowest for what it provided the city and its fans. Aside from the Blue Jays, Peddie had a hand in all the teams — Leafs, Raptors, and Toronto FC — that have fared so poorly.

Peddie was brilliant at harnessing the interest in the teams to build a bunch of condos and a sports bar in a real estate market that was already one of the most robust in North America. It didn't exactly take an über-genius to figure out that condos would sell around the Air Canada Centre. Or that a sold out building had a market for a great sports bar serving fans without tickets, or a place for those with tickets to drink before and after games.

What Peddie managed to do perfectly was to change the definition of what makes a sports franchise successful. Sure, winning is nice — he often said that popcorn tasted better when the teams were doing well, but never mentioned that the popcorn cost $5.50 a bag when he left, almost double what it had cost when the ACC opened. It's just a small example, but it's a perfect snapshot in how the Peddie regime created an environment where winning didn't really matter: the profits kept rolling in regardless.

Smart and shrewd, Peddie for the most part didn't say anything too controversial when speaking publicly and inspired loyalty in those around him. If high-level MLSE executives, Leafs GM Brian Burke, and Raptors boss Bryan Colangelo ever thought that the company was a bit too focused on issues other than winning, they've never said it for public consumption. But there were times when Peddie let his guard down. His comments about hiring John Ferguson Jr. being a mistake made him look incredibly out of touch with the business of hockey. It was a shockingly dumb thing to say. Peddie's remarks and his decision to hire Ferguson, just as much as Ferguson's questionable decisions, hurt the Leafs because rival GMs soon began to perceive Toronto's chief hockey man as not being up to the job.

Courtesy of Getty Images.

RICHARD PEDDIE'S STEWARDSHIP OF MLSE PRODUCED ENORMOUS PROFITS BUT ZERO CHAMPIONSHIPS FOR ANY OF THE COMPANY'S FOUR SPORTS TEAMS.

When federal GST legislation led to a modest reduction in ticket prices in 2006, Peddie used the occasion to muse aloud that perhaps MLSE wasn't such a big, bad corporate entity after all because they lowered their prices in accordance with the smaller GST. It was seemingly lost on Peddie that the GST reduction had no ill effect on ticket revenues for his company and that finally holding the line on prices followed several years of increases.

In 2011, after Bell and Rogers emerged as new owners, Peddie took his leave fairly quietly, but a few media reports as he made his exit were enough to make Leafs fans' blood boil. First, he remarked that he was taking his first vacation that exceeded two weeks — as though Leafs fans should somehow feel badly for him — but a few of the self-congratulatory zingers were especially insulting.

Peddie talked openly of the need to franchise the Real Sports idea around North America, and also, in an interview with *Canadian Business Journal*, crowed about MLSE creating and following a budget instilling "culture and values" conducive to good business. Again, Peddie's definition of success apparently had little to do with winning. It wasn't until another interview with the Globe's *Report on Business* magazine that came several months after he left the job that Peddie finally took full responsibility for the competitive failings of MLSE's sports teams. He would have little choice: by the time he gave the interview the Leafs had flamed out of the Eastern Conference playoff race, the Raptors were rebuilding (again), and TFC was on its way to a record losing streak to open the season under new manager Aron Winter. To not be anything but fully and completely humble would have made Peddie look like a clueless clown. And the man is no dummy.

❖　❖　❖

One night in April 2006, I was at the Ricoh Coliseum, just a couple of kilometres down the road from the ACC. The Toronto Marlies were in the playoffs, that night facing the Grand Rapids Griffins, Detroit's AHL affiliate. The Leafs' season was finished by then, and Pat Quinn had already been fired by John Ferguson. Perhaps Richard Peddie was like me, looking for more hockey action that night, given that the Leafs had missed the playoffs. But he didn't look like a man either disappointed in the big club or happy to be taking in that night's match involving the minor league affiliate. He was talking to someone I took to be a Marlies employee, completely ignoring the play that was going on nearby. I'd seen something like this before at the ACC. When I'd seen him there, I'd got the feeling the smile on his face was more because of seeing people spending money than interest in the action on the ice.

I once saw Peddie strolling about the ACC's upper level on the night of the Leafs breast cancer awareness game when arena patrons were encouraged to wear pink. Peddie, wearing a pink tie, ducked in behind the area near the Raptors practice court and pecked away incessantly on his BlackBerry. Another time, I saw Peddie at the Real Sports Bar & Grill standing near a model version of the Stanley Cup. He didn't seem to even notice the mock trophy.

They are just a few examples, but the man always gave off the impression that he was always working, or trying to find ways to make the business run smoother. Perhaps that is evidence of his no doubt tireless commitment to the job. But it also never seemed to have anything to do with the actual action on the ice, on the court, or on the pitch.

Some day, many decades down the road when most of us are no longer encumbered with our earthly lives, it's not hard to imagine citizens of the day finding a box somewhere under where the ACC, Real Sports, or Maple Leaf Square now stand. The box found under Maple Leaf Gardens contained, among other items, a book of hockey rules, a municipal handbook, a stock prospectus, a small red ensign flag, and a small ivory elephant. What might those Torontonians find in a box under the MLSE building? I wouldn't be surprised if that box contained some sort of document detailing the profits that were expected to be made inside the great entertainment complex. The thought must bring a smile to Richard Peddie's face. But nothing can change the fact that during his time in charge of MLSE, none of its teams seriously challenged for a championship. The dichotomy has never been satisfactorily addressed.

16

CORPORATE WONDERLAND

THE FACILITY THAT RICHARD PEDDIE HELPED MAKE INTO ONE OF THE best money-making complexes in the entire world of North American professional sports has five seating tiers. The platinum tier is the most expensive and closest to the ice. Gold is next, followed by red.

In a stroke of strategic brilliance, because it allowed for more tickets to be priced at the more expensive gold level, there are very few red seats along the sides of the Air Canada Centre; the few that are there but tightly up against the luxury boxes perched behind them. The result is that almost all red seat holders are behind the nets or in the corner, seriously lessening the vantage point for what should be a prime lower bowl placement, especially since netting behind the nets became a requirement at all NHL rinks.

The platinum–gold–red setup makes up the ACC's lower bowl. Every Leafs ticket in that area sells for close to $200, often more. That's too expensive for a typical fan, and, as a result, the vast majority of people occupying lower bowl seats are doing so because of some sort of connection to a corporation or business that owns the seats. The relative few who aren't are often connected to a participating player, because it's in this area of the building that they are allocated their two tickets to each game.

The upper bowl is where most regular people watch games. Just like at Maple Leaf Gardens, greens dominate the upper bowl and are replaced by blues on the ends. Greens are roughly half what it costs to sit down below and often offer a better sightline to the play. It's generally accepted that seats in lower greens are the best budget-wise in the building, just like they were in the Gardens.

Purples run around the top of the ACC and are the last tier of seats completing a platinum–gold–red–green–purple pattern that would probably make Conn Smythe spin in his grave.

One thing that hasn't changed — or, more accurately, has returned to what it was like when Smythe used to rule the Gardens with an iron fist — is an apparent strict code of conduct, especially for those sitting in the lower bowl.

Smythe would often personally accost patrons for not dressing properly. Or at least not dressing how the "Major" thought they should while attending a hockey game in the arena he built.

If you attend any more than a few games a season at the ACC, you may feel as though Smythe's iron fist was still doling out punishment, because it's not uncommon to witness a fan being ejected from the building for offences that would be considered borderline at worst in other buildings.

I can't honestly say that I've witnessed that many incidents of this type — perhaps a half-dozen or so in total where I was close enough to clearly see what happened — but I do know beyond certainty that in virtually every case I've witnessed a fan get booted, it was for an offence that was pretty much the norm at the Gardens — once Mr. Smythe had left his earthly coil, of course.

To be fair, the Leafs brain trust is now faced with little alternative. The ACC is the biggest bar in the city aside from perhaps the Rogers Centre, and anyone who has ever witnessed the stringent application of Ontario's liquor laws knows that it doesn't take much to attract unwanted attention and then to face the punitive penalties that are on the books. The ACC has landed in hot water for relatively minor transgressions and has paid the price, including having to halt the serving of alcohol. A lot of people feel that Ontario's liquor laws are the single biggest reason why the Buffalo Bills' foray into Toronto has been such a bittersweet experience — you simply can't create the same festive tailgate atmosphere outside in Toronto that you can in New York State, where the rules are not nearly as strict.

The Leafs play in a building that isn't just a hockey rink, basketball court, and entertainment complex; it is also the biggest meet-and-greet of corporate hobnobbers in Canada. Corporate bigwigs love to be seen and to do business at Leafs games, but it's bad for business to be utterly legless at them. And with that high-flying clientele, the Air Canada Centre almost never fails to make the same impression on a first-time visitor.

"Wow, this is beautiful," said my wife's stepbrother, visiting from Calgary during a game between the Leafs and the Buffalo Sabres on December 21, 2009. "But, ah, it kinda sucks the noise out of the fans, doesn't it…? You could hear a pin drop in here."

Ah, we know, we know.

It is certainly quite appropriate that the ACC is located essentially at the foot of Bay Street. It's as if the great moneyed crowds that populate the nerve centre of Canada's business elite have their playground at their feet forty-one times a year. If you work in the downtown core, you don't even need to go outside to walk to the ACC because virtually the entire inner grid is connected by the PATH system, a vast labyrinth of tunnels lined with shops and restaurants.

The scene between 6:30 and 7:00 p.m., especially on midweek game nights is predictable throughout the hockey season: Bay Street types hurry down the PATH to the ACC with tickets that are almost certainly provided for free by clients or are part of the stash controlled by their company, and which they don't pay for out of their own pockets. Such a large percentage of the ACC's regular clientele, at least for Leafs games, are people who work in this relatively small geographical area that vehicle traffic around the great grey edifice that is the ACC/Union Station complex is only marginally heavier on game nights.

And that is not exactly a triumph of Toronto's overextended public transit system, either. Only a scattering of hockey fans come down to the ACC using public transit. Back in the good old days of Maple Leaf Gardens, at least half the crowd would arrive on the subway, lending a carnival air to the area surrounding the old building as the crowds milled about before eventually filing inside. Back then, it was part sporting event, part party, even when the Gardens itself started to become filled with too many corporate suits in its later years.

Midweek games are the worst for seeing the corporate types in great numbers, but even many weekend contests see the area infected with a corporate gloss. After intermissions, it's also not uncommon to see acres of wide-open seats as many of those people can't be bothered to hustle back to their seats in time for the second and third periods to start.

Courtesy of Graig Abel.

Courtesy of Graig Abel.

THE DIFFERENCE IN CROWD MAKEUP BETWEEN THE ACC (TOP) AND MAPLE LEAF GARDENS. THE NEW FACILITY IS A SPRAWLING SPACE FULL OF LUXURY AMENITIES.

Aside from games against the Montreal Canadiens, the occasional Saturday night tilt with another Canadian team, or a rare visit by the Detroit Red Wings, my guess is that less than half of the people stuffed into the ACC are true hockey fans. At least half are there for some sort of quasi-work purpose: entertaining clients, sitting in seats provided by clients, or showing up merely to be seen in the midst of Toronto's high-flyers. The hockey game is an incidental occurrence to a night out. To stroll through the lower bowl of the ACC, but especially to visit the areas that cater to the upper-crust set such as the Platinum Lounge or Air Canada Club, could shake your faith in human nature. It's like several thousand people have chosen a sporting event to show off their sense of self-importance.

One woman who sat beside me during the Leafs game versus the New York Rangers on January 14, 2012, was a classic study in this sect of Toronto crowds that dominate the atmosphere here. The mother of two young girls, she was sitting in her husband's company seats with her oldest daughter for the Saturday night game. The woman, white, late thirties, was impressively dressed, with a head of dark, salon-perfect hair. Her daughter was about seven and an impossibly cute kid with a sunny disposition and massive brown eyes. That night was the fifth installment of the Leafs tribute to the Canadian Forces. Almost five hundred season ticket holders had donated their seats for the use of the armed forces and the ACC was dotted with a wide and varied collection of military personnel, all clad in uniform. During the pre-game ceremony the Leafs honoured a few military men who had been away from home during seminal moments in their daughters' lives. These men had missed births, confirmations, graduations, and the like while serving far from home. It was a touching tribute, effectively voiced by Leafs PA announcer Andy Frost and presented with the type of nuance that often is lost when sports teams honour the military.

As the men were being honoured with their daughters at centre ice for the ceremonial puck drop, the mom beside me had tears in her eyes as she hugged her beautiful daughter close to her. It was a nice moment and the highlight of the night in what was an otherwise drab game where the Leafs got hammered 3–0.

The woman seemed to be a decent person, with just a hint of big-city coolness about her. Once the official puck dropped and play began, she fell right back into the precise mode that so many in the lower bowl do. Her head tilted equally between watching her daughter on her left and her iPhone clutched in her right hand.

"I like following the game on Twitter instead," she said, turning briefly my way on her right, "because I can't really see the puck or follow the play."

Great, so, ahem, why are you here?

Her daughter became a bit distracted about five minutes into the second period with the Leafs now down 1–0. It was obvious that the little sweetheart was not long for the game, just like it was soon clear it wasn't going to be the Leafs' night. Mom managed to perform a few strategic tricks to hold her daughter's attention longer — playing with her hair, handing her the iPhone a couple of times — but when the Leafs fell down by two goals late in the second period, that was it.

"We're going home. It's been a long night and we're going to the symphony tomorrow," she said. With that, she tucked her daughter into her pink bulky ski jacket, put on her own trendy overcoat, and both were off just a shade ahead of the crowds that float away after the period ends.

Though a weekend game, I was immediately struck by how much this interaction reminded me of one at a midweek game between the Leafs and the Washington Capitals on October 29, 2007. The Caps had not yet arrived as a high-profile team and were more a collection of young, unproven players with one legit star, Alexander Ovechkin, then in his second NHL season. They were still coached by Glen Hanlon, who would soon walk the plank and be replaced by former Leaf Bruce Boudreau, who himself has since been fired.

Unlike the Leafs–Rangers game, where I had an up-close vantage point by sitting in the lower bowl, I was high above this time. Just as the third period started, I glanced down from my seat in the second row of section 309 to the bank of seats below (it was the section where I sat for the Rangers game almost five years later). I instantly recognized the blond locks of a guy who had virtually the entire section to himself.

"Hey, I know that guy," I called out to no one in particular. "He's my RRSP guy!"

An older man, who all night had been complaining aloud about the play of Alex Ponikarovsky, heard me.

"Well, you're sitting here and he's down there in the best seats in the house," said the man who I would describe as a friendly grump. "Have you ever thought you might pay him too much money?"

My RRSP guy's name is Allan Small, and he's pretty handy with financial and investing advice and can be seen and heard on various Toronto media outlets offering his opinion on such matters. That description may make Allan sound like the type of person who should be sitting in the platinum seats with only a passive interest in the game. In fact, Allan is a good guy and a pretty dedicated Leafs fan. I noticed him only because he was acting so *unlike* most of those who occupy those seats. He didn't hear me call to him. Instead he was watching the game and during breaks in play he was trying to get the attention of someone in the section beside him as if to point out to them that he had a whole area of expensive seats all to himself.

The Leafs put in a wretched performance, losing 7–1 on home ice. I fired off an email to Allan the next day telling him that I'd seen him, sharing my angst about the game and asking where all his friends had gone.

"I know," he replied. "I get the seats from a client once a year and don't like to miss too much of the game. No one seemed too concerned with getting back to their seats."

These examples and Allan's comments are a micro indication of a macro conundrum the hockey team is caught in.

This is an entertainment company that, like any business, strives to make money. In order to do that, you should have to win hockey games (and basketball and soccer contests as well). But if you can create a business model where the dollars still roll in with little regard to winning and losing, why not go along with it?

Of course, if the Leafs make the playoffs it will be even better, because that's more revenue for games where the players aren't being paid.

Though not alone in this category, Toronto is somewhat unusual in that the Maple Leafs appeal to virtually all segments of the population. And while it's true that many people are willing to pay top dollar for hockey tickets, many of the Leafs' season tickets have migrated into the hands of corporations and ticket brokers.

In the end, corporate high rollers spend massive amounts of their companies' money on tickets that price most of the building out of reach for true hockey fans. The people who go to the games only have a passing interest in what's happening on the ice and often none at all. They are there to drink, be seen, hang out with like-minded people, and generally act how people on expense accounts often do — like upper-crust toffs. That's why true fans like Allan Small sit in vacant sections watching games, wondering where the hell everyone has gone in what is supposed to be a sold-out arena. Leafs tickets have become a commodity, primarily available only to those willing to pay with someone else's money.

A friend of mine is often asked to find tickets for clients who make no secret they expect to be taken to Leafs games, seated in platinum seats, and wined and dined throughout. As a result, this friend goes to roughly ten games a year. He's fortunate if he sees one period of play per visit. The rest of the time is spent in the various lounges tucked into the area behind the platinum and gold seats nearest to the ice.

Forced to watch and endure the bonfire of the vanities before him, he has one rule he enforces on himself: he keeps his BlackBerry switched off for the entire game, so as to not offend some of his more prima donna clients who insist on his undivided attention, but also to be careful he's not giving the impression he's as bad as the worst offenders himself.

The sheer expense of these junkets can make your head spin, especially when you look at the corporate boxes. Bar bills often run into several thousand dollars there as companies spare no expense in entertaining clients.

Even in regular seats, the prices for corporate outings can make you question whether you're viewing one too many digits on the left side of the decimal point. For example, my friend's firm recently brought two important clients to a game on January 23, 2012, a Monday night, versus the New York Islanders. Their party had three people in total and they needed to have the tickets secured before the week previous to the game in order to confirm plans before everyone took off for the weekend. In the end, it cost almost twice face value for three gold tickets priced at $210 each for a total bill of $1,200 from a local ticket broker. They ate in one of the lounges, where my friend signed for a bill that was a shade more than $650 with tip. Total cost: $1,850. Interestingly, he was grateful and relieved because both clients were decent guys to watch a game with and had to leave right after, given the long work week ahead. Without the early departure, the bill would have nudged past the $2,000 mark. It also ended up being a good game with a surprisingly lively crowd as the Leafs won 3–0.

The same friend is fond of telling a story about a time his boss wanted one more drink after their box attendant had shut the bar for the night near the end of the third period. For some reason, a single shot wasn't possible but if he wanted to buy the whole bottle, he could get his final, final drink that way. Some $300 later, my friend's boss had his last call; a few others helped out, but the bottle was left behind three-quarters full — licensing laws prevent customers from taking the alcohol away.

Another example: for the January 7, 2012, game versus Detroit, a firm doing business primarily with local municipal governments mostly in Central Ontario offloaded its two gold tickets — face value $420 — to an elected official. It's certainly good business practice to keep local politicians happy, especially when they control the purse strings to lucrative contracts. But the local pol realized after accepting the invitation that he couldn't make the game and handed off the tickets to one of his grown children, who attended with a guest. The firm ensured that the pair charged their dinner and drinks in the ACC Club to the client's account. In the end, the young couple treated themselves to a menu that includes $68 prime rib, $31 burgers, and $20 sundaes — named for former Leafs star Wendel Clark, no less — with tax and tip extra. Eaters need not worry about compromising their ethical standards as the "Senior Director of Culinary and Executive Chef" leaves a lovely note at the bottom of the menu assuring them they're munching on the "best locally grown, responsibly farmed ingredients." It's all enough to make you want to drink more, of course, and the couple made sure that they each took two beers to their seat before the start of each period at almost $15 a pop. In the end, the couple signed for a bill that was virtually identical in price to the face value of their tickets. In total, it was an $800 night for a little more than three hours in the building. The two people who enjoyed the festivities weren't paying, of course, and the company that did pick up the tab will surely write it off as part of doing business.

As these numbers suggest, MLSE's smooth hospitality operation and its catering to high-end clientele is a virtual licence to print money. In fact, the financial stakes are a notch higher in the Platinum Club downstairs in the bowels of the ACC. Technically, access is supposed to be controlled, but in reality, if you look the part — a suit jacket helps and make sure not to look too awed by the high-powered surroundings — you can gain entry. The place has the feel of a high-end restaurant that could be found anywhere around Bay Street. It's a nice place, to be sure, but not overwhelmingly so. The service is professional, prompt, and by the book, right down to the precisely measured glasses of wine served. A clock over the main entrance counts down intermission breaks so patrons have a sense of when the puck will drop, but it's often ignored. Crowds thin out somewhat once play resumes, but one image from 2010 remains with me and perfectly sums up the atmosphere and most of the bar's clientele: I was scrambling to pay my bill in time for play to begin, but the normally helpful bartender couldn't do much to make it happen — he was tied up trying to explain to a slightly edgy customer the wine and cheese offerings available as me and a few other customers waited to settle up.

How did it come to this? Aside from free-market forces, there are some unique elements of the Leafs season-ticket subscriber base that have contributed to the vastly changed makeup of the team's crowds in the past ten or fifteen years. In addition to the estimated 15,000 or so season-ticket subscribers, the Leafs have also maintained a waiting list that is decades long. A typical story of a multi-season's ticket holder goes like this: The tickets were bought early on and long before the ACC was even built and remain either in family or company hands. The sheer cost and grind of going to games week-in, week-out, season after season, lost its appeal years ago, especially when the lockout hit and the Leafs have iced mediocre teams. But because of their value, they are sold on to either a corporation or a ticket broker at a profit and usually before the season starts, ensuring that you're insulated from the various Leaf swoons that could hurt their value.

Once the ACC was built, seat licences allowed people to effectively skip the waiting list. And now many of those people have done precisely the same thing: they hang on to the tickets waiting for the price to be right to sell the seat licences, which could yield a four- or five-fold return on the original investment. In the meantime, they use the tickets only sparingly themselves, if at all, selling the rest to brokers or corporations. The final result is that a block of about 15,000 seats is controlled by a group of people that numbers only a few thousand. In the process, Leafs tickets might have become the city's ultimate commodity, perhaps even more desired than Yankees and Red Sox tickets are in New York and Boston, or Lakers tickets are in Los Angeles.

The makeup of crowds at Leafs games started to change in the last few years at the Gardens. More and more corporate types started to show up at games as the Leafs emerged from the post–Harold Ballard years. The construction of the ACC, with a few thousand more seats that were gobbled up by the seat licence buyers, pushed the price to get into games much higher and made the mucky-muck set a permanent fixture of the new arena right from the very beginning of its existence.

There are other newly ingrained elements: manufactured noise, silly scoreboard prompts to "make noise," and a general malaise and stilted atmosphere. It all takes place while the fan is watching NHL hockey, a sport where home-ice advantage is considered a valuable factor. But how valuable is home-ice advantage for the Leafs? I was struck by this thought during the television broadcast of a Leafs–Winnipeg Jets game on February 7, 2012. The Jets have likely had the loudest fans in the NHL since their return to the league. That night, the Jets won the game 2–1 even though the Leafs looked very much the better team. The Jets may well have benefited from the enthusiasm of their home crowd. Having been in the ACC as much as I have over the past seven seasons, it's hard to recall even a handful of times when the Toronto crowd willed the Leafs to play better. Sure, some of the more entertaining games have a fairly raucous feel to them, but it's a pretty rare occurrence for a Toronto crowd to be *the* story. I'm not suggesting there is a direct link to the loss in Winnipeg and the Leafs' collapse that took place soon after. But if the Jets crowd was the deciding factor in that particular game, it does illustrate some of the disadvantages the Leafs face by playing to such dead crowds at home.

Leafs crowds are basically indifferent. So indifferent, in fact, that they tend to not view kindly those rare occasions when true fans display genuine passion.

Of all the cases I've witnessed where raucous groups of fans end up petering out because those around them simply don't care to join in; or worse, of individuals being kicked out for minor indiscretions, came during a Saturday night game late in the 2006–07 season against the Ottawa Senators. The Leafs were trying to mount a playoff charge and were coming off a 5–1 thumping in Ottawa a few nights earlier. It was an up-and-down barnburner that the Leafs eventually won in overtime after erasing a couple of two-goal deficits against a team that would make a visit to the Stanley Cup final later that spring. During a stretch in the second period, a man in his twenties and clad in a Montreal Canadiens jersey did what many Habs fans do, especially with the help of a few drinks: he began to taunt the crowd in his immediate vicinity. It's not unusual for Habs fans to turn up at the ACC even when their team isn't in town. They are instantly recognizable by their crimson jerseys and the odd shape of their craniums. They seem to think that because they support a team with such a glorious past, they have the right to poke fun at Leafs fans in their own building. This Habs fan became so overtly belligerent he began to physically interfere with other patrons immediately around him. One shudders to think what the reaction would be in Madison Square Garden or, for that matter, Montreal's Bell Centre. An ejection, a broken nose, perhaps worse, or at the very least a prompting to sit down, would be the likely reaction such an interloper would get at pretty much every other sports arena in North America. The young drunk continued his contrarian routine for the better part of the middle period as the Leafs were struggling to come back against the Sens. Finally, one Leafs fan had had enough. Fuelled by both rage at the game taking place in front of him — the Leafs were losing despite outplaying the Sens — and also a bit of liquid courage himself, he snapped at the Canadiens fan. He was much bigger than the Habs supporter and could have pummeled the smaller man before security guards arrived. Instead, what followed was a clumsy attempt to shut him up, to instill a little physical intimidation. It was pretty benign stuff and the Leafs fan barely touched the Montreal fan, who, frankly, deserved to have his ass kicked.

Other Leafs fans were horrified — on behalf of the Habs supporter! They called to have the man who took action himself tossed from the building. The offending Leafs fan, his blond hair flapping about, was demonized. On cue, the yellow-jacketed ACC Mafioso arrived, including one chap whose job seemed to be to stand back and jot everything down on a notepad — imagine a police officer at the scene of a fender bender. With a handful of his security mates on hand to perform the wet work involved in such altercations, the security guard with the notepad scribbled madly while various shouts and catcalls demanded that the offender — the Leafs fan — be ejected. Not enjoying his humiliation, nor the instant sobriety it brought about, the hometown fan sheepishly made his way to the exit of his own accord. It was the hockey fan's equivalent of a perp walk. All the while, the Habs fan, enjoying his newfound infamy, proceeded to try to pump up the crowd, exhorting them to cheer as the fellow was drummed out of the building. A scattering of cheers and a few boos followed, the irony seemingly lost on the crowd that one of the biggest surges they could muster all evening was for the ejection of one of their own at the behest of a fan of their archrival.

Why did security act in such a way? Why did they not throw both men out? They were clearly unaware that the situation had been stirred up by the Habs supporter. His mugging to the crowd was merely interpreted by security as him being the victim and getting his revenge. Whatever the case, the message from both security and those cheering their actions was clear: we'll take your money but behave yourself, or you risk embarrassment and humiliation, to say nothing of ejection from your expensive seats. Given how entrenched the Leafs' season-ticket base is in the hands of brokers and corporations, it's hard to imagine it changing any time soon.

There is more. After that Leafs–Rangers game where my seats suddenly became much roomier because they were vacated due to the looming mommy-daughter date at the symphony, I made arrangements to meet a colleague later that night. My wait was going be about an hour, but there was no way I was ever going be able to put in the time in the Real Sports bar near the ACC's main outside entrance on the west side of the building — it's always packed with a huge lineup to get in.

I decided to cool my heels, alone, in e11even, another MLSE-owned eatery so named for the number of Stanley Cups won by the Toronto Maple Leafs. A bit more upscale — if you can imagine, given that Real Sports is perhaps the most highbrow sports bar most people have ever seen — it admittedly tends to attract a pretty urbane crowd on any night, whether it's a game night or not. But the great appeal of el1even is that you can almost always get in without walking the extra distance down Bremner Boulevard to the more mid-level places such as Hoops.

I took my seat at the end of the bar and struck up a conversation with a man with whom I had worked with a bit in the past. He was doing precisely what I was — waiting for a friend — but he had the luxury of living behind the ACC and was debating leaving before I walked in. As we were chatting, we realized that the second *Hockey Night in Canada* game was not on the television. Given that we were in an MLSE-owned establishment and almost all of the people in the bar had just attended the Leafs game, not having the late game on seemed a bit odd.

It may come as a surprise, but we were the only ones clamouring for the game. One staff member explained that the restaurant didn't get Sportsnet One, a secondary channel that to my knowledge didn't even show Leafs games but certainly wasn't connected to Saturday night CBC broadcasts. After numerous queries and enduring a bunch of requests to provide our business cards by staff who were attempting to acquire as many as possible for some internal el1even staff contest, we finally managed to speak with a manager, who quickly changed the channel.

The Calgary Flames were playing the Los Angeles Kings, a Sutter-on-Sutter battle as Darryl was returning to his old club still coached by brother Brett. The Kings were handing it to the Flames, but just as we both were expecting our respective friends to arrive, the channel inexplicably changed.

"It's on a timer," said a bartender, who didn't seem too concerned with changing it back to the hockey game.

My friend's mate arrived. We took one look at each other and then took stock whether it was going to be worth it to try and get the channel changed back.

"Forget it," he said. "Let's go to Hoops."

With that, having each left behind about $50 for drinks (and our business cards), we went down the street to catch the third period of the hockey game.

17

THE MAN IN CHARGE

WHEN I WAS IN UNIVERSITY IN THE MID-1990S WATCHING TSN'S *That's Hockey* with my university floor mates, they used to joke that it looked like Brian Burke got dressed for work *before* he went to bed at night.

When Burke was NHL VP in charge of discipline, long before he came to Toronto, a typical Leafs fan was more familiar with him explaining a suspension, usually looking slightly flustered on screen as he did so.

Just as television tends to make everyone look a bit heftier, it also has a way of making someone look a notch grumpier than they are in person. In those days, the combination of Burke and the cameras seemed to accentuate his foul mood and how desperately he needed an iron.

BRIAN BURKE CAME ONBOARD IN LATE NOVEMBER 2008, BUT THE RESULTS WERE MIXED THROUGH HIS FIRST FOUR SEASONS.

Today, Burke cuts a rather suave figure. The closest he comes to letting his fashion guard down is to slightly loosen his tie and occasionally having it untied around his neck.

My lone up-close impression of Burke occurred on an unseasonably warm, early spring night in Barrie, Ontario, in April 1999. The Barrie Colts were one of the best junior hockey teams in Canada and were locked in a spirited battle in the Ontario Hockey League playoffs against the Oshawa Generals (who they eventually lost to in a huge upset). Junior hockey is virtually ignored in Toronto, but these types of games are a huge deal in communities such as Barrie and dozens more across Canada. Further, news had broken that day that Wayne Gretzky was going to retire. With the New York Rangers out of the playoff chase, Gretzky had confirmed that a game that night in Ottawa was his final one in Canada. The hockey world at all levels was abuzz because its best player was going to bow out three days later, after a home game against the Pittsburgh Penguins in New York. So there was a nice three- or four-day window for fans and the media to discuss Gretzky's departure and his legacy. I was at the Barrie Molson Centre in my role as a cub reporter for the *Barrie Examiner*. My duties included getting comments about Gretzky from some of the NHL scouts and personnel who were sure to be in the arena that night. More so than usual, I had my antenna up for the various scouts and executives I knew were going to be there.

Like all junior teams, the Colts make arrangements for media and scouts to get their required work done before, during, and after games, but unlike in the professional rinks, it often means that both rub shoulders in the same room. It's not uncommon to see a prominent NHL GM such as Burke at an arena in a place like Barrie, or Lethbridge, or Rimouski as they travel around to watch prized prospects play. It is one of the great contradictions of the hockey world that in order to get an up-close look at a prominent decision-maker, you often have to go to a non-NHL building to do it. The guy beside you using the mustard dispenser could be a figure you recognize from TV. Experienced media personnel often highlight marquee junior games in their area, knowing they tend to bring out the type of hockey royalty only common at semi-annual GM meetings in far-flung places like Florida or at the summer NHL Draft.

This was one of those nights. One of the few holdovers from the Generals' league championship squad from two years earlier was Bryan Allen, a draft pick of the Canucks and a player who is still considered to be a solid NHL defenceman. Burke was relatively new in the Canucks gig back then, having taken over after Pat Quinn was fired and returning to the city where he was previously the team's Number Two hockey man. Allen was considered a prime piece of the puzzle in Burke's effort to build the Canucks into a contender and Burke was there to see him play.

Twenty-five or thirty various NHL people were shoe-horned into a small hospitality room when I looked up and saw that distinctive figure come barreling through the door. Burke appeared especially hot and bothered this night. He *was* hot — it was ten or twelve degrees outside in early April — and the clear feeling of winter giving way to spring was in the air. Burke was dressed for much colder weather, and his face was as red as it had ever been barking into the microphone of a media mob. Burke looked to be in dire need of a seat and perhaps a cold beverage. As he went to fling his overcoat over the back of a chair, out of the corner of my eye I saw something fly through the air, but I didn't equate it to anything other than the dizzying whirl of a crowded room. A split second later, that *thing* landed in my lap. I looked down, quickly realized it was someone's wallet, and looked around to try to figure out what the hell had just happened. I opened the wallet and there was the unmistakable face I had seen so many times on the television screen and now in this hot, crowded room.

It was Burke's wallet, identifiable by his driver's licence, which was prominently displayed inside along with his mug shot.

"Sir, is this for me?" I asked him, entirely in jest.

He snatched it from my hand without saying a word — he didn't need to, because the look on his face said it all. He was a guy who was annoyed that some smart aleck had his wallet.

Let's just say that I didn't ask him for a comment about Gretzky that night.

Later, as he waited for Allen outside the Generals' dressing room, I walked past Burke and tried to make eye contact with him. He stared right through me.

❦　　❦　　❦

Burke took charge of the Leafs on November 29, 2008 — the day of my son's first birthday party — and four words characterized Burke's arrival in Toronto: pugnacity, truculence, belligerence, and testosterone. He famously used those words to describe how he felt his teams should play to be successful and they became a catchphrase for much of his first two years as GM.

Big problem: the Leafs have rarely played like a team living up to those qualities as the kind of personnel required to do so has largely been absent from the roster.

Even bigger problem: September 18, 2009. That's the day Phil Kessel arrived in Toronto. Kessel is a gifted offensive player with a sniper's precision, an underrated set-up ability, and blazing speed that make him a threat even if he's not playing well. What's not to like, then?

Well, it was the small matter of the two first-round picks that Toronto surrendered in the transaction. They turned out to be Tyler Seguin and Dougie Hamilton. Of course, both players are from the Toronto area — how often does this story need to be told?

Seguin has been compared to Steve Yzerman and he is also a right-handed centre, which aside from a multi-dimensional defenceman, is likely the toughest type of elite talent to find in hockey. Did I just say something about a multi-dimensional defenceman? Hamilton came a year later, taken ninth overall by the Bruins at the 2011 NHL Entry Draft and soon after became regarded as the best all-around defencemen in Canadian major junior hockey. He's also the son of two former Olympians — Doug, a bronze-medal-winning rower, and Lynn, the starting point guard on Canada's 1984 women's basketball team, which finished fourth. His older brother Freddie is a draft pick of the San Jose Sharks, finishing his junior career as one of the country's best two-way players — and, of course, passed over by the Leafs in the 2010 Entry Draft.

The sight of Doug, now a Toronto lawyer, and Lynn hugging their son on draft day after being taken by a team that just won the Stanley Cup seemed like just the 3,245th occasion in which Leafs fans were forced to watch a good, young, and local player go elsewhere. There's more: in the Hamilton household hangs a pair of photos; one is of a young Freddie, the other of Dougie at the same age, both taken after each boy had won a skills competition as a peewee. The prize? Participating in the Leafs skills competition. The photos taken at those events hang in the Hamilton basement, as well, along with an impressive collection of other swag won by both the boys and their parents during their respective athletic careers.

Now Kessel is a great player and a fine lad by all accounts, if a little odd, media shy, and one-dimensional. It's never a player's fault who he is traded for, but the Kessel deal hangs like a pall over Burke no matter how high your opinion of the player he got in the deal. Burke had no way of knowing the two first-round picks were going to be second- and ninth-overall selections when he made the trade. Making it as he did was also confirmation that Burke didn't think his team would be missing the playoffs both years, the first by such a wide margin. Overall, the Kessel deal will have an especially pungent odour to it if he leaves as a free agent when his contract expires in 2014.

Most of all, the Kessel trade is the biggest example of how Burke has been a man of contradictions in Toronto. He's been on the losing end of one of the most lopsided trades since the lockout and yet other deals Burke has made provide hope that the Leafs will finally find their way out of the malaise they've been stuck in for almost a decade.

There are other examples that make Burke something of a walking paradox: he possess a razor sharp intellect and yet comes across at times like a guy who can't help himself from speaking aloud before he stops to think what it is he's saying. He's a veteran Stanley Cup–winning GM who replaced a neophyte in John Ferguson Jr. and yet Burke's competitive record is considerably worse than Ferguson's in roughly the same time on the job. Burke has also made admirable public contributions to the greater good in Toronto, most notably speaking out against all forms of discrimination, but also supporting other community causes and especially the Canadian military. And yet there are times that Burke seems like a dinosaur, holding press conferences lamenting the demise of tough guys because he was forced to put one of his many mistakes, free agent Colton Orr, on waivers.

Burke's bluster was well known before he came to Toronto and was even quite entertaining to watch back then, but also at times since he's been in charge of the Leafs. Even if his tendency for grand pronouncements have come back to bite him, there have also been some beneficial effects of Burke's reign.

First, the Kessel trade, even if it turns out as badly as it might, Burke has swung other deals that have helped the Leafs significantly and given very little up in return. Team captain Dion Phaneuf is the biggest example, arriving in Toronto from Calgary for Ian White and little more than bad contracts. Joe Colborne, Cody Franson, Jake Gardiner, Matthew Lombardi, and Joffrey Lupul were all acquired in a series of deals, with the biggest assets going the other way being an underperforming Francois Beauchemin and a declining Tomas Kaberle — the Stanley Cup he won in Boston aside.

As that roll call indicates, Burke's trading has been a net-plus even if the tendency is to focus on the ever-evolving Kessel trade. Burke has also created a certain degree of depth in the Leafs organization, partially through trades, partially the draft, that was sorely absent before his arrival. Colborne, Gardiner, Nazem Kadri, Carter Ashton, and Ben Scrivens are five solid prospects (three forwards, one defenceman, one goalie) that are expected to help the Leafs moving forward. With a reasonable degree of depth both in the American Hockey League and among its prospects in junior and college, the team no longer has to rely on the likes of Robbie Earl and Justin Pogge like it did when the organization was so thin on young talent before Burke's arrival. The Toronto Marlies run to the 2012 Calder Cup final is affirmation that the young players in the Leafs system could have considerable upside in the coming years.

It's still a bit too early to judge Burke on the drafting front. Former junior star Kadri split the opinion of scouts in his draft year in 2009 and he appears to have had a similar effect with Leafs fans. Tyler Biggs and Stuart Percy both were taken in the first round, but only time will tell how they turn out. Others such as defencemen Jesse Blacker and Korbinian Holzer have now been playing for the Toronto Marlies for a while but are expected to eventually become full-time Leafs someday soon.

Courtesy of Getty Images.

DION PHANEUF IS THE MOST RECENT LEAFS CAPTAIN, BROUGHT TO TORONTO IN A LOPSIDED TRADE FROM CALGARY, ALMOST TWO DECADES AFTER THE LEAFS GOT ANOTHER CAPTAIN FROM THE FLAMES: DOUG GILMOUR.

All told, Burke and his scouts haven't been awful at the draft table, but they haven't exactly set the world on fire either, in part because of those two high first-round picks they gave up in getting Kessel.

For some, there is also another uncomfortable element to the Burke regime: nationality. The Leafs have almost as many Americans as Canadians in their lineup most nights. The NHL average, on the other hand, is more than 2:1. Burke-haters and the conspiracy theorist types, the ones who love to call in to radio shows in the wee hours, cite the Leafs GM's ongoing role with USA Hockey as somehow being in conflict. Something about him giving jobs to Americans in order to help the development system of that country's national team. Overall, though, Burke's man-crush on U.S. players is likely just one of those odd cyclical quirks that happen in sports — a majority of Canada's NHL teams were once captained by Scandinavians, after all. It also should be noted that the Leafs have among the NHL's highest percentage of Canadians on their roster during Burke's tenure. If Burke has a bias, it's in being pro–North American, and the way he stocked his teams before coming to Toronto also displayed that tendency.

Courtesy of Getty Images.

NAZEM KADRI IS ONE OF THOSE RARE TORONTO MAPLE LEAFS: A HIGH DRAFT PICK WHO HAS BEEN ALLOWED TO DEVELOP WHILE SPLITTING TIME WITH THE BIG CLUB AND THE MARLIES.

Where the American-in-Canada was a legitimate issue was with Ron Wilson and his odd connection to his native country (Canada) and his adopted one (U.S).

Ah, Wilson and his charming personality and tact. Wilson, though born here, always seemed to have a chip on his shoulder about Canada's fascination with hockey. It was almost as if he couldn't accept Toronto wasn't Anaheim, or Washington, or San Jose, where he previously coached away from the intense media glare ever-present in Hogtown. Though Burke eventually fired Wilson — two years too late — his iron-clad defence of his coach was tough to stomach, even to reasonable folks who don't like jumping to odd conclusions. We all should be as lucky to have a boss with such loose standards. Though he's now long gone, there's another critical element to Wilson not getting more out of the Leafs squads he coached: the Kessel trade would look a hell of a lot better if the Leafs didn't have to give up such high draft picks that turned into Seguin and Hamilton. Viewed through that lens, maybe the deal isn't so much Burke's mistake but Wilson's.

Despite the continued disappointment on the ice — and therefore with his job performance — Burke does bring an intangible to the job that even his harshest critics have to acknowledge. A Maple Leafs GM (and coach) should have a personality consummate with the job. Burke has it. It's an aura, an air of know-how, a presence.

In putting together this narrative, I sniffed around the areas of Toronto that Burke is known to frequent when away from the ACC to get a sense of the impression he leaves on average Leafs fans. It has to be said that, until roughly early February 2012, he left an incredibly positive impression. I heard numerous anecdotal stories, many of which were impossible to confirm for certain, but two stood out. The first took place at a Starbucks near his mid-Toronto home, where Burke came to the defence of employees one day when an unreasonable customer crossed the line from being annoyed with his service to being downright rude and disrespectful. In the second, he put up for bid the opportunity to follow him doing his job for a day in order to raise money for his children's school. Two men split the prize and the school raised several thousand dollars in the process. Perhaps those examples are too anecdotal and even out of context, but Burke has that certain quality needed to lead a hallowed institution like the Toronto Maple Leafs. If you think otherwise, ask Montreal Canadiens fans if they saw that same leadership in former GM Pierre Gauthier or Leafs fans' thoughts about Wilson.

Though not everyone likes Burke — with the continued losing, many media and now fans think he's all shirt and no trousers — he has a sensibility that's suitable for Toronto and for a Canadian market. He's an American who has taken out Canadian citizenship. He has a genuine respect for this country. He seems to know what makes Canadians tick; he's taken the time to understand us and, indeed, become somewhat like us, even if he's an American first and foremost.

In the aftermath of the Vancouver Olympics, Burke had to be in some form of emotional purgatory knowing how close the team he built got to winning the gold medal in the very building where he had spent so much time as Canucks GM. Team Canada dominated the gold medal game. But Burke's (and Wilson's) American players were opportunistic and very nearly won the game. The U.S. was but an inch or two away from gold when Joe Pavelski very nearly scored early in the overtime period.

Burke's behaviour after the overtime was a study in class. Though obviously disappointed, he credited Team Canada and said they deserved to win, whereas Wilson moaned loudly about Sidney Crosby's goal being, if not fluky, the result of a good break. Burke took the opposite tack, saying publicly that Crosby's winner was a skillful play by the best player in the game.

More importantly, Burke at the time was going through a personal hell that no parent should ever have to endure. His son Brendan had been killed in a car accident just a few weeks earlier, not long after he had publicly revealed the fact that he was gay. Burke had stuck by his son when he came out, answered every question thoughtfully and truthfully, and stated over and over again that loving one's offspring was unconditional and not worthy of praise just because he happens to be gay.

There are no hard and fast ways to measure things such as acceptance and diversity, but Burke's support of Brendan and then his pain at losing him in such a tragic way is perhaps the single biggest motivator the North American sports world has seen for all those in it seeking true equality.

It's now a troubling question as to what kind of hockey legacy Burke will leave behind in Toronto. Even if it continues to go pear shaped and Burke's reign in Toronto ends badly, leaving behind a legacy of acceptance is a reasonable consolation prize.

But here's the very itchy rub: Burke needs to start winning. He has the personality and he has certainly made some good moves, along with one spectacularly bad trade and a few horrendous free-agent signings.

In Toronto, there is always the danger that the focus gets lost. Too often in this city it becomes about the background noise and not the one thing that should be focused on in the foreground — playing and winning games. Of course, if Burke can help advance various social causes, do it in a style all his own, and have a bunch of punchy sound bites and public displays in the process, that's great. But it's not why he's the general manager of the Toronto Maple Leafs. Burke is in Toronto to mould the Maple Leafs back into their previous form of a glorious hockey team that has now been absent for the better part of two generations. Do that and all that other good stuff in the process — we can all dream, can't we?

18

HYSTERIA

My plane had just touched down in Edmonton on a frigid January morning in 2008, the type of day that the fine people of northern Alberta don't notice but the ones from slightly warmer climes such as Ontario never forget.

I was in the Alberta capital as part of my regular job, taking in the Top Prospects Game, the annual contest between the Canadian Hockey League's top forty eligible players for the NHL Entry Draft that spring.

The city of Edmonton gets a bad rap from certain visitors, many of whom are NHL hockey wives and girlfriends who are not enamoured of the city's climate and, apparently, its lack of designer shops. After arriving at Edmonton International Airport, I noticed that the facility didn't particularly help the cause. It felt like it hadn't been given a spit and polish since the Oilers last won the Stanley Cup.

First impressions aside, it was clear something else was going on that was putting a damper on things. The flight I had arrived on also had a number of people connected to the game and to the wider hockey community on it. People were anxious to fire up their phones and by the time they were allowed to turn them on and the email started flowing in, the pall in the air was carried all the way to the baggage area. One person clearly in some form of angst was Doug Gilmour, who was in Edmonton in his role as John Ferguson Jr.'s assistant. It was clear judging by how fast he made a beeline for the ticket counter that Gilmour had had news that necessitated a sudden change of plans. Another colleague, Terry Doyle, who was also on the flight, had managed to glean from his phone that Ferguson had just been fired back in Toronto.

Too many losses, too many cumbersome salary-cap-killing contracts, and just a general feeling of not really having a plan beyond the next move eventually cost Ferguson his gig. The firing was wholly deserved, but to a fan, it seemed like Ferguson was put into a situation where he was almost set up to fail by the board at Maple Leaf Sports and Entertainment. Perhaps it was entirely his own fault, but Ferguson always gave off the vibe that he was never really in charge in the true sense of the word. He was forced to prove himself each and every year. You could look at his situation as a combination of on-the-job training and a *Hockey GM for Dummies* exercise that was typical of the way MLSE guided everything on both the hockey and basketball side until Bryan Colangelo and then Brian Burke came to town.

As I sat waiting for my own bags and started to mentally review his four-plus years on the job, I realized that Ferguson was a bit like Edmonton: he made a bad first impression but in a better situation, who knows what he could have done. It also should be noted that had Ed Belfour's health allowed him another season or two of his Hall of Fame standard, the Leafs disastrous post-lockout record wouldn't be quite so bad.

Ferguson, having assumed control of a decent team that had stumbled out of the playoffs in 2003, went all in before the lockout to give the Leafs the best shot at winning in 2004 with a group that was starting to get a bit long in the tooth. It all ended when the Philadelphia Flyers' Jeremy Roenick scored in overtime of Game 6 of the conference semifinals. I hated to admit it then, but the better team won that series. The fact that Darcy Tucker had run the Flyers Sami Kapanen with a questionable hit just before Roenick scored likely meant there was a bit of karma in the air, as much as it disappointed me.

The lockout wiped out the following season and the Leafs returned to action with the rest of the NHL having shot their bolt. Having dealt so many prospects, draft picks, and what few young players the club had, Ferguson had to go into band-aid mode. Unfortunately, the new reality made the Leafs look a bit like the guy who shows up for hockey year after year in Cooperalls, still thinking they were cool and cutting edge.

Though they were close to making the playoffs in the first year after the lockout and especially so the second season, Ferguson's firing was the indication that something had to change. The jig was up.

❧   ❧   ❧

While I was at the Top Prospects Game in Edmonton, the Leafs managed to do something they didn't do enough of while Ferguson was GM: they won a game, beating Washington. What followed soon after, when I was back in Toronto, was precisely the type of false bump that has played with Leafs fans' minds since the Harold Ballard era. It took a few weeks but *it* began again: the completely and utterly delusional way in which I, like tens of thousands of other Leafs fans, actually believe that a bad hockey team can somehow become good overnight, put together a win streak, and make the playoffs. If there is one thing that unites all Maple Leafs fans, it's their capacity to believe in this common cause underpinned by such flawed logic that it makes Chicago Cubs fans blush.

That false hope was washing over me when I stepped off the plane from Edmonton. *Sure, the team is eleven points back but that's only five wins, plus another extra point for losing in a shootout. We can make that up in, what, seven or eight games, right?*

For me, the false hope really kicked in at a rare Saturday afternoon home game against the Detroit Red Wings, the team that eventually won the Stanley Cup that spring. The Wings, like every other elite team in the NHL, were trying to get through that tricky part of the NHL schedule that falls after the All-Star Game but before the real push to solidify your playoff spot begins. Good teams simply try to not fall on their face or have anyone injured during this time. A Mike Babcock–coached team would never take any opponent lightly, but if there was a game where even a squad like the Red Wings would let their guard down, it would come against a team that had won just twenty-two of fifty-six games. That was the Leafs' record heading into that game on February 9, 2008.

The Leafs were coming off a solid win in Montreal two nights earlier and the dreamers weren't quite in full fantasy mode. Until that day. That's because the Leafs beat the Red Wings in overtime, and suddenly the situation started to look a little different. Head coach Paul Maurice had finally taken the advice of hundreds of thousands of Leafs fans and accepted the fact that Andrew Raycroft was not the starting goaltender. With Raycroft stapled to the bench, Vesa Toskala was playing literally every single game and looking okay in the process. And now the Leafs had beaten the Habs and the Red Wings, two teams that at that point looked like a Stanley Cup final preview for later that spring.

Could something be in the air here? Seriously, that's what I was thinking when I left the Air Canada Centre that day. I mean, c'mon, they just beat two of the best teams in the NHL, Ferguson had been fired, guys were playing for their jobs, a miracle run made sense, didn't it?

Well, no. The Leafs lost their next two games, and I briefly vacated that horrible head space no one wants to be in: that of a delusional Leafs fan.

But then it started again. Toskala continued to play well and the Leafs won six of their next eight games, with one of the losses coming in overtime. That's thirteen of a possible sixteen points and all of a sudden the Leafs were in that zone: just a few points back of a playoff spot.

But let's step back to reality for a few seconds. Quests such as that the Leafs were on have been made even more complicated and difficult by the NHL's introduction of the three-point game. No matter how a team wins, be it in regulation, overtime, or a shootout, the prevailing side is always awarded the same two points. If a team can extend a contest to overtime or a shootout, but ultimately loses, it gets one point. In other words, no matter what happens in every NHL game, one team is going to get two points and between a quarter and a third of the games award a consolation marker to the losing side. The effect, as all hockey fans know by now, is that even late in the season, as many as twenty-three or twenty-four teams are within a few games — four to six points — of earning a playoff berth. In the old days of the pre-lockout NHL, that type of gap was possible to close. But even back then it would often take a sustained run of good play over a dozen games and often more. A six-point deficit in the context of the current NHL setup is almost impossible to close once the calendar passes February 1.

Consider this fact: In the first seven seasons played since the new system was put into place and therefore fourteen different conference playoff races, there have been just three cases of a team erasing significant deficits. The first took place in the 2007–08 season when the Washington Capitals lit up the stretch run and snuck into the Eastern Conference playoffs. Another took place in 2010–11 in the Western Conference when the Anaheim Ducks put together roughly the same type of run. Not only did the Ducks reach the playoffs, they also earned home-game advantage in the first round by getting all the way up to fourth place in the Western Conference standings. The last case was the St. Louis Blues. They tore up the final two months of the 2008–09 schedule to squeeze into the playoffs, but were swept in the first round by Vancouver.

That's three successful examples stacked up against at least a dozen (hello, Calgary Flames) that ultimately fell short. Notable too about both the Capitals and Ducks making a successful charge was that each team had a few legit star players and likely shouldn't have been so far back in the first place. Anaheim had Corey Perry, Ryan Getzlaf, and Bobby Ryan in its lineup, and they were helped by having goaltender Jonas Hiller return late in the season as well as emergency signing Ray Emery, who played well in his absence. So, while impressive, glancing at the Western Conference heading into play that season, the Ducks looked about the fourth-best team on paper. They finally started playing like it.

Washington was an interesting case because everyone knew that it was a team on the cusp. Alex Ovechkin, Nicklas Backstrom, Mike Green, and Alex Semin were either all big-ticket players or well on their way to becoming ones. Washington also fired its coach, Glen Hanlon, early on that season and replaced him with former Leaf

Bruce Boudreau. Boudreau basically let the Caps play all out — they didn't really have a choice, they were so far back in the standings — and it paid off.

Corey Perry, Ryan Getzlaf, Bobby Ryan, Jonas Hiller, Alex Ovechkin, Mike Green, Nicklas Backstrom, and Alex Semin. Are you picking up on a key difference between the Caps and Ducks and the Leafs chasing a far-flung playoff berth?

Let's see. The Leafs still had the splendid talent of Mats Sundin. Tomas Kaberle was still a very good defenceman, as was Bryan McCabe (more on him in a moment). But Nik Antropov, a spent Darcy Tucker, Matt Stajan, and Jason Blake? Does that sound like the type of roster that the Capitals had a season earlier or the Ducks would three years down the line?

I didn't think so. But don't think for a second that sober reflection ever enters into the equation once the Leafs win a few games. A pair of losses to the New Jersey Devils in early March temporarily took the edge off, but with their record a neat and tidy 30–30–10, the Leafs welcomed the Philadelphia Flyers to town in early March for a home-and-home set.

Remember what I said about good teams just trying to stay out of the way while gearing up for the playoffs? Well, the Flyers were showing signs of ascending the ladder and, given the eventual results, you have to wonder whether the Leafs benefited from that odd phenomenon that takes place when good teams play bad ones late in the season. The Flyers got up 3–0 during the first game in Toronto. It looked like the Leafs were dead in the water, but they came storming back and the mood in the ACC went from tomb-like to once-or-twice-a-season loony. When Pavel Kubina scored in overtime to secure a 4–3 win for the Leafs, I left the building honestly believing the Leafs could make the playoffs. Watching the Leafs win 3–2 the next night, I distinctly recall turning the television off wondering where I was going to get my playoff tickets. Seriously. Wins in three of their next four games and the playoff push was on.

The end came rather quickly, however. With thirty-five wins and eighty points and six games left, the Leafs hadn't been getting the type of results needed in games involving other contenders (another more subtle reality of the three-point game era). Because of that unfortunate development, they needed to sweep the Boston Bruins in a home-and-home series and then they would likely need to take seven of a possible eight points available the rest of the way.

Put it this way: the Bruins quickly saved me the dilemma of finding playoff tickets. In a clinical display that, if I was honest with myself, showed what capable teams can do to not-so-capable teams when it really matters, the Bruins took 6–2 and 4–2 wins and the fairytale run was over in the space of twenty-four hours. It had been six weeks since that Saturday afternoon when the Leafs beat the Red Wings and two months since Ferguson had been fired, but the playoff run to nowhere was over. And soon so were Sundin, McCabe, and Tucker's time in Toronto.

Though I didn't always think this way, I now believe that McCabe was treated unfairly in Toronto. With his goofy hair and general cocksure attitude, the much-hyped one-timer gave the impression that he was a bit like a twenty-first-century version of Al Iafrate, the Leafs defenceman from the 1980s who earned the nickname "Planet Al" for being just a bit eccentric. McCabe's "can opener" move, where he would put his stick between the legs of onrushing opponents to slow them up, only added another layer to the package. Provided the team was winning, McCabe brought a talented, slightly off-the-wall element to a good hockey team. But like so much with the Leafs, McCabe's act started to wear thin after the lockout when the team was no longer that good. Suddenly, things were different with everyone, but with McCabe especially. Further, with the new rules and different interpretations of old ones, his trademark can opener was a surefire penalty every time. McCabe's time in Toronto ended with probably as much negative press as any player in the modern era. He was *the* story in 2007–08, aside from Sundin and even more than Ferguson's firing.

As a defenceman, McCabe made some shockingly bad decisions. He was careless in his own zone, a habit that occasionally led to the puck ending up in the back of his own net. But McCabe was also

Courtesy of Graig Abel.

BRYAN MCCABE'S DEPARTURE FROM TORONTO IS AT ODDS WITH HIS PERFORMANCE. HE WAS ESSENTIALLY RUN OUT OF TOWN, BUT HIS PLAY WITH THE LEAFS WAS LARGELY FIRST-RATE.

victimized by some incredibly bad luck and by perhaps trying to do too much, especially once he signed a mammoth contract that paid him almost $6 million a season on average. In the space of a couple of months during the 2007–08 season, McCabe, among other things, hand-delivered a pass to Canadiens defenceman Mike Komisarek. The move led to the Canadiens' game-winning goal in overtime. It was an ill-advised play that many junior defencemen would not have attempted. The fact that Komisarek was able to skate the length of the ice with no one catching him shows how out of position McCabe's boo-boo had put not just himself, but the three other Leafs.

McCabe also skated into his own net — something that in the more than 120 games I've witnessed live at the ACC I had never seen done before. And most stunning of all, during a game in Buffalo he scored on his own net with just four seconds left in overtime. This latter error was more bad luck than anything else. McCabe was trying to clear the puck and he had Sabres forward Ales Kotalik behind him, who would have swatted the puck in for the winner had McCabe not attempted to do something with it. McCabe simply misjudged the bouncing puck and it ended up going into the Leafs goal. The one-on-top-of-another mistakes just contributed to McCabe's *out there* persona.

Ferguson's decision to sign McCabe to a five-year, $28.75 million contract played a role in his firing, after which Cliff Fletcher took over on an interim basis. Perhaps Fletcher's most astute move in his limited second go-round with the Leafs was getting rid of McCabe and his contract by moving him to the Florida Panthers. The Leafs got back a very capable Mike Van Ryn in the deal, though his career was eventually cut short due to injuries he suffered while playing in Toronto. Getting a player back of Van Ryn's status also showed that the NHL community hadn't soured on McCabe anywhere near to the extent that Leafs fans had.

Two additional facts underscore how underappreciated McCabe was in Toronto, his grating ability to make untimely gaffes aside. The first is that he remains the lone Leaf to play for Canada in the past two Olympic Games. Second, when McCabe was hurt in January 2006 and eventually missed nine games, the Leafs lost eight in a row, effectively killing their playoff chances that year, notwithstanding the late push (with McCabe back in the lineup). More significantly, in the lead-up to that slump, the Leafs won six games in a row to sit comfortably inside the playoff bracket, with McCabe playing as much as half the game some nights. When you consider that the Leafs eventually fell just two points shy of the playoffs, it's not beyond the realm of possibility that McCabe's nine-game absence was the decisive factor.

McCabe is just one of several examples of Leafs fans getting their dander up on a player who was not nearly as bad as their anger suggested. Kaberle, for another, was certainly not run out of town, but never got the respect he deserved in Toronto. I would also throw Aki Berg's name on to the same list. Though not as much as McCabe, Berg could rankle Toronto fans even though he did some yeoman's work on the back end. Berg was also good enough to make his country's Olympic team twice, winning a silver medal in 2006 and a bronze in 1998, with Finland beating Canada at both tournaments. Given his considerable contributions to his national team, doesn't it seem odd that Leafs fans generally had little regard for Berg during his time in Toronto?

♣   ♣   ♣

What about the other side of the coin, that classic Hogtown trait of building up a player who perhaps benefits a bit too much from all the positive attention?

Hello, Darcy Tucker.

The same season that Bryan McCabe was being skewered, Tucker was in the first season of a four-year contract but playing dramatically below the form expected when he signed the new deal. He's now retired, but if you were to gauge fans' reaction when he is shown on the ACC's video scoreboard, you would think he was a surefire Hall of Famer. Further, to listen to some of his devoted followers, you'd think he had descended into the ACC from Mount Olympus, spawned from some sort of modern-day hockey Zeus.

Courtesy of Graig Abel.

THAT TROUBLING TORONTO TRAIT: DARCY TUCKER WAS ONE OF THE BEST EXAMPLES OF A TORONTO PLAYER IDOLIZED BY HIS OWN FANS BUT QUESTIONED BY OTHERS. TUCKER'S LEAFS TENURE ENDED WITH A CONTRACT BUYOUT.

The dichotomy between McCabe's and Tucker's treatment is striking, especially with both players now out of the NHL. Tucker has landed back on his feet and makes frequent appearances at events, filling the role of celebrity Leaf. To be perfectly blunt, I would also say this about Tie Domi, another former Leaf remembered in irreverent tones by many, the adulation is mostly unwarranted. Tucker and Domi simply didn't perform on the ice the way they are remembered.

Tucker and Domi did bring their share of gifts to the Leafs' table during their careers in Toronto. Tucker, when he was on, was a solid two-way player and averaged twenty-four goals in four of his final five seasons as a Maple Leaf. Domi was not to be messed with when he didn't have his gloves on. He even scored fifteen goals one year and thirteen in another, both during seasons in the so-called dead-puck era before the lockout. But by the definition of NHL hockey players, both were run-of-the-mill talents, plain and simple; valuable, sure, but as supplementary pieces to a much bigger puzzle. Key cogs now to be remembered as hockey gods? C'mon, what does that say about Leafs fans? Are our standards really that low?

I still remember the first time I saw Domi in Toronto. It was around the time Harold Ballard had died and Domi was shown in press reports in the same photo as Wendel Clark down at Maple Leaf Gardens. Clark at the time was the Leafs' best player, already a legend in town and perhaps the lone reason why hockey fans had any hope left at all given the madness of the man who had just died.

Domi had played just two NHL games to that point but there he was, right beside Clark. Years later, rumours of Domi's penchant for creating friendships with the most important people in the room seemed to have the ring of truth to it given how he always seemed to land in such a good situation. His good fortune with the Leafs ended when he was mercifully bought out at the end of the 2005–06 season.

Just before that, at the 2006 trade deadline, Domi, who ought to have known how ineffectively he had played in what turned out to be his final season, told the Toronto media that he would retire instead of report to another team. The comments were moderately controversial, and it could be argued that a player who had given a decade to the club had earned the right to not be moved and to say so publicly. But Domi never bothered, or at least the media didn't ask, to address the fact that it was extremely unlikely anyone would even want him. By that point in his career, he no longer fought, was rarely physical, and was on his way to a modest sixteen-point season. Not exactly the type of guy that NHL GMs are looking to add to bolster their lineup, and that's before considering the fact that fighters rarely have a role in post-season hockey.

There was another perfectly logical reason why Domi didn't want to go anywhere during his final season. It came on March 4, 2006. That was the night he was honoured for playing one thousand career games. Domi deserved to be honoured as others have been when they reach that milestone, but there was something that was just off about the way it all came together. The ceremony dragged on and on before the start of the Leafs–Senators game that night, televised for all watching *Hockey Night in Canada*. It had the feel of being staged and his speech will never be found among the great oratorical deliveries at sports arenas. To be completely honest, I was (glad to be?) spared watching it on television; from my seat way up high in section 321, the ceremony almost put me to sleep. It was like listening to someone's old Uncle Chester drone on and on at a wedding. At weddings, you nudge the person beside you to share in your angst. At the ACC that night, I simply repaired to the closest bar, but just as I was descending the stairs, I heard Domi make an awkward remark about fans being his "friends."

Really, Tie, your friends? It was well-known that Domi ran in the rarefied circles of Toronto's elite. It was classic Domi, trying to send a tailored message to the great unwashed that he was one of them. Aside from the fact he was well past it as a hockey player by then, I always found Domi's playing both sides of the fence — the everyman and the well-connected man — the most grating thing about his whole persona. Forever snorting and sneering at television cameras when he didn't like the question of some nosy reporter was also at odds with Domi's apparent leadership role with the team.

Courtesy of Graig Abel.

TIE DOMI WAS A TOUGH GUY WHO SKATED IN MORE THAN A THOUSAND GAMES, BUT CRITICS CITE HIS POPU-
LARITY AS DISTINCTLY A TORONTO PHENOMENON WHERE A PLAYER ASCENDS TO A LEVEL FAR GREATER
THAN HIS ACTUAL PERFORMANCE.

Someone in the Leafs front office should have known better and streamlined the ceremony. There had even been a recent precedent. I had been in the building two years earlier when Leafs Gary Roberts and Tom Fitzgerald were honoured for playing their one thousandth games. It was a much shorter and appropriate ceremony for two players who were much better players than Domi, Roberts especially so. Then again, a couple of weeks earlier, at the trade deadline, Domi should have kept his mouth shut, but common sense and proportionality didn't prevail then, so why on the night of his thousandth NHL game?

Domi and Tucker may have said all the right things about being flattered by all the attention, but they also didn't seem too opposed it, either. I like to think I saw through Domi's and Tucker's acts. But I'm as guilty as any Leafs fan when the same psychosis takes hold about faux playoff pushes, or honestly believing the team has the ability to seriously contend when, if I were honest with myself, its lineup was so full of holes that there was no realistic chance.

I believe there is something way more honourable in hoping in the face of all reasonable facts when it applies to your favourite team. Just as in the wider world, hope is what makes the sporting world go 'round. Blowing smoke up the posteriors of players such as Domi and Tucker is not just rewarding the individual over the team; I would argue it's precisely what has contributed to the hubris that has crippled the Leafs franchise for so many years.

Despite being in just the first year of a four-year deal that was worth $12 million, it was soon obvious that Tucker was not long for Toronto. Ron Wilson at his introductory press conference later that spring praised Tucker — for his play in previous years — but hinted strongly that he had no plans for him. Fletcher bought him out soon after.

Two glorious Leafs heroes, two inglorious contract buyouts. You would never know it for how they are remembered.

The Tucker buyout is the gift that keeps giving for Tucker: he got a nice $1-million annual kiss-off for six years. Tucker's buyout lives on as one of the worst examples of a contract unfulfilled in the post-lockout NHL.

Tucker doesn't appear to be bothered by the whole thing. He is a frequent sight at various public events. Heading into the Leafs home opener on October 6, 2011, I was going up the escalator at the west end of the building and spotted a guy ahead of me wearing a Leafs jersey with "Tucker" on the back. It's not an unusual thing to see, even as the years tick by from when he last played in Toronto. There was one notable exception this time: it *was* Tucker. He was garnering a fair bit of attention and appeared gracious in signing a few autographs and posing for at least one picture. In that sense, he was acting like the plain-spoken Albertan he is. Fans called out, many who were already well immersed in liquid refreshment, and none seemed too concerned that Tucker was still costing the Leafs some serious dough, both of the real kind and the salary-cap variety. A cheeky friend, an avowed Leafs hater, loved the story when I met him after the Leafs 2–0 victory over Montreal.

"Seriously, you mean Tucker was walking around in his own jersey?" my friend asked.

Yep, he was.

"And fans were happy, even though the Leafs are still paying him, and no one said anything?"

Yep, they were.

What does that say about Tucker? Perhaps nothing, just like anyone with the means or the connections, he had the right to be in the ACC that night. He may have even had a role to play there. I hate to be cynical, but I wouldn't think Tucker, or any other former player still essentially on the team's payroll, would be so quick to stroll through the home opener of the Philadelphia Flyers, or the New York Rangers, or the Canadiens. Fans in those cities are a bit more edgy when it comes to remembering players who didn't exactly live up to the expectations dictated by the monetary terms of their contracts. I'm not suggesting that things should have gotten unruly on this night or that Tucker deserved to be pelted with rotten fruit. But it just seemed so pathetic that Leafs fans would embrace a player who essentially bottomed out during his final season, which led to the Leafs exercising their right to buy out the remaining three years of his contract.

In Toronto, Tucker had 319 points in 531 games. Not bad, especially when you factor in the guy had a bit of sandpaper as well. But to put it into perspective, his career numbers are very similar to Nik Antropov's and a small notch better than Matt Stajan's.

Are Antropov and Stajan remembered for anything other than being supporting players, first on good Leafs teams, then some pretty bad ones? And yet, aside from Sundin, the most talented Leaf by a wide margin, Tucker and Domi are likely the two most popular players to have suited up in blue and white in the past decade. In fact, it can be argued that Tucker and Domi are more popular than Sundin because of the oddly mixed legacy the Swede left behind. Being popular and being talented are two different things, of course. McCabe and Kaberle also played during that time but don't conjure up anything like the warm-and-fuzzy feelings that Tucker and Domi do even though the former two were much better players.

Domi's contract buyout was much less painful, both financially and for its cap hit. But he sleepwalked through his final year with the Leafs. Perhaps he was injured, who knows, but what was undeniable was that he was no longer an NHL-level player, goon or otherwise. He signed on to work at TSN but he wasn't very good on camera and that arrangement soon ended. Domi has faded away a bit since then, occasionally seen in the platinum areas of the ACC, surrounded by his children or high-powered friends and looking a little more like a corporate-type than the feared NHL tough guy he once was. Put another way, Domi wouldn't be wearing his old Leafs sweater the way Tucker did because it would be tough to get it over his expensive tailored suit jacket.

However, there is a happy developing story with Domi; It's his son, Max, a legitimately gifted junior hockey player who looks a lot like his dad but some day soon will be an infinitely better player. The younger Domi is considered a can't-miss NHL prospect and reminds many scouts of Patrick Kane at a similar age. The youngster is also universally liked by both his London Knights teammates and fans, who marvel at both his talent and dignity, developed while growing up with a surname that was surely just as much of a hindrance as it was a benefit.

❧   ❧   ❧

Let's finish as we began, with another trip to Alberta. I was attending the 2012 World Junior Hockey Championship in Calgary. The tournament was notable for its massive crowds, six-figure 50/50 draw prizes, and thrilling elimination-round games, one of which involved an epic comeback attempt by Canada against the Russians that fell just short. The tournament was now drawing to a close and various NHL scouts and other management types were cooling down, gathered in the media centre around television sets before the gold medal game between Sweden and Russia.

An interesting conversation ensued with a prominent NHL scouting director who shall remain nameless because he had no way of knowing that I was in the process of writing a book. While poking fun at me for electing to eat the massive piles of red meat on offer, he offered his own piece of information that I've chewed on ever since. He said that when he analyzes both current NHL players and the teenagers he regularly scouts, there is an intangible element that his staff pays particular attention to. He said it's a quality that is just as important as whether a kid can score, pass, or shoot.

"It's a humbleness while still being confident," he said, making the point with a hand adorned with a Stanley Cup ring. "All the great ones have it. You would never know [how good they are] talking to them, but when you see them play, you know they are something special. In this sport, as soon as a player starts taking himself too seriously, he's in trouble.

"[Hockey] is a very provincial sport," he continued. "You need to have players that your fans can identify with, look up to, but they better be good ones who have *that* quality."

Up until then, I had struggled to put into words what bothered me about certain Leafs players over the years. Sure, many decent players had come through town, even very good ones. But some always seemed to have a tendency to appear as if they thought they were just a little more important than their ability warranted.

Blue and White disease, it's been called.

After talking to this learned hockey man, I have a better understanding of this odd hysteria that tends to grow around certain Maple Leafs, with Tie Domi and Darcy Tucker being the best recent examples but certainly not the only ones.

Later that night I took the red-eye home from Calgary. After landing, I got some work done at my office near Toronto's airport. Having not eaten on the plane and now having spent the morning at work, I had a mad craving for a burger at a particular greasy spoon — Apache Burger — to cap off the long week. The restaurant was only a couple of kilometres away. It's a bit of a legendary spot, with perhaps fifteen or twenty photos on the wall of various celebrities, most of whom are Leafs players but also other NHLers who are Toronto natives. There are even a few shots of players who had brought the Stanley Cup into Apache (none of those are Leafs, of course).

Gazing at the wall, I realized there was one guy whose image popped up more than any other: Domi. It suddenly dawned on me how, especially given the conversation I had had the previous night, it seemed appropriate that a player who was never much more than a fourth-line fighter always seemed to be in the picture, in the frame. It had first happened more than twenty years earlier, when Domi was beside Wendel Clark in that photo printed in the aftermath of Harold Ballard's death. Sure, there was a perfectly logical reason why Domi continued to be a focal point; he was one of the most popular Leafs players. He clearly liked stopping in at Apache for a bite to eat, likely on the way home from a road trip given the proximity to the airport and because he was always with his Leafs teammates. So, yes, it made sense he was plastered all over that wall. But there was another message there. It had something to do with Toronto needing to shake this odd tendency, the one that allows players who are, by NHL standards, mere role players, to be feted as if they are so much more.

It's acceptable to have false hope; it's another thing entirely to have false heroes.

19

SOMETHING'S GOTTA GIVE

I KNOW THAT I'M JUST AS GUILTY AS ANYONE, EVEN MORE SO THAN your average Maple Leafs fan. When I think of how easily I filled my life when NHL hockey was not played during the fall of 2004 and the winter months that followed, it's a bit embarrassing to think that I haven't found a way to stop spending my time and money watching the Leafs. But saying no would be the easy way out, wouldn't it?

I've instead taken the hard road, buying tickets with my own money to one hundred games over the past seven seasons. During that time, I have at least matched the expense of tickets with how much I've spent on food, drink, parking, and transportation costs both inside the Air Canada Centre and at various venues that surround the building. Hell, I've even gone on the road three times during that span to watch the Leafs, and I subscribe to Leafs TV.

My reward? About a quarter of the games I've seen live were truly entertaining, with roughly that number again moderately so. At least twenty five were complete snorefests, which would have been easier to stomach had the Leafs been on their way to making the playoffs in any of those seven seasons. The hockey club hasn't done that, of course, not even once.

In total, I would estimate that I've spent $25,000 on my Leafs habit, with roughly half going into the team's coffers directly, the other half to related expenses. For that, I've seen exactly zero playoff games at the Air Canada Centre.

I should know better, but I accept that dichotomy and even have an answer to why it exists both with me and for many thousands of other Leafs fans.

I also know how completely shallow the words are of various Maple Leaf Sports and Entertainment executives when they profess their undying commitment to building a winner. Richard Peddie may have inspired the confidence of the various interests that owned the Leafs, but it was obvious to me soon after Peddie opened his mouth publicly that the man didn't know the first thing about assembling a winning hockey (or soccer and basketball) team. If you think otherwise, you're welcome to peruse the stewardship of John Ferguson Jr., Rob Babcock, or Mo Johnston when they were in charge of their respective clubs under MLSE's watch. Peddie was the man in charge for all three hirings. If that doesn't convince you, you're welcome to troll back to the old, pre-lockout NHL and re-educate yourself on how the Leafs decided to always spend enough to be competitive but never enough to put themselves over the top, even if they could easily have afforded it.

I have significantly more faith when Brian Burke proclaims his commitment to winning because Burke has proved to be a capable hockey executive, even if his tenure so far has been a failure.

But one thing I have come to understand is that the wait for the team to finally start winning is at least part of the reason I keep the faith. Had the Leafs won the Stanley Cup during my lifetime and contended for it more often than they have over the past four decades, it might loosen my resolve to support the hockey team.

Though not as passionately, I have followed the Toronto Argos, Blue Jays, and New York Giants fairly closely since I was a little boy. All three teams, though spectacularly bad during parts of my lifetime, have also won many championships. Every year I maintain hope that the Argos, Jays, and Giants will be winners, but when they show themselves otherwise, I don't obsess over it. I simply tune the misfortune out and move on. Having experienced eleven league championships as a fan of those three teams, plus a handful of other occasions when they either lost in their league final or got awfully close to getting there, subconsciously I knew the next run was just around the corner. As far as the Toronto Raptors go, I don't dislike basketball, but it simply doesn't excite me the way hockey, football, or baseball do. I have a bit more time for soccer, but my interest in Toronto FC is more casual than passionate.

Besides, both the Raptors and TFC only further remind me how utterly incompetent MLSE can be in running sports teams, or at least producing winning teams, and you can only take so much heartbreak during a calendar year.

Nearly two decades of essentially listless results are starting to put the Jays into the same category as the Leafs, but at least I have fond and vivid memories of them winning, and winning often. Frankly, I'm not sure that people under the age of twenty-five realize what they missed when the Jays used to make one of their patented charges virtually every year from 1985 to 1993. But answer me this: let's assume for a second that the Jays had never won the World Series, or even got close. Let's say for the sake of argument that their World Series championships in 1992 and 1993 ended in the American League Championship Series and therefore roughly matched what the Leafs did at almost the same time by making it to consecutive conference finals.

Sure, there would still be acres of empty seats at the Rogers Centre, especially when the roof is closed for dreary midweek games in April, May, and later in September. But it could also be that the Jays fans would have wanted more. They would have seen their team come oh so close and would be rooting for it to take it to the next level. We all know that thirst was quenched with World Series victories over the Atlanta Braves and then the Philadelphia Phillies in 1992 and 1993, respectively. Had those glorious wins not happened, the two decades that followed could have been much different because the burning desire to win would still have been there. No matter how discouraging the Jays' situation is right now and has been for much of the past twenty years, the fact remains that the only other team to win the World Series in back-to-back years is the New York Yankees (who won three consecutive titles from 1998 to 2000). That fact may be the single biggest reason why fans simply aren't interested in going back in large numbers to the SkyDome — now Rogers Centre — until the team gets better and gives us reason to be excited.

Been there, done that.

With the Leafs, the longing to win has been bubbling beneath the surface for more than four decades. And sure, the longing is taking place in a city with a more natural connection to the sport than Toronto does to baseball, or basketball, or soccer. Hockey is almost a religion in Canada, a bond that ties us all together and even makes us hate one another a bit when, say, the Leafs are playing the Vancouver Canucks.

With that type of backdrop, the Leafs' sad record on the ice and the blind loyalty are sometimes two sides of the same coin. One begets the other.

The sad decline of the Montreal Canadiens is more acute than the Leafs. The team with twenty-four Stanley Cup titles has not had a realistic shot at winning another since 1993, the Habs' last victory. The Canadiens were somewhat close in the spring of 2010 but eventually fizzled out. The season before that was trumpeted as perhaps the best Habs squad since the 1993 team but Montreal fell by the wayside with a whimper. What have Habs fans done? They don't blindly go back to the Bell Centre — they demand answers and results, even if none of the right ones have been forthcoming in the past twenty years. There have been Molson product boycotts and non-sellouts at the Bell Centre over the past ten or fifteen years — an unthinkable development in Toronto. Besides, what, or who, can Leafs fans boycott?

Even acknowledging hockey's hold on the rest of Canada, there have been clear signs from other cities besides Montreal that fans aren't willing to blindly follow a loser. In Vancouver, Canucks tickets were very easy to come by as recently as ten years ago even if today they are almost as scarce as Leafs ones. Mass sellouts are, in fact, a relatively recent phenomenon in all other Canadian NHL rinks.

Aside from Winnipeg and the Leafs, all Canadian NHL teams have given the current generation of their fans much to be happy about. Edmonton has seen a dynasty created and another visit to the Stanley Cup final; Calgary has one Stanley Cup win and another appearance in the final; and Vancouver has made three trips there, though without hoisting the silver vase. Even Ottawa, as bad as the early Senators were right after entering the NHL, have been to the final. In Winnipeg, you can be sure that a prolonged run of non-competitive teams in this Jets incarnation will create many of the same issues that helped them leave town in the first place.

Leafs fans? We keep trudging back to the ACC, completely lost to the fact that there is almost no real motivation for the corporate masters who own the team to institute real change. What I and so many other Leafs fans have is that one impossible-to-quantify ingredient that keeps us returning: hope. Hope is the one thing that always keeps us coming back.

And if that hope is ever fulfilled by the Leafs winning their fourteenth Stanley Cup? The immediate joy is tough to imagine, but what about once the dust settles? Who knows, the desire to see it happen again may not be nearly as strong.

But there are other emerging issues with the Leafs and their hold on the vast sea of followers that should be real concern to the folks who count the money and construct the business plans. The first is

Courtesy of Aaron Bell/CHL Images.

TORONTO'S THIRTEEN STANLEY CUP BANNERS HANG HIGH UP IN THE AIR CANADA CENTRE. IT'S BEEN MORE THAN FOUR DECADES SINCE ONE HAS BEEN ADDED.

that the hockey team has benefited greatly from another one of those great unknowns that, like hope, is a bit tougher to gauge. I'm talking about the undeniable feel in the ACC's upper bowl in the past few years that people are there as part of a night out just as much as the lower bowl is occupied by the corporate types doing business.

The upper bowl attracts a completely different type of fan. Up there, it's groups of mostly thirty- and forty-something men and the occasional couple in that age group and even a bit younger. Many are from Toronto but many others hail from places like Barrie, or Dundalk, or Dunnville. Going to the ACC and watching the Leafs is part of the experience of being in Toronto for the day, or even overnight. A bit like going to the theatre. They drive in, perhaps stay at a hotel, or drive home, or even take the GO Train back after the game. These are not people on expense accounts; these are real people willing to spend their own money. They are essentially the people I have sat among since 2005; they come once or twice a season and may or may not come back the next. What I've found increasingly in the last few seasons is that these people are interested in the game, but not overwhelmingly so — certainly not to the degree the pre-lockout fans who sat in these areas did, or even the ones who showed up the first few years after the work stoppage. This group's declining interest has contributed to the stale atmosphere at the ACC in recent years because even some of these upper-bowl areas now have a jaded feel to them.

Perhaps this can be explained by the Leafs' poor record since 2005 but, frankly, I doubt the losing explains everything. I really sense that people feel ripped off, sick of watching losing teams, yes, but also sick of tickets priced so high. Sick of paying for $15 beers, $6 slices of pizza, and $5.50 bags of popcorn. Sick of being told to make noise by some dummy on the scoreboard, when the team on the ice is incapable of making you want to do it naturally.

It all takes place in a building that, sure, is nice, but doesn't hold any of the emotional appeal of the Gardens; this vast swath of people seem to be tiring of going to a venue that feels like it exists solely to separate them from the contents of their wallet without an emotional return on that investment.

I'm loathe to cite scalpers and ticket brokers as a source for solid information — I can't tell you how much I've haggled with both over the past seven years — but every single one I speak to has been saying pretty much the same thing since about 2008: the spending geyser of that usually dependable fan base is not spouting nearly as high as it used to. I've heard it so much from these guys that I'm actually starting to believe them.

People are starting to say no. Or at very least they aren't saying yes as much as they used to. And I have to admit, maybe I have something to learn from them — I haven't been saying no as often as I should.

That brings me to my last point, one that may define what the Maple Leafs have become in an ever-changing city and an ever-changing media marketplace.

The next generation. Where does it fit in?

Ticket prices have for almost a generation precluded families from attending Leafs games together. That's true, not just in Toronto, but in pretty much every other Canadian NHL market. But a storm could be brewing — the next generation of potential Leafs fans could grow up disconnected from the hockey team. Virtually all of them have parents who can't afford to bring them to a game. In fact, some of those parents, especially in the case of new Canadians, have never been.

Is this a brewing problem, or a solution, depending on your perspective? Consider my experience: I would estimate that since 2006, I've helped people find Leafs tickets about a hundred times. Some are friends who have tagged along with me to a game; others are people I've helped get tickets for clients, or for a guys' night out. Not a single friend or acquaintance has ever asked me for tickets to a game in order to bring their child. Not once.

The Leafs, in becoming the ultimate commodity, have also priced themselves out of reach for large swathes of people in the Greater Toronto area. It could be a blip, it could be a warning sign, I'm not completely sure.

But I know this: if my experience says anything, it's that the Leafs aren't as popular or as in demand as some of the mythmakers tell you. Yes, the hockey team is incredibly popular to guys like me, who have the inclination and financial resources to pony up the cash. The Leafs certainly have Bay Street and other corporate crowds hooked as they fawn all over themselves in the swankier areas of the ACC and occupy most of its lower bowl.

Those groups, though, don't exactly represent growth, do they? They all represent a flat line at best. And with condos built and swanky bars opened, it's tough to see growth in ancillary revenue.

Believe me, as much as I may have sounded like a hopeless buffoon at times, pissing away my money watching a crappy team, the end is nigh unless I start seeing some return on my money (though I will always be a fan).

What happens when today's kids grow up? Not many will have had the chance to go and watch a live game the way my generation did. And those who did will have done it at the ACC, not the Gardens. For all the new facility's appeal, it's pretty obvious that it's not leaving its mark on the next generation the way the Gardens did on previous ones. Manufactured noise and some fake hillbilly in a cowboy hat don't hold a candle to what today's generation of kids has to entertain them.

The longer the losing continues and as the kids grow up without the emotional touchstones that even we who lived through the horrible Harold Ballard years had, the tougher it will become to make an everlasting connection.

I still remember the noise the pucks would make off players' sticks at the Gardens. The sound would cut through the air like a machete — it was a natural sound of the game taking place, and the crowd reacted to it. Today's experience can't hold a candle to that unmediated combination. I doubt my son will even remember being told to make noise by some yahoo on the ACC big screen — probably just as well, as it's not the kind of thing that makes for a childhood touchstone.

If that wider emotional connection isn't made, will this new generation spend their money supporting a team that has not given back nearly as much as it has taken? It may seem like a contradiction, but I hope that they take a longer look, ask more questions, and don't just follow blindly down the same path my generation did. That's the only way things can change.

And if real change does take place? Well, maybe, just maybe, that fourteenth Stanley Cup banner will find its way up to the rafters of the Air Canada Centre.

APPENDIX

THE JOURNEY

THE BIGGEST "YOU HAVE TO BE KIDDING ME" MOMENTS IN LIFE generally involve money matters. It's especially true if you're a Leafs fan.

The hockey club has the most expensive tickets in the NHL, which, given that demand is just about the highest is a testament to the merits of a free market system. A cynic could argue that a clogged-up season-ticket subscriber base dominated by corporations and brokers gives rise to the resale market, inflating prices in the process and skewing real demand. But I digress.

Since my first visit after the lockout that cancelled the entire 2004–05 season, I have kept reasonably detailed records of most games I attended and the cost to secure tickets. Less exact is the money spent once inside the ACC, but the estimates here are fairly close.

Also, I took particular care to not include money spent outside the ACC, such as bar visits before and after games, though those discretionary expenses are difficult to avoid. Three Leafs road games — two in Montreal, one in Ottawa — are also not included here because the money I spent did not go into my team's coffers.

Of course, the true expense of Leafs games is much higher than listed here, because I've only listed my own costs. Roughly double it to bring a guest, triple or quadruple etc. for families. Also, I took great care to educate myself about the ticket-buying landscape and generally bought only the least expensive seats in the ACC. I may be a fool to love the Leafs but I'm no dummy when it comes to negotiating with scalpers.

I've witnessed a 49–38–12 home record over seven seasons, not horrible but not the hallmark of a very good hockey team and about on par with how the Leafs have played overall during that time. Frankly, I didn't know whether to laugh or cry while compiling this material. One parting shot of advice: if you choose to embark on a journey like the one I started in 2005, make sure you have an understanding spouse. Divorce is about the only thing more expensive than being a Leafs fan.

Here's the rundown:

2005–06

October 8
Montreal 5, Leafs 4
Ticket: $180; Drink: $80
* I give myself the green light to spend this type of money given the euphoria of having NHL hockey back. I didn't realize that I'd still be spending it seven years later.

March 4
Ottawa 4, Leafs 2
Ticket: $50; Food and drink: $50
* Tie Domi's 1,000th career game commemoration; Eric Lindros is injured, ending his season and brief Leafs tenure. If you listen closely, Domi may still be giving his speech — or did it just seem to last that long?

March 14
Leafs 5, Boston 4 (SO)
Ticket: $45; Food and drink: $40
* Mats Sundin scores twice and still has his post-Olympic glow after leading Sweden to the gold medal a couple of weeks earlier. How the big Swede is anything but universally loved in Toronto is beyond me.

April 18
Leafs 5, Pittsburgh 3
Ticket: $140; Food and drink: $20

* Mats Sundin's two goals and two assists upstage Sidney Crosby's goal and assist; Leafs win their 41st game, their highest total in seven seasons of post-lockout hockey.

Season Record: 2–2–0   **Estimated Cost: $605**

2006–07

October 4
Ottawa 4, Leafs 1
Ticket: $50; Food and drink: $50
* Home opener and the Leafs are never really in the game against a team that would lose in the Stanley Cup final that season.

October 7
Montreal 3, Toronto 2 (SO)
Ticket: $90; Food and drink: $50
* The Leafs lose Andy Wozniewski on his first shift — and still lose.

October 9
Leafs 2, Florida 1 (SO)
Ticket: $50: Food and drink: $0
* A Monday night game with the Panthers in town helps cure almost 20,000 people's insomnia issues.

October 18
Colorado 4, Leafs 1
Ticket: $50; Food and drink: $80
* First disturbing sign of goaltender Andrew Raycroft's inconsistency leads to increased bar bill. There would be many more disturbing signs and inflated bar bills.

November 18
New Jersey 2, Leafs 1

Ticket: $50; Food and drink: $50
* Darcy Tucker breaks Martin Brodeur's shutout late in the third period and celebrates as though he's just won the Stanley Cup.

November 20
Leafs 4, New York Islanders 2
Ticket: $160; Food and drink: $30
* Lower bowl excursion is rewarded by Leafs win.

November 25
Boston 3, Leafs 1
Ticket: $125; Food and drink: $100
* Dreadful game; my dog took off just before I was heading to the ACC with family, including my mother-in-law. We found the dog but I never managed to lose my mother-in-law.

November 28
Boston 4, Leafs 1
Ticket: $50; Food and drink: $25
* Leafs are clearly slumping; good start now a faint memory.

December 5
Atlanta 5, Leafs 2
Ticket: $90; Food and drink: $50
* Leafs lose fifth game in a row; it becomes clear that Hal Gill will not win the Norris Trophy during his first season in Toronto.

December 16
Leafs 9, New York Rangers 2
Ticket: $80; Food and drink: $80
* Kyle Wellwood's first career hat trick comes as the Rangers look like they may have forgotten to go to bed the night before.

December 19
Florida 7, Leafs 3

Ticket: $45; Food and drink: $30
* Why did the Leafs not re-sign Gary Roberts (two goals) again? Hey, is that Wayne Gretzky dressed up as Josef Stumpel (four assists)?

December 23
Washington 3, Leafs 2
Ticket: $90; Food and drink: $50
* The combination of Alex Ovechkin on the other team and Andrew Raycroft in goal never turns out well for the Leafs. Never.

December 30
Ottawa 3, Toronto 2 (OT)
Ticket: $80; Food and drink: $40
* Tough night but not as bad as Saddam Hussein's day over in Iraq: he was hung.

January 1
Leafs 5, Boston 1
Ticket: $150; Food and drink: $40
* Happy New Year, the Leafs are undefeated in 2007!

January 9
Carolina 4, Leafs 1
Ticket: $50; Food and drink: $25
* For a man nicknamed "Razor," I can only hope Andrew Raycroft is more adept with one in his hand than he is in goal. If not, I fear for his safety.

January 13
Vancouver 6, Leafs 1
Ticket: $100; Food and drink: $40
* Andrew Raycroft is making a serious case to become the first Calder Trophy winner to have his award recalled.

February 10
Pittsburgh 6, Leafs 5 (SO)
Ticket: $170; Food and drink: $75
* Tough loss + lost wallet = angry Leafs fan.

February 13
New York Islanders 3, Leafs 2 (SO)
Ticket: $45; Food and drink: $20
* Geez, I hope this lost point doesn't mean anything when it comes to the final playoff seeding. Wait…

February 17
Leafs 4, Edmonton 3
Ticket: $45; Food and drink: $40
* The 1967 Stanley Cup champions are honoured to little more than golf claps. Noble gesture but it only shines spotlight on how long it has been since the Leafs last won it all.

February 20
Boston 3, Leafs 0
Ticket: $45; Food and drink: $40
* My annoyance with Andrew Raycroft briefly subsides about a month later when I realize that I finally managed to impregnate my wife just before leaving for the game. Seriously.

March 10
Leafs 4, Ottawa 3 (OT)
Ticket: $140; Food and drink: $50
* Another rare foray into the lower bowl is rewarded with an equally rare comeback win. Darcy Tucker scores the winner and his eyes look like they are going to pop into my lap when he's awarded first star.

March 13
Leafs 3, Tampa Bay 2

Ticket: $50; Food and drink: $10

* The Leafs post consecutive wins for the first time in a month.

March 27

Leafs 6, Carolina 1

Ticket: $50; Food and Drink: $25

* Leafs catch a break when Carolina goalie Cam Ward plays poorly. The loss effectively eliminates Carolina from playoffs.

April 3

Leafs 3, Flyers 2 (OT)

Ticket: $30; Food and drink: $40

* The Leafs come through in must-win game; one word of advice to those buying obstructed-view tickets: don't.

April 7

Leafs 6, Montreal 5

Ticket: $300; Food and drink: $100

ANDREW RAYCROFT CAME TO TORONTO FROM BOSTON IN RETURN FOR ONE OF THE BEST GOALTENDING PROSPECTS IN TUUKKA RASK. HE NEVER SEEMED COMFORTABLE IN HIS ROLE AS A STARTING GOALTENDER AND HAD A TENDENCY TO PLAY HIS WORST IN IMPORTANT GAMES.

* Leafs eliminate Canadiens in most entertaining game to take place at ACC in post-lockout era. Raycroft is pulled but is spared the indignity of being benched in the playoffs when the New York Islanders prevail in a shootout the next day and take back the final post-season berth.

Season Record: 10–11–4   Estimated Cost: $3,300

2007–08

October 6
Leafs 4, Montreal 3 (OT)
Ticket: $95; Food and drink: $50
* Tomas Kaberle scores overtime winner, shutting up Habs fan beside me who seemed to believe that Jean Beliveau was still playing.

October 11
Leafs 8, New York Islanders 1
Ticket: $120; Food and drink: $30
* Mats Sundin breaks the Leafs all-time scoring record — twice. First when he's credited with an assist in the second period, later nullified, then by scoring for real in the third.

October 13
Pittsburgh 6, Leafs 4
Ticket: $95; Food and drink: $50
* First clear signs that this could be a horrible year for Bryan McCabe as he seems confused that the puck does not explode on impact with the blade of his stick; Sidney Crosby scores twice.

October 23
Atlanta 5, Leafs 4 (SO)
Ticket: $55; Food and drink: $10
* Burning by Atlanta: Ilya Kovalchuk torches the Leafs in regulation (three points) and with shootout winner.

November 10
New York Rangers 3, Leafs 2 (SO)
Ticket: $95; Food and drink: $40
* Brendan Shanahan scores shootout winner and gives nifty fist pump; almost makes me forget he grew up about two long clappers from the ACC.

November 13
Montreal 4, Leafs 3 (OT)
Ticket: $55; Food and drink: $30
* Bryan McCabe gives me pause to think that going to games while having a heavily pregnant wife at home hurts my chances of winning husband of the year award; his giveaways imperil his hopes for a Norris Trophy just as much.

November 17
Leafs 3, Ottawa 0
Ticket: $95; Food and drink: $10
* Wow, the Leafs aren't so bad after all.

November 20
Boston 4, Leafs 2
Ticket: $95; Food and drink: $10
* Forget point above. Oh, and by the way, that Tuukka Rask kid in the Bruins net wouldn't look too shabby in blue and white, would he?

November 27
Montreal 4, Leafs 3 (SO)
Ticket: $90; Food and drink $0
* Not sure of the logic in this but I choose to view Bryan McCabe skating into his own net as a sign something was about to change in my life. Wait…

December 4
Leafs 3, Nashville 1

Ticket: $90; Food and drink: $50

* My son, approaching a week old, moves to 3–0 as a Leafs fan. My attempts to retroactively change his name to "Vesa" are rejected out of hand by Mrs. Robinson.

December 10
Leafs 6, Tampa 1
Ticket: $90; Food and drink: $40

* Seriously, this fatherhood thing is really helping the Leafs. No longer unbeaten but he's 5–1–0.

December 29
Rangers 6, Leafs 1
Tickets: $160; Food and drink: $30

* If my wife reads the dollar figure above she will want to kill me, which is roughly the same feeling I had when watching Andrew Raycroft try to stop a puck on this night (I was sitting directly behind the Leafs net). Never again.

January 1
Leafs 4, Lightning 3 (SO)
Tickets: $45; Food and drink: $20

* If every day was like New Year's Day the Leafs would be like the 1980s Edmonton Oilers.

January 15
Leafs 5, Carolina 4
Ticket: $45; Food and drink: $10

* Decent game but I spent half it impersonating Darcy Tucker's scary face from the ticket sleeve to the amusement of the eight-year-old boy beside me. The kid eventually tells me to stop it and grow up.

February 2
Leafs 4, Ottawa 2
Ticket: $95; Food and drink: $45

* Nice win but if someone finds Darcy Tucker wandering around somewhere, can they please tell him that the season started about four months ago.

February 9
Leafs 3, Detroit 2 (OT)
Tickets: free; Food and drink: $75
* Leafs beat the eventual Stanley Cup champion, but by picking up a $600 stroller on the way to the ACC — it was a rare afternoon tilt — it gave me pause to consider that perhaps my spending priorities were out of whack even if these tickets were free.

February 19
Leafs 3, Columbus 1
Tickets: $90; Food and drink: $40
* If there isn't already a rule against it there ought to be: you can't brag about beating Columbus.

February 21
Buffalo 5, Leafs 1
Ticket: $45; Food and drink: $25
* With the trade deadline looming, I've accepted that my man-crush on Chad Kilger is likely to take on a long-distance feel. Fingers crossed that Dominic Moore doesn't leave as well (he doesn't).

March 11
Leafs 4, Philadelphia 3 (OT)
Ticket: $90; Food and drink: $50
* Awkward moment when former Leaf Chad Kilger is pictured on ticket despite being traded a couple weeks earlier and then not reporting to sunny Florida. Must have been *pretty* serious personal issues.

Season Record: 11–4–4   Estimated Cost: $1,855.00

2008–09

October 21
Anaheim 3, Leafs 2 (SO)
Ticket: $80; Food and drink: $25
* Perhaps putting Curtis Joseph in goal for *just* the shootout wasn't such a good idea, Mr. Wilson, though we know that you're smarter than the rest of us.

October 28
Tampa Bay 3, Leafs 2
Ticket: $40; Food and drink: $25
* Nothing, just an early and subtle reminder that the Leafs are not going to win the Stanley Cup come spring.

November 1
Leafs 5, New York Rangers 2
Ticket: $95; Food and drink: $40
* John Mitchell plays the role of hero with two Leaf goals as Toronto storms back from being two goals down; perhaps that's why the Rangers picked Mitchell up when the rose came off the bloom in Toronto.

November 25
Atlanta 6, Leafs 3
Ticket: $95; Food and drink: $30
* The Leafs are on their way to their second prolonged losing streak and it's not even December yet. Brian Burke is on the verge of becoming the new GM; I haven't had warm and fuzzy feelings for a man with ginger hair since watching *Happy Days*.

December 6
Washington 2, Leafs 1
Ticket: $165; Food and drink: $40
* Alex Ovechkin remains a great draw but his and Washington's

tendency to beat the Leafs in low-scoring, dull games is getting annoying. As is Ovechkin hurting Luke Schenn.

December 8
Leafs 4, New York Islanders 1
Ticket: $95; Food and drink: $5
* The Leafs win, and I manage not to have a single refreshment, a rare occurrence on both counts.

December 16
Leafs 3, New Jersey 2 (SO)
Ticket: $55; Food and drink: $35
* Some drunk guy wearing a Marty Brodeur jersey must be upset that a) Brodeur is not playing and b) the Devils lost. So he tries to fight me in the stairwell. I remind myself I'm no longer twenty-one, now a father, and turn the other cheek.

December 30
Leafs 4, Atlanta 3 (OT)
Ticket $55; Food and drink: $55
* Pavel Kubina repays John Ferguson's faith in him by scoring the overtime winner. Wait, sorry, JFJ, a year too late. I also conclude that Jonas Frogren, despite wearing the same No. 24, is the anti–Bryan McCabe — he doesn't leave his own zone and tries *not* to touch the puck.

January 31
Leafs 5, Pittsburgh 4
Tickets: $165; Food and drink: $45
* Hard to believe that the Penguins rolled into town and weren't very good. Harder still, by winning, the Leafs got within shouting distance of them.

February 14
Leafs 6, Pittsburgh 2

Ticket: $95; Food and drink: $40

* The Leafs give Michel Therrien a real sweetheart Valentine's Day present: they beat the Pens, who fire Therrien as their coach. Dan Byslma is hired the next day and is now seen as the last piece in the eventual Stanley Cup championship that Pittsburgh wins that spring. Does that mean the Leafs sort of won the Cup, then?

February 25
Leafs 2, New York Rangers 1 (SO)
Ticket: $150; Food and drink: $40

* I watch the game wearing a heart monitor as per conditions of a medical checkup, and when I notice Rangers coach John Tortorella with his hand on his heart during the U.S. national anthem, I think he is sending me a message. I ask my doctor later if she could cross-reference if my ticker skipped a beat when Nikolai Kulemin scored the shootout winner. She didn't get the joke.

March 3
New Jersey 3, Leafs 2 (OT)
Ticket: $50; Food and drink: $35

* A four-game winning streak snapped and with it the faint whispers of an unlikely playoff push fall silent, blessedly. The guy who wanted to beat me up earlier in the year is nowhere to be found, but Brodeur does pick up the win.

March 7
Edmonton 4, Leafs 1
Ticket: $55; Food and drink: $30

* The Martin Gerber era begins not very well in Toronto as Dwayne Roloson continues to confound the Leafs despite being the oldest and longest-serving career backup since Gump Worsley.

March 14
Leafs 8, Calgary 6
Ticket: $100; Food and drink: $50

* Mikhail Grabovski is originally awarded a hat trick and then his third goal is taken back after review. Many hats are lost for no good reason, as is Calgary's late playoff push.

Season Record: 8–4–2   **Estimated Cost: $1,785**

2009–10

September 26
Leafs 2, Detroit 1
Ticket: $95; Food and drink: $50
* Just an exhibition game but Jonas Gustavsson shows a lot of heart — prophetic given the medical condition the new Leafs goaltender brought with him to Toronto.

October 10
Pittsburgh 5, Leafs 2
Ticket: $95; Food and drink: $75
* Sidney Crosby and his mates blow into town and confirm the Leafs are no longer merely unlucky through the first three games — they are a bad team as well.

October 13
Colorado 4, Leafs 1
Ticket: $95; Food and drink: $40
* Darcy Tucker (two points) is finally found: he's on the other team and causing the Leafs defeat. It's all a bit too familiar because he contributed to many Leafs defeats two seasons earlier — while playing *for* Toronto.

October 17
New York Rangers 4, Leafs 1
Ticket: $210; Food and drink: $40
* Apparently Vesa Toskala had his labrum fixed over the summer; we couldn't tell.

November 10

Minnesota Wild 5, Leafs 2

Ticket: $95; Food and drink: $45

* It's one thing to lose to the Penguins, even the Rangers, but to get hammered at home by the Wild?

November 30

Buffalo 3, Leafs 0

Ticket: $95; Food and drink: $45

* Kerry Fraser and Ryan Miller. What a treat for Leafs fans, especially when Miller taunted the crowd when he was picked first star. I swear, I saw that he was keeping the five-hole open all night long (Sid, did you hear that?).

December 16

Phoenix 6, Leafs 3

Ticket: $100; Food and drink: $60

* I recall a $15 prime rib sandwich served by a woman named Lovely to start the evening. It soon got really un-lovely from there: Twitter star Paul Bissonnette scoring a goal and celebrated like he had just cracked 1,000,000 followers. A team that was essentially a ward of the NHL state hammers the Buds.

December 21

Buffalo 3, Leafs 2 (OT)

Ticket: $95; Food and drink: $75

* Entertaining family in from Calgary; they are treated to a Colton Orr giveaway that leads to the tying goal by the Sabres in the third period. They laugh, I cry, we all repair for Christmas cheer.

January 5

Leafs 3, Florida 2

Ticket: $40; Food and drink: $10

* I ignore my mantra of not buying standing-room tickets and the Leafs reward me with a win. I wasn't even supposed to be here but

the flu bug ravaged the Robinson household and cancelled my World Junior trip. Small miracles.

January 12
Carolina 4, Leafs 2
Ticket: $95; Food and drink: $20
* Leafs lose their fourth in a row as Gustavsson appears shaky; legit argument can be made that the only reason Ron Wilson still has a job is that he's working with Brian Burke at the upcoming Vancouver Olympics.

January 14
Leafs 4, Philadelphia 0
Ticket: free; Food and drink: $50
* Friends treat me to one of the best played games by the Leafs in the post-lockout era; Tyler Bozak shows that he may have some game — if Leafs fans are patient. Make that really patient.

January 26
Los Angeles Kings 5, Leafs 3
Ticket: $95; Food and drink: $10
* Dreadful season continues; I start making plans to offload my tickets that I have left in my "Ultimate Hockey Pack." The Leafs have now lost twenty more games (37) than they've won (17).

February 8
San Jose 3, Leafs 2
Ticket: $95; Food and drink: $50
* The Leafs organization mourning the loss of Brian Burke's son, Brendan, in a car crash; Nazem Kadri called up and shows flashes.

March 2
Carolina 5, Leafs 1
Ticket: free; Food and drink: $20
* Two days after Olympics, the world returns to normal and the

Leafs do their part: they play a horrible hockey game.

March 9
Leafs 4, Boston 3 (OT)
Ticket: $95; Food and drink: $10
* Scalpers are offering literally pennies on the dollar for tickets, and postings to sell on websites get no response. I'm essentially forced to *use* my tickets.

March 11
Leafs 4, Lightning 3 (OT)
Ticket: $95; Food and drink: $50
* I trade my Ice Box tickets that weekend against Edmonton for Thursday night platinum seats straight up; it proves a shrewd choice — Leafs win and Steven Stamkos is impressive to watch.

March 18
Leafs 2, New Jersey 1 (SO)
Ticket: $95; Food and drink: $25
* A scalper offers me $20 and subway tokens for my tickets, honestly; another proposes a trade for two Esso gas cards. I think he was joking.

March 20
Leafs 3, Montreal 2 (SO)
Ticket: $95; Food and drink: $50
* Aside from the Philadelphia game, this is the only tilt worth the price of admission all year.

April 1
Leafs 4, Buffalo 2
Ticket: free; Food and drink: free
* A friend gets me into his company box and he proceeds to invite everyone walking by to come in as well, including a retired judge and his wife. The Leafs play well, it's a lovely spring night, and

because I don't want my one remaining game to leave a bad taste over the summer, I sell my last pair for that weekend against Boston at a $30 loss.

Season Record: 7–10–1   Estimated Cost: $2,500

2010–11

October 18
New York Islanders 2, Leafs 1 (OT)
Ticket: $95; Food and drink: $40
* John Tavares scores the winner to beat the Leafs who are still technically undefeated. Is it just me or was that rule created to further distance Leafs fans from reality?

October 21
New York Rangers 2, Leafs 1
Ticket: $95; Food and drink: $25
* Now living about 75 minutes from the ACC, I'm hopeful the travel time eliminates impulse visits. It doesn't. Leafs repay my loyalty by twice losing after starting with four consecutive wins.

November 2
Ottawa Senators 3, Leafs 2
Ticket: $150; Food and drink: $60
* About 13 months later Brian Burke holds a press conference lamenting the demise of heavyweights. Funny, I was doing the same watching Colton Orr this night. Memo to Burke: don't ask your long-suffering fans to feel sorry for a player being paid $1 million a season *not* to play for you.

November 18
Leafs 3, New Jersey 1
Ticket: $95; Food and drink: $25

* Leafs catch the Devils in the midst of the franchise's worst troubles since Wayne Gretzky called them bad names.

November 22
Leafs 4, Dallas 1
Ticket: $50; Food and drink: $100
* Attending game with good friend Tim, an oil patch worker on so-called turnaround leave, turned a staid Monday night game into a bit of a blur. I do recall that the Leafs played well, though, and Mrs. Robinson not being happy at the state of her husband on a Tuesday morning.

December 9
Philadelphia 4, Leafs 1
Ticket: free; Food and drink: $50
* I'm struck by the hockey knowledge of the graceful woman sitting directly behind me — it turns out to be Brian Burke's wife. A section or two over some knucklehead throws breakfast food on to the ice as the Leafs are about to lose.

December 20
Atlanta 6, Leafs 3
Ticket: $100; Food and drink: $10
* Leafs, about to take a five-day Christmas break, decide to make it six. Proving that even men whose knuckles drag watch the news: someone throws waffles on to the ice in protest. Monkey see, monkey do.

January 6
Leafs 6, Blues 5 (SO)
Ticket: $105; Food and drink: $10
* A friend invited me down to his company box where his inebriated client tilted his head all night at the very same 45-degree angle as his pint glass; he never spilled a drop, never completely passed out, and never watched the game. Mikhail Grabovski scored a shootout winner for the ages. Still, the drunk guy's dexterity given his condition was more impressive.

January 20

Leafs 5, Anaheim 2

Ticket: $105; Food and drink: $10

＊ First game with my father since New Year's Day in 2007; I found it tough to convince a retired man on the leisure side of sixty that it's not good form to be spilling his peanut shells everywhere, you know, that allergy and all. Leafs play well and win going away.

February 3

Leafs 3, Carolina 0

Ticket: $105; Food and drink: $20

＊ Leafs were very impressive and this game was the first real sign of the playoff push, albeit a late one, that would come later in the month.

February 7

Leafs 5, Atlanta 4

Ticket: $160; Food and drink: $25

＊ Good Leafs win and it was notable to sit beside Norman Stewart, father of the Thrasher's Anthony (and St. Louis Blue Chris). The constant hum of "puck pressure" spoken with a Jamaican accent right beside me gave off a different vibe than the normal ACC canned noise.

March 14

Tampa Bay 6, Leafs 2

Ticket: $40; Food and drink: $25

＊ The unofficial dagger in the Leafs' playoff hopes. I pledged to stay away after this game and only wavered with thoughts of bringing my son for the first time, but he was sick. The self-discipline arrives six years and more than $10,000 too late.

Season Record: 6–5–1   Estimated Cost: $1,500

2011–12

October 6
Leafs 2, Montreal 0
Ticket: $115; Food and drink: $15
* Leafs do the rope-a-dope and win a game after starting poorly. I'm sat beside TSN host Michael Landsberg in the greens; a fine fellow by the way. And I soon realize that the guy that looks exactly like Darcy Tucker coming up the escalator had good reason to: he *is* Darcy Tucker.

October 19
Leafs 4, Winnipeg 3 (SO)
Ticket: $60; Food and drink: $40
* Welcome back Winnipeg. It was a pleasure to give the Jets a standing ovation in the first period even if the Leafs play the first 40 minutes like they still think Winnipeg is an AHL team. Rookie Matt Frattin scores a shootout beauty.

December 22
Leafs 3, Buffalo 2
Ticket: free; Food and drink: $75
* A friend gets me back for a game last season and we watch the game from the lower bowl sitting directly behind a group of four middle-aged Americans who are either related to Phil Kessel (the jerseys and accents were a dead giveaway), or just happened to like the thought of spending the holiday season in Toronto.

January 14
New York Rangers 3, Toronto 0
Ticket: $150; Food and drink: $50
* My car breaks down and strands me in a friend's Leaside house while he's away for the weekend. I do what any self-respecting Leafs fan would do: spend too much money watching them getting their hats handed to them.

January 23

Toronto 3, New York Islanders 0

Ticket: $110; Food and drink: $75

* One great mystery: they've been utter crap for most of the past two decades but the Islanders have a way of bringing out the best in ACC crowds. A solid game and one of the first where I've noticed the platinum set actually returned to their seats in a timely manner. They likely think Mike Bossy is still playing.

February 6

Leafs 6, Edmonton 3

Ticket: $65; Food and drink: $20

* Leafs play well, win, and Mike Brown crunches Ryan Nugent-Hopkins body and his Calder Trophy hopes into the boards in the third period. Tough break but perhaps karma bit the Leafs back as they soon go on an epic slide that kills their playoff hopes. I go into hiding in order to dull the pain and to write this manuscript.

Season Record: 5–1–0   Estimated Cost: $820

NOTES

CHAPTER 2

1. Michael Farber of *Sports Illustrated* first hung that label on the Leafs and they later made that publication's list of most-hated teams of all time.

2. Vasicek later won a Stanley Cup with the Hurricanes in 2006 and went to play in Russia not long after. He died in September 2011 when a plane carrying the Lokomotiv Yaroslavl club crashed, killing all members of the squad.

CHAPTER 3

1. Leeman may have struggled in Calgary but he made out just fine at his next NHL destination, Montreal, where he was part of the Canadiens' 1993 Stanley Cup win. In one of those bizarre twists in the Gilmour trade, the Leafs won the lopsided deal, but Leeman soon won the Stanley Cup. Gilmour's lone Stanley Cup win came in 1989 in Calgary, when Risebrough was an assistant coach.

CHAPTER 4

1. Fraser was now required — kicking and screaming, no doubt — to don a helmet, by the terms set out in the new collective bargaining agreement between the NHL and its officials association.

CHAPTER 8

1. Bremner Boulevard's growth is powered in large part by MLSE's ancillary businesses — condos, the Real Sports Bar, and the e11even restaurant.

2. E11even is a play on the Maple Leafs eleven Stanley Cup triumphs, a bold move given that the team won its last in 1967. Real Sports' opening during the summer of 2010 was generally well-received, but cynical fans couldn't help but notice the replica Stanley Cup near the bar entrance.

3. Working the phones and pooling inventory among younger scalpers is also out of necessity; a byproduct of not having had as many years to secure a line on as many regular seats.

4. The Leafs entered the game with eight overtime or shootout losses, a staggering number considering that they hadn't hit the mid-point of the schedule yet.

CHAPTER 10

1. Four months later Cooke would cold-cock Boston Bruins centre Marc Savard, earning personal infamy, seriously hurting Savard, and putting the concussion debate firmly front-and-centre in the hockey community and media.

2. Buble's mugging for the in-house camera that night is often played on the "Carlton Cam" segment that runs on the scoreboard during television timeouts.

3. The four-year deal was a disaster for the Leafs, but buying him out was not. Tucker had just 40 points in 134 games for the Avs and was clearly a spent force. His game versus the Leafs was one of few impressive efforts in his final season.

4. Chicago, of course, broke its drought by winning the 2010 Stanley Cup, leaving the Maple Leafs with the longest championship-free stretch of the Original Six teams.

5. In his end-of-season press conference Burke acknowledged that the horrible start scuttled any hope of making the playoffs. The Leafs first win came nine days after this against Anaheim, but not before another loss to Vancouver. Given the time difference from the West Coast, and the drab Monday date, it meant that Leafs fans had to wait until well past midnight and

for 25 days in total since opening night for the first victory of the season.

CHAPTER 12

1. To be fair, the Royal York did an outstanding job of hosting much of the festivities of the 2007 Grey Cup, including the great green masses from Saskatchewan, a province whose people are about as diametrically opposite to Torontonians as you can get.

2. The media mob was mostly made up of news reporters on this day, wanting to get comment from the Great One about an emerging gambling scandal that had ensnared his assistant in Phoenix at the time, Rick Tocchet. Gretzky, or his wife Janet, were rumoured to somehow have been involved. He wasn't, and neither was Janet, but Tocchet eventually pleaded guilty to a misdemeanour charge of running a betting ring.

CHAPTER 13

1. John Tavares scored in overtime to win, Matt Moulson scored the Isles' first goal — both are Toronto-area natives.

2. Assuming the type of form he failed to show in Toronto, Cunningham sailed passed the century mark after being traded to Dallas in 2008.

3. The *Hockey Night in Canada* broadcast started at 4:00 p.m. Pacific time in order to take advantage of the prime-time audience back east.

CHAPTER 15

1. In researching a feature on the Memorial Cup program, I became interested in Ballard's involvement with elite junior teams and I set out to try and find more information. I couldn't find any tangible evidence of Ballard having a hands-on role with any of the teams he was listed as an executive. Memorial Cup–winning captain Billy Harris told author Jack Batten (in

Batten's book *The Leafs*) that Ballard would only show up for the team picture.

2. The long list of charges Ballard was convicted for included buying a motorcycle and falsely claiming it as a business expense from Brown's Sports in west Toronto, a store that still stands at Jane and Bloor, a short walk from the former Smythe homestead in Baby Point.

OF RELATED INTEREST

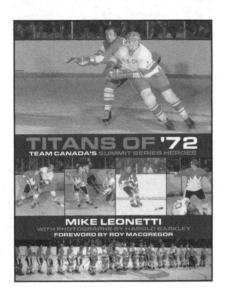

Titans of '72
Team Canada's Summit Series Heroes
Mike Leonetti
9781459707665
$14.99

Phil Esposito, Ken Dryden, Frank Mahovlich, Yvan Cournoyer, Bobby Clarke — these are some of the Team Canada hockey heroes who struggled to defeat the Soviet Union in the September 1972 Summit Series. Here are profiles of each Canadian who played on that fabled Team Canada, showcased with superb photographs by Harold Barkley.

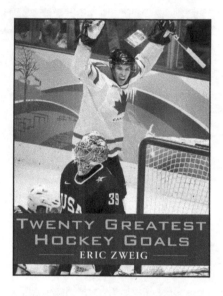

Twenty Greatest Hockey Goals
Eric Zweig
9781554887897
$24.99

Every hockey fan remembers certain goals scored that stand out
from all others. But if one had to name just twenty as the greatest
ever, what would they be? Eric Zweig serves up a slice of exceptional
hockey moments, including Paul Henderson's game-winning goal in
the 1972 Summit Series and Sidney Crosby's "golden goal" in the
Vancouver 2010 Olympics.

VISIT US AT
Dundurn.com
Definingcanada.ca
@dundurnpress
Facebook.com/dundurnpress